Anti-Racist Feminism

Anti-Racist Feminism
Critical Race and Gender Studies

edited by Agnes Calliste and George J. Sefa Dei
with the asistance of Margarida Aguiar

Fernwood Publishing • Halifax, Nova Scotia

Design and production: Beverley Rach
Printed and bound in Canada by: Hignell Printing Limited

A publication of:
Fernwood Publishing
Box 9409, Station A
Halifax, Nova Scotia
B3K 5S3

Fernwood Publishing Company Limited gratefully acknowledges the financial support of the Ministry of Canadian Heritage and the Canada Council for the Arts for our publishing program.

Le Conseil des Arts | The Canada Council
du Canada | for the Arts

Canadian Cataloguing in Publication Data

Main entry under title:

Anti-racist feminism
    ISBN 1-55266-032-X

1. Minority women -- Canada. 2. Racism -- Canada. 3. Feminism -- Canada.
I. Calliste, Agnes M. (Agnes Miranda), (date) II. Dei, George J. Sefa (George Jerry Sefa), 1954-

HQ1453.A57 2000   305.48'8'00971   C00-950045-6

Contents

Chapter Seven
**"Making" White Women through the Privatization of Education on
Health and Well-Being in the Context of Psychotherapy**

Chapter Eight
**Nurses and Porters: Racism, Sexism and Resistance in
Segmented Labour Markets**

Chapter Nine
Anti-Racist Feminism: A Conclusion to a Beginning

Contributors

Agnes Calliste is Associate Professor, Department of Sociology and Anthropology, St. Francis Xavier University. Her academic research has focussed on anti-racism and feminism in employment, immigration and education. She has several scholarly publications in refereed journals, most notably her work on nurses and the health care system and social histories of Black porters.

Maria Castagna is a Master's graduate of the Ontario Institute for Studies in Education, University of Toronto. She has been a high school language teacher in the Greater Toronto Area since 1988. In her commitment to minority students she has taken on the responsibility as teacher-facilitator for both African Heritage and Anti-Racism groups within the schools she teaches, some of which have received recognition both at a board and community level. Her professional practice includes social activism beyond the walls of the classroom.

George J. Sefa Dei is Professor and Associate Chair, Department of Sociology and Equity Studies in Education at the Ontario Institute for Studies in Education of the University of Toronto (OISE/UT). He is also the Director of the Centre for Integrative Anti-Racism Studies at OISE/UT. He teaches in the areas of Anti-Racism Studies, Indigenous Knowledges and International Development.

Enakshi Dua is Assistant Professor, Department of Sociology at Queen's University. She works on the intersections in race and gender, as well as post-colonial studies. She is currently working on a project that explores the ways in which Canadian nationalism, British imperialism and the Indian anti-colonial movement combined to discursively construct the category of "Indian" women in the Canadian context. She has published articles on the historical construction of race and gender in Canada. She has also co-edited *Scratching the Surface: Canadian Anti-racist Feminist Thought* (The Women's Educational Press, Toronto, 1999).

Patience Elabor-Idemudia is Associate Professor, Department of Sociology at the University of Saskatchewan. She has written extensively in the area of women and development, and immigrant women in Canadian society, and has published several scholarly papers in refereed journals.

Usha George is Associate Professor, Faculty of Social Work/University of Toronto. Her scholarship focusses on the development of culturally competent social work practice. Advancing beyond cultural and ethnic diversity, her major

theoretical orientation has been the broader concept of "difference" that includes the intersecting and interlocking oppressions of race, gender, class, age,
sexual orientation and differential ability. Her research interests are in the areas
of newcomer settlement and adaptation, organization and delivery of settlement
services, and community work with marginalized communities.

Helle-Mai Lenk received her M.A. in Adult Education from the Ontario
Institute for Studies in Education of the University of Toronto in 1998. She
teaches English-as-a-Second-Language at McGill University. From 1991–1993,
she worked as a cooperante with Oxfam in Egypt.

Sherene Razack is Professor, Department of Sociology and Equity Studies at
the Ontario Institute for Studies in Education, University of Toronto. Her books
include *Looking White People in the Eye: Gender, Race, and Culture in
Courtrooms and Classrooms* (Toronto: University of Toronto Press, 1998) and
*Canadian Feminism and the Law: The Women's Legal and Education Fund and
the Pursuit of Equality* (Toronto: Second Story Press, 1991). She has also
published extensively on race, space and prostitution; the race to innocence and
hierarchical relations among women; Canadian national mythologies and immigration policies of the 1990s; and the Somalia affair.

Kerstin Roger has taught at the University of Manitoba and is currently
teaching in the Social Work faculty of the University of Calgary. She continues
to be involved in community-based development and research that reflects
intersections between race and gender.

Acknowledgments

We offer many thanks for the assistance obtained in the publication of this book. We particularly dedicate this book to the many students, educators and community workers whose struggles, sacrifice and devotion to work and duty have been a source of inspiration to us. Our academic scholarship has benefited a lot from our close association with many community workers, and students in Ontario and Nova Scotia and other parts of the country. The list of names will be too extensive to mention here. But we will include a special thank you to Margarida Aguiar of the Department of Adult Education, Community Development and Counselling Psychology of the Ontario Institute for Studies in Education of the University of Toronto (OISE/UT), to christine connelly, Marcia James, Leeno Karumanchery of the Department of Sociology and Equity Studies, OISE/UT, and to Debbie Murphy of the Department of Sociology and Anthropology and Tauja Hinds of the Biology Department at St. Francis Xavier University for their invaluable comments on the text and the tremendous amount of time and work put in to ensure that the book came to fruition. We are indeed honoured by the decision of the various contributors to hang in and bear the pain of long delays as we went through all the requirements for the publication of this collection. We deeply appreciate the integrity of the publisher and editorial staff of Fernwood Publishing for carrying through the commitment to see this work in print. Finally, our warm gratitude goes to all those anonymous reviewers who commented on drafts of this work. If this book is favourably received it is a testament to the fact that the collection builds on other works that have preceded this volume.

Agnes Calliste and George J. Sefa Dei
Toronto, October, 1999

Introduction

Anti-Racist Feminism
Critical Race and Gender Studies
Agnes Calliste and George J. Sefa Dei

In collaboratively putting together this collection our objective and fervent hope is that we can contribute to a widening of the boundaries of debate on anti-racist feminism and social difference. Contextualized and emerging from within broad personal, political and academic experiences, the book addresses important questions of anti-racist feminist theory and its connection with difference in a variety of social, historical and institutional contexts and practices. Anti-racism for most people has primarily been associated with questions of school-ing and educational change. However, we continuously engage with each other in knowledge-generating activities in multiple formal and informal learning sites outside of the classroom. Consequently the papers in this collection seek to advance anti-racist, feminist discourse far beyond spaces in schools to the media (historical past and present representations), women's national and international identity, employment and immigration, social services, the field of psychotherapy and to nursing in hospital settings.

Today, the need to theorize insurgent responses to racialized and gendered discourses of "nation" and "democratic citizenship" is widely recognized. This collection adds to our understanding of how gendered and racially minoritized bodies can and do negotiate their identities and politics across several historical domains (see also Dua and Robertson 1999).

Many academic works have contributed to our understanding of race, gender, class and sexual orientation as primary categories that inform the complexity of human experience. The individual is a multiple self with no single dimensional identity. Individuals are socialized into identities corre-sponding to our shared and contested meanings of race, gender, class and sexuality. For the purpose of this "Introduction," rather than rehash many of the insightful discussions interrogating multiple identities and oppressions (see Brand 1985; Brewer 1993; Carby 1986; Collins 1990, 1993; Dei, 1996, 1999; Dua and Robertson 1999; hooks 1981, 1984; Mirza 1997; Ng, Staton and Scane 1995; Razack 1998; and Stasiulis 1990, to mention a few), we prefer to raise some key questions about anti-racism discursive politics and the understanding of difference with the intersection of gender.

In myriad ways, the papers in this collection explore the relational aspects of difference and the implications for reconceptualizing anti-racism discourse and practice. In acknowledging situational and contextual variations in intensities of oppression, a key issue is how social movements, and politics can be mapped broadly enough to acknowledge multiple oppressions and at the same time still retain specific agendas at the centre. The manuscript raises some key theoretical questions in the attempt to reframe anti-racist practice for social and community work that is centred on women and race. By offering a grounded analysis of intersecting and interlocking oppressions we can hope to pursue meaningful politics for genuine social transformation. Critical anti-racism discourse examines ways "difference" both fractures and enhances the understanding of community for anti-racist practice. Integrating race and gender analyses in anti-racism discourse allows for exploration of multiple and, perhaps, conflicting meanings of "community."

The relevance of understanding race, gender, culture and power in progressive politics for social change cannot be underestimated. Understanding gender and race relations is knowing about power relations in society. Race and gender as social identities frame the construction of [social] difference and how identity is connected with knowledge production. Gender is recognized as an important aspect of identity as well as political organizing. As Dei and connelly (1999) point out in another context, the possibilities for revisiting "gender and race" outside of the [dominant] frame of "gender and race" are not necessarily visible simply through a comparative analysis concerning the male gaze. This is particularly the case as the line of fault masking women's everyday/everynight lives as problematic (Smith 1987: 49) is not registered when participants speak through a male-centred discourse as though it were naturally a neutral and objective frame for explicating the everyday. Smith describes the need for disrupting an objectifying process of theorizing the "subject" by resisting the superimposition of external theoretical frames describing or explaining behaviour and instead viewing the "knowing subject" as "located in a lived world in which both theory and practice go on, in which theory is itself a practice, in time, and in which the divide between the two can itself be brought under examination" as ontological constructions of ordered and ordering activities (see Smith 1999: 75).

In working with the concepts of race and gender as categories of difference, anti-racist feminism raises questions about how to support "difference" without simply reiterating an objectifying framework constituting problems of patriarchy and racism, but in terms of the possibility of taking up "difference" more subjectively in terms of human agency and creativity to recreate and occupy multiple, shifting, alternate socio-political and cultural positions beyond conventional categories such as "gender and race" (Dei and connelly 1999). The project of supporting a discursive paradigm shift away from conventional problematic readings of social relations requires a "double reading and writing" of the power relations informing social dynamics engendering societal participation. For the anti-racism feminism project this entails not only a process of exposing or naming the master's structures and strategies as they construct frames for viewing and naming difference, but also a viewing and a suggesting of resistances and transformative possibilities beyond the frame.

A critical reading/writing of "anti-racism experience" in part means re-reading "gender" and "race" from subordinate perspective(s) in terms of the ways in which dominant or normalized notions of "gender" and "race" correspond with dominance, or in terms of the dynamics at the nexus of "gender," "race" and other "forms" of social organization which sustain racialized heterosexual male privilege through the mobilization of authority to regulate and subordinate women's bodies in terms of "female innocence." For example, this reading/writing at the intersection of "gender" and "race" might involve a strategy, which is not presumed to be neutral, of uncovering and disrupting the hidden relations of power inherent to "engendering" and "deracializing" to create new, non-linear, different and sometimes alternate/relational meanings of "gender" and "race" that move beyond the conventional frame to support the possibility of bringing other less hegemonic possibilities into view (see also Dei and connelly 1999).

Furthermore, change that moves us towards an anti-racist, non-sexist society has been a subject of intense scholarly research and writing for some time now. Academic works have emerged from diverse theoretical, epistemological and ontological foundations drawing attention to the enormous range of possibilities and constraints in promoting change in societies marked by divisions along racial, gender, ethnic, class and sexuality lines. Despite knowledge generated and insights gained from theoretical analysis and frameworks, we still strive for greater understanding of the institutional practices and social processes that contribute to create, sustain and ferment the glaring disparities and inequities structured at least along the lines of race, gender, ethnicity, language, religion and class. The recognition that "Western" society is fundamentally structured along the relations and dynamics of difference, coupled with the awareness that these structures and practices are contrary to a just and equitable society, has not concurrently moved us from the idea of an anti-racist, anti-sexist society to the application of the necessary changes in institutional practices, social processes and relations. As we have been struggling concretely with these international, national and local practices, the ground on which we have been seeking to negotiate these relationships of power has continuously shifted within and outside of national boundaries.

In rethinking anti-racism, critical scholarship must consider how to begin to attend ethically to the social construction of relations which constitute racial minorities and women's possibilities for participating both within and beyond the ideologies serving a system of national and global economic/political interests aligned as they are with a white hetero-patriarchal Western/Northern elite. Emergent from this scholarship are questions concerning access and social equity, and how to respond to the legitimate claim of diverse social groups to the valued goods and services of society, and to active participation in framing and structuring what is valued. Critical anti-racism and feminism scholarship is beginning to carefully examine alternative discursive frameworks for critiquing and understanding how social capital can solidify dependencies and subordinations through internal and external power relations. To problematize the notion of "democratic citizenship," critical scholarship now asks the following questions: How do human dignity and welfare connect to labour and political/economic/cultural/historical contexts of development? How do the experiences of migration, agency, resistance, and the reclamation of multiple identities and representations inform understandings of social integration and human survival/reproduction in contested spaces? How do differences, multiplicities, ambivalences and contingencies inform anti-racist [political] practice in society? How does anti-racist, feminist discourse attend to questions of power, language, identity and representation in supposedly "post-colonial" contexts? What are the differential responsibilities of state, local governments, international finance capital, schools, colleges, universities and other institutional settings in the pursuit of non-hegemonic knowledge for human survival/ reproduction? The search for answers to any of these questions calls for a critique of the status quo and the problematic assumptions underlying individual merit, achievement and what constitutes success. There are profound limitations of contextual spaces in which those minoritized by race, class, ethnicity, sexuality, language, ability and religion have been inimically inscribed in prevailing societal discourses through subject/object relations of disempowerment in education, schooling, social work, nursing, law, immigration and employment training.

Additionally, this book raises an important question: As Dei and connelly (1999) note in another context, in the unmasking of our constructed positions of knowledge/power, particularly in the voicing of barely tenable positions of difference within or from the "margins," how do we begin toward voicing difference/transformation beyond the dominant discourse while the dominant persistently intercedes in the imagination of possibilities for conceptualizing change (see also Fanon 1963)? It would seem that these "slippages" between dominant and alternative discourses indicate important contradictions or tensions that emerge as significant indicators of the negotiation of power and knowledge. We believe that an important contribution of this collection is the call to attend critically to reading sites and sources of oppression differently and to seek possibilities beyond re/invoking the notion of the marginalized as quintessential victim. Admittedly, those marginalized by racial, gender, ethnic, class, ability and sexuality differences continue to be subordinated to social, economic and political forces constructing human subjects as labourers and incidental reproductive bodies constantly under siege by the authorities, violations and regulations of the ruling classes. Nevertheless there is agency and resistance on the part of the subordinate.

The historically situated knowledges of minoritized groups have often been discounted, although not without a challenge. In other cases, the futures and identities of racial, ethnic, class and sexual minorities and women have been constructed for them by the dominant. Against this unscholarly pursuit, no one would deny the constant struggle and resistance of the marginalized to assert their agency and indigenous identity. Critical anti-racism seeks to affirm agency as both the possibility and necessity of racial minorities to actively determine the direction for social change through participation in the sites and the structured settings of local resistance and political, economic and social transformation. Critical anti-racist feminism locates the dialogue in the reality of women's lives and at the intersection/s of race, gender and class. Racism, patriarchy and colonialism continue to dominate power relations in North American society and within institutional settings it appears few resources have been allocated to supporting forms of intervention that are not merely reproductive of the alienation, oppression, marginality and exploitation of marginalized groups. Sites of women's work are often better located to bring material inequities and alternative values to the foreground.

Positively, the essays in this book stress the need to attend more carefully to the transformative possibilities of postmodern and post-colonial theory for critically reading the multiple, shifting, dynamic voices of subordinate groups across borders of class, nationality, regionality, gender, ethnicity, ability, sexual orientation and race. Critical anti-racist feminism must seek to support possibilities for those minoritized as actors and agents of change with reference to the specifics of the everyday reality of women, to ancestral histories, critical traditions and local knowledges through the struggle for identity, power and possibility in the context of externally-regulated social demands.

The book supports possibilities toward an ongoing consideration of the relations of identity, power and difference in North American society. In considering the multiple voices of racial minority women working for anti-racism change, the book contributes to the possibility of continuing to engage in a process of discursive critique around alternative readings of social change. The various authors present alternative anti-racist approaches to the construction of knowledge and the inter-subjectivities of racial, gender, sexual, class and ethnic minority groups within critical scholarship and social practice. They collectively affirm possibilities toward claiming voice/agency in difference for social change that has still not gained prominent ground in conventional knowledge production. The authors acknowledge the fact that social justice work from the margins, initiated through local knowledges at the intersection of race, gender, class, sexuality, ethnicity, culture, language and different abilities, has received minimal attention or acknowledgement in Western scholarship concerned with redressing race and gender inequity. To help promote change, critical anti-racism discourse must explore the implications of racial, gender, class and sexual minorities' ways of making sense of their everyday experiences. In beginning from a structuralist discourse to theorize the context of multiple social oppressions in terms of individual and collective agencies, critical anti-racism helps explore the meanings of location and power.

This collection brings important contributions to the anti-racism discourse and practice. The essays also help us to understand how we can begin to claim a language around the socio-cultural situating of knowing bodies in terms of racialized/engendered/class-regulated histories. The book advances the need for continued inquiry toward deconstructing and transforming sites of oppression, marginalization, alienation, subordination, subjugation and exploitation. Within the limited site of these pages, the authors' seek to move through various places where the conditions of women's work/lives and women's identities are negotiated.

In fact, the strength of the book lies in its centring the experiences of racial minority women within a variety of social sites, thereby seeking to incite the reader to broaden the examination of social spaces through the lens of an anti-racist feminist scholarship and practice. Admittedly, much work remains to be done in other sites of difference. From diverse social locations these authors have taken up the question of difference and the intersection of anti-racism theory and practice. It is our hope that with this collection we have made a contribution to the broadening of the dialogue/s on anti-racism and feminism.

Maria Castagna and George Dei's jointly authored paper provides an historical analysis of the application of the race concept in social analysis. The authors examine the processes and dynamics of racial categorizations, race differentiation and the implications for understanding human relations and conflict. A key concern is the interrogation and understanding of the historical specificities for the reproduction of "races" in racially structured situations. In positing the analytical and conceptual relevance of the race notion, this paper provides new meanings of the race concept and its relevance for current questions of social identity/identifications and representation.

Sherene Razack's chapter explores the general subject of race and knowledge production through an examination of the position of racialized immigrant women in the academies of the North. She argues that the academies of the North are primarily interested in the racialized immigrant woman as a symbol—an "Authentic Third World Woman"—who can be a native informant. In this position, "Third World" women scholars in the "First World" are expected to help the "First World" save the "Third World," or, in other words, manage the natives. This argument is explored through an examination of the author's own subject position and research on asylum claims based on gender persecution. She suggests some of the ways in which we might begin to subvert the nNative informant position and practice a truly transnational feminism. Accountability and complicity are key concepts which she proposes.

Increasingly questions of race/ethnic and gender/class identification in constructions of nationhood and citizenship have come to the fore as important areas of critical anti-racism and feminist studies. Enakshi Dua's work joins the debate in identifying the links between the discourse of racial and social purity and the institutional manifestations of systemic racism and patriarchy. The author examines the ways in which the social construction of Canadian nation-building and its concomitant racial politics—that certain races were [un]suited for citizenship—historically constructed notions of what constituted gender for South Asian–Canadian women. She argues that the discourse on nation-building, in the early twentieth century, was intimately tied to racializing gender for both Anglo-Saxon and South Asian Canadian women. Whereas Anglo-Saxon women were socially constructed to be "mothers of the nation," South Asian–Canadian women were initially excluded from immigration because they were socially constructed as "creators of undesired ethnic communities," and became desirable later only as spouses for South Asian men in order to contain/direct Asian men's sexual activity and create segregated ethnic communities. Dua suggests that the legacy of this discourse has continued to shape the structural relationship that South Asian women have with the Canadian economy and society.

Helle-Mai Lenk's examines newspaper coverage of a particular incident. In the fall of 1994, a Montreal high school student, Émilie Ouimet, was sent home for wearing an Islamic headscarf or *hijab*, allegedly in contravention of the school's dress code. This event unleashed a considerable media debate. By mapping, annotating and analyzing the development to the *hijab* controversy in four newspapers (*La Presse, Le Devoir*, the [Montreal] *Gazette* and the *Globe and Mail*) over a three-month period, the essay shows how racism and sexism become articulated within these discourses and how these articulations in turn attend to different political projects relating to nationalism. Particular attention is directed to the use of news schemata (headlines, quotations) in the articles that "broke" the Émilie Ouimet story and the argumentative strategies of editorials. The essay proposes that the intensity and volume of the debate, and its telling silences, arose out of a need to make sense of an incident for which the dominant narratives of a culture did not work.

Patience Elabor-Idemudia points out that employment plays a key role in the integration of newcomers in most societies, and economic survival through labour is a predominant reason for the migration of most "Third World" African families to Canada. Yet, African immigrants and refugees to Canada, especially women, face severe discrimination in the Canadian labour force because of their race, gender and non-recognition of their foreign credentials. Utilizing the findings of a case study carried out in Toronto in 1994, she demonstrates that many African/Black immigrant women with substantial educational backgrounds relative to the Canadian standard are either marginalized in the labour force or are forced (due to limited choice) to engage in low-paying jobs under poor and difficult working conditions upon arrival in Canada. She suggests that African immigrant women and other women of colour should fight for their human rights through racially specific community-based agencies which have provided more effective, responsive and equitable services to minority communities than mainstream institutions have done.

Usha George's chapter examines the importance of race and ethnicity in social work and locates racism at different levels of social work practice preventing access and equity to services by immigrant and visible minority communities. She describes the possibility of an anti-racist/feminist social work practice comprising of three interrelated components: individual, organizational and structural. George explores the elements of individual competencies in anti-racist social work. It would consist of different "layers of understanding" and would be a creative blending of knowledge, skills and values that should be part of social work education and training. She suggests that at the structural level, coalition building needs to take place for a comprehensive anti-racism strategy.

Kerstin Roger's paper explores how the professional practice of psychotherapy, and the identity of the white woman as a psychotherapist, shapes hierarchical relations of race within the helping professions. The author demonstrates that psychotherapy is a privatized and elite site through which the social service professions have continued to provide Western white women with a contemporary privilege based on the historically negotiated presence of the racial "Other." Moreover, psychotherapists are invested in being seen as kind and innocent through this more elite helping work—either helping people of colour or other whites. She suggests that given most psychotherapists are white women, and psychotherapy is a form of privatized health education that hopes to resist patriarchy and psychoanalysis, the broader implications of this article are to understand how shaping white women as elite helping professionals marks a reproduction of historical relations of race, class and gender.

Finally Agnes Calliste's paper provides a comparative analysis of African Canadian women's resistance to professional exclusion and marginality in nursing in the 1970s to 1990s and sleeping car porters' anti-racist struggles on Canadian railways in the 1950s and early 1960s. The work is significant in that it brings together anti-racism theory and segmented labour theory showing how these theories inform each other to provide a more integrated and in-depth analysis of the workplace. Using research data from interviews with a group of nurses and oral history interviews with porters and former porters, the author extends the discussion of anti-racism to the workplaces of both manual (porters) and professional (nurses) workers and to the labour movement. Calliste raises the important dimension of pro-active "resistance" to anti-racism praxis. She suggests that groups representing racialized minority nurses should unite and organize a strong lobby group to fight racism and marginalization in the health system. By including the labour organizing struggles of porters alongside the present working conditions of nurses in the health care system together with the inclusion of a historical perspective on employment and immigration polices, she thrusts the discussion on anti-racism into a broader social context.

Chapter One

An Historical Overview of the Application of the Race Concept in Social Practice

Maria Castagna and George J. Sefa Dei

In the field of social science, arguably, one of the most hotly contested concepts is the notion of race. Academic debates over the notion of race have historically centred on its conceptual and analytical significance in understanding social relations and conflict. This paper provides an historical analysis of the application of the race concept in social analysis. It examines the processes and dynamics of racial categorizations and race differentiation and the implications for understanding and interpreting human relations and conflicts. A key concern is the interrogation and understanding of the historical specificities for the reproduction of "races" in socially and racially structured situations. Our intention is to provide a historical account for the contemporary ideological, material and social meanings[1] of the race concept. Elsewhere Dei (1996) examines some of the theoretical approaches to the study of race.

The race concept is important for its social and political consequences. To deny the race concept is to deny the lived historical realities of many peoples. The idea of race has both theoretical and operational meanings in everyday practice. It is therefore extremely problematic to dismiss the race category as empty. The race concept is not based on a false consciousness. Race is an ideological and political construct with both subjective reality and a material base. Unlike others who argue to the contrary (see Miles and Torres 1995), we[2] point out that the race concept has analytical and conceptual usefulness. The relevance of the race concept lies in its social significance and meanings. We also believe that avoiding the analytical relevance of the race concept can obscure important distinctions between the production of racism and its reproduction of social oppression. The production of racism refers to its origins, while reproduction refers to the continual manifestation of racism in society. This distinction is important in order to account for the fact that the function of a phenomenon does not necessarily account for its origins. While the reproduction of racism can be rooted in contemporary social, political and economic forces, the production of racism may well lie beyond these forces, extending to an ideology that supports white supremacy for its own sake, without being driven by economic interests necessarily. This includes not only the obvious example of hate groups, but the various manifestations of cultural superiority pervasive in our society. White Western values are continually reinforced while experiences and knowledges of people of colour are often devalued, ridiculed or dismissed.

Histories are dynamic, and in the process of telling and retelling, new ideas and conceptions about race are created. There is an obvious connection between dominant ideas about race and the socio-political and economic contexts in which the ideas are produced and disseminated (see Banton 1977). Omi and Winant (1994) have described a process of "racial formation" in which "race is understood as a fluid, unstable and decentered complex of social meanings constantly being transformed by political conflict" (p. 59). The historically specific meanings ascribed to race contribute to the difficulty of establishing a general theory of race. Yet, there is what can be termed the reality of skin pigmentation as a powerful, visible marker for distinguishing between groups. This knowledge has implications. While there are limitations to a historically specific analysis of racism focussing only on skin colour through time, its recognition does offer an important theoretical space for critical anti-racists to articulate the saliency of skin colour racism over other forms of racisms (Dei 1996). While different forms of racism are manifest in society, racism is more frequently and more harshly manifested against those who are furthest from the "white skin colour norm," regardless of whether or not they fit into the dominant value systems [i.e., class, language, faith]. If, for example, one takes a long view of historical time, religion and culture appear to challenge the norms of the dominant culture less than does skin colour.

Towards a Definition of Race

Social scientists, and particularly early researchers on race, expressed the difficulty of defining and operationalizing the race concept. The problem was, and continues to be, the lack of clarity and the intellectual dangers of using conceptual and analytical categories that are themselves social constructs. Historically, disagreements among social scientists have been on two fronts: firstly, about the criteria and number of races into which human groups can be classified; and secondly, disagreements among those who have argued that race does not exist because groups of the human species do not fit neatly into definite racial categories (see also Reynolds and Lieberman 1993: 110–14). Today, questions surrounding the taxonomic validity of racial categories and the arbitrariness of the race concept have been superseded by discussions about the materiality of race as a social, ideological and political category in human social life. To understand some of these initial conceptualizations of race we need to examine the ideas espoused in early racial discourses. In this exercise, we must ask, for example, how has the race concept been constructed historically and in the biological and social sense? The brutal records of economic history and the harsh realities of contemporary society clearly demonstrate there are, and have been, ideological, political and material consequences to race.

In this paper we operationalize the race concept as a social-relational category defined by socially selected real or imagined physical, as well as cultural, characteristics (see also Wilson 1973). As a socially constructed category, race lacks any "scientific" validity. Yet the concept continues to gain in social currency because of its utility for distributing unequal power and privilege. It has become an effective tool for the distribution of rewards and punishments. The concept has been used to "divide and rule" peoples, a practice that is itself assisted by the human propensity to categorize individuals and social groups. Talking about race in the context of critical anti-racism studies is not about a need to categorize. Rather, it is to make sense of (and rupture) and contribute to the elimination of racially constructed power relations in our world.

So far, the intellectual ambiguity surrounding the term "race" has not rendered it a meaningless category. Its power, as well as social and political relevance lie in part in the persistence of racisms. Rather than rejecting concepts of race, it is more appropriate in the contemporary sense to speak of the processes of "racialization," that is, the myriad contexts and "instances where social relations have been structured by the signification of human biological ... [and cultural] ... characteristics in such a way as to define and construct differentiated social collectivities" (Miles 1989: 75). While the process of racialization cannot be understood with reference only to race, it is important to acknowledge the centrality of historically specific meanings of the race concept in the process of racializing groups for unequal treatment.

Our analytical approach should be based on the multiple political and social constructions of race. Race is not a reductive, biological "essence" (King 1994: 5). Race must be understood as the result of historically specific processes (see Omi and Winant 1986; Miles 1989). This knowing calls for a non-reductionist, historically specific analysis of racism which touches on the internal character of racism. This approach gets beyond the reducible questions of economic and material concerns. In effect, contemporary critical race studies are characterized by a shift from biologistic and assimilationist conceptualizations of race to a discussion of race in the social, historical, ideological and political sense. These theories do not assume racial categorizations as "natural" or "given." The thinking on race "in terms of racial formations rather than eternal or essential races is an important step in the comprehension of new forms of racisms as well as the historical expressions of racialized identities" (Carby 1990: 85; see also Omi and Winant 1994; Morrison 1992; and Ware 1992, cited in Ferber 1995: 5). Current conceptualizations of race recognize the multifarious forms of racisms (Goldberg 1990, 1993). They provide for an important theoretical distinction between the possibility of all people holding racist beliefs as a form of ideological conditioning, and the actual practice of racism with significant material consequences for people.

The Question of Historical Origins

History and contexts are important for understanding the analytical and conceptual "terms that mythologize our differences and similarities" (Grewal and Caplan 1994: 138). There have been substantial scholarly discussions on the origins of the race concept and how it manifests its significance in the everyday practices of society. In fact, numerous academic essays continue to broach the subject of race and racisms, each offering valuable insights into the social, ideological, biological constructions and abstract formations of race and the practice of racisms in society (see Omi and Winant 1993; 1994; Banks 1994; Miles 1989; Cox 1976; Goldberg 1993; West 1987, 1992; Rattansi and Westwood 1994).

Dei (1996) argues that the idea of race may have been an essential feature of early societal formations, especially as individuals searched for social explanations about the nature and consequences of human differences. Still, the origins of the race concept can appropriately be tied to Western European philosophical and belief systems, and particularly, the colonial and imperial expansion activities of the Western powers and economic capital in the seventeenth century (Reynolds and Lieberman 1993). Some writers may put this date around the early years of the sixteenth century (see Goldberg 1993). Race, at the time, was a powerful and useful concept for sorting out human variation observed by European explorers, conquerors and colonizers. In fact, as Reynolds and Lieberman (1993) argue, a self-righteous racial ideology was developed to legitimize the ruthless exploitation and subjugation of non-Europeans. Since the seventeenth century, the race concept has been applied, to varying degrees, by social and natural scientists in the course of everyday reasoning and research about human social relations and interactions (Miles 1989).

Historically, the study of racial diversity has tended to reify racial categories. A review of the social construction of races and racialized identities in various historical contexts reveal the mixing of biological and cultural "facts," as well as a shift in the privileging of biology to culture. In the biological sense, the race concept was based on a categorization of people on the basis of perceived differences of intelligence. One justification for the enslavement of African[3] peoples was viewing Africans as a "sub-human" species, like cattle. They supposedly did not have the "same" capacities for language, communication and culture as their European oppressors. Most of this discourse occurred within what was perceived to be the imagined objective and rational science of biology. In its social conception, the term "race" was/is argued to be a social, political and ideological construct. Notwithstanding the fact that there are still important forces in society who argue for biological differences in intelligence, the powerful social meaning of race today rests on the knowledge that the concept cannot be defined biologically. Rather, as many have pointed out, race is a product of specific socio-historical and political contexts (see Omi and Winant 1994; Lopez 1995). Goldberg (1993), in fact, wrote about the "different racisms in the same place at different times; or different racisms in various different places at the same time" (p. 91). For example, while southern Europeans were racialized in the North American context during the 1900s, as colonizers in South America and Africa, they imposed their own racial hegemony over the peoples they colonized as well as over more disenfranchised groups in North America.

Biddiss (1979) pointed out that the development of racial theories was central to the dominant ideas of European bourgeois civilization and aesthetics (e.g., ideas of intelligence, character, physical prowess and beauty). Eighteenth and nineteenth century ideas reified the race concept within a theoretical framework of biological determinism. Connections were made between supposedly scientific and mystical approaches to race. Racial ideas were presented as pseudo-religious thought, later adapted to a more secularized society (see Biddiss 1979). In fact, the role of the Church in maintaining a race differentiation through definitions of "un-Christian," "savage and unholy practices" in European expansion was paramount during these periods. For many scholars of the time, what was worth stressing was the importance of racial biology for maintaining/enforcing human and social relations. Racial typologies were devised to categorize humans on the basis of perceived phenotypical differences with the understanding and implication that there was little hope for changes in "racially behavioural models" (Macchiusi 1992/93: 60). Racial typologies, buttressed by a Eurocentric view of the world, were critical in justifying European practices of cultural, economic and political genocide of non-European peoples (see also Eke 1997). As Macchiusi (1992/93: 50) additionally points out, in the biological formulation of racist doctrines, the oversimplification of race and racialism in biological facts also denied the role of human agency.

The acceptance of race as biologically determined restricted the understanding of racism. Furthermore, the failure to conceive of race relations as ostensibly power relations, or, as relations of domination and subordination, prevented any critical discussion about human resistance and agency and their emotional, symbolic, physical, intellectual and social complexities (see Foucault 1980). Eighteenth and nineteenth century race theorists simply adopted biologically determinist and essentialist positions on race and racism. Seeing race and racism as including questions beyond those of biology, skin pigmentation and other phenotypical differences allows us to capture the nuances and dynamics of racializing groups for unequal treatment. In examining racism from a comparative and historical perspective it can be argued that the roots of racist practice predate the sixteenth century. In fact, early practice of discrimination was on the basis of culture and religion, not on biologistic definitions of race. This can be seen, for example, even in the literature of the fourteenth century. Dante's offensive depiction and imposition of torture on the Prophet Muhammad and on other Muslims in his *Inferno* (see Said 1979: 68) testify to racism on the basis of culture and religion during this period. Europe as the centre in the white imagination would create the term "Orient" (meaning "East of" the centre). Consequently, those included in this "imaginative geography" became "outsiders," as Europeans constructed images of heathenism, indolence, despotism and sensuality (Said 1979: 102). Europeans could not reconcile their biases with the evidence of seven centuries of Muslim influence, which had brought Europe out of its "Dark Ages." Ironically, Columbus' 1492 voyage to the "new world" was in large part funded through the confiscated wealth of the Muslims and Jews who were expelled from Spain (Moghissi 1994).

Groups came to be racialized in the notions and hierarchies of inferiority and superiority on the basis of social organization and cultural and technological accomplishment. European supremacy was espoused and defended through the conscious and unconscious negation and erasures of the accomplishments of other peoples (see Eke 1997). This provided a basis and justification for the later colonizing practice of Europeans as they sought to impose/propagate their religion and culture on other peoples. The racist beliefs that white people were to rule the world (Manifest Destiny) and that certain people were to be subservient (Hamlite Rationalizations) [see Banton 1977] were powerful colonizing tools.

Thus a powerful ideology of racism emerged from a combination of social, cultural, economic, biological and religious factors. Blackness subverted the moral and rational order of Europeans and whiteness. There was an overdetermination of Blackness with immorality, sin, evil, criminality and inferiority. First Nations were also depicted as "savage" but "salvageable." That is, whites viewed themselves as adults, at times "white saviors," and conceptualized "people of colour" as children or "sub-human." This is not to say that non-European peoples did not have their own views of Europeans. The Chinese, for example, viewed the English as "red-haired barbarians" (Wolf 1982: 252). The Hausa and Yoruba people of northwestern Africa had their own terms for early Europeans they encountered, viewing them as "people without skin." For example, the Hausa term "bature" (ba = no; ture = skin) referred to the light-skinned Europeans and Arabs.[4] The Yoruba term "oyinbo" (bo = to peel off; a person whose skin has been taken off) was a similar way of viewing the first whites encountered (Adebayo 1996).

European views, however, would "justify" a racist history of genocide, exploitation and subjugation of non-Europeans: and various white Canadians, whether educators, clergy people, workers or government officials, also engaged in this exploitation. The Canadian government, for example, at times [see La Violette 1961: 40–42] attempted to ban cultural practices that challenged Eurocentric norms. Some practices (and consequently people engaging in these practices) were criminalized. This was the case of the potlatch on the West Coast and sundance ceremonies on the Plains where First Nations engaging in these practices were imprisoned. White norms of private property viewed potlatch as the wanton giving away of goods and both potlatch and sundance as barbaric impediments to the assimilation of First Nations (see Francis 1993: 98–101).[5] While the potlatch law was not always enforced,[6] its existence and petitions against the potlatch law by various West Coast bands (see La Violette 1961: 57, 70–71) nonetheless demonstrate the attempted imposition of white Christian norms. [It became enforced with more consistency after Duncan Scott became deputy superintendent of Indian Affairs in 1913; see Francis 1993: 99–100].

"Scientific" Theories as a Mechanism of Racial Oppression

In addition to Hamlite Rationalizations and Manifest Destiny, whites created different "sciences" and "scientific" theories to justify, legitimize and maintain the existing social order, "theories" which are still being espoused by many today. Polygeny, craniometry and intelligence testing functioned to fulfill the racist agenda of keeping "subordinates" in their place as hewers of wood and drawers of water. As race became reified, so too was "intelligence," which achieved status as a measurable entity (see Gould 1981: 24, 157). Under the guise of "science," test results acquired objective validity. Polygenists maintained that different races were separate biological species (Gould 1981: 39). Typologies were created leading to books such as *Account of the Regular Gradation in Man* (White 1799, cited in Gould 1981: 41) and *Types of Mankind* (Nott and Gliddon 1854, cited in Gould 1981: 34). Polygenists claimed objectivity, even though diagrams of skulls were purposely distorted to create the impression that Blacks might rate lower on the "intelligence" scale than chimpanzees (Gould 1981: 32). Some polygenists disclaimed any political motivation for the ranking of humans along a hierarchical scale; it was merely to appreciate differences and out of curiosity.[7] However, there could be none other than political motives (both conscious and unconscious) for the categorizations/typologies created by pseudo-scientists. Those professing objectivity often made recommendations regarding social policy:

> No man has a right to what he is unfit to use.... Let us beware of granting too much to the negro race in the beginning, lest it become necessary to recall violently some of the privileges which they may use to our detriment and their own injury. (Agassiz 1863, as cited in Gould 1981: 48)[8]

To "prove" their polygenist theories, white Europeans and Americans went about gathering, or rather, fabricating "hard data." Thus began the measuring of skulls, craniometry. The study of cranial capacities and racial brain theories were methodologically flawed. A priori assumptions, miscalculations and convenient omissions together provided "data" that was so desperately needed by whites to justify the existing social order and to fuel further "research" for sorting human lives. For example, polygenist and craniometrist Samuel George Morton often included or deleted large subsamples of skulls so that group averages would correspond with his prior expectations (Gould 1981: 68).

The next step to "measuring intelligence" was the formulation of intelligence tests (again, the misguided belief, unfortunately still held by many, that intelligence was a measurable entity). Particularly well-known by now are the American army tests, which led to the American Immigration Restriction Act of 1924 (Gould 1981: 157). Tests, proclaimed as being objective, were of course culturally biased and whites who interpreted the tests dismissed the differences in educational opportunity. When differences appeared in test results between northern and southern African-Americans, these differences were not attributed to educational opportunity, but rather, to "selective migration."

Of course, not everyone bought into the theories of the ultra-hereditarians. Numerous articles appearing in the *Journal of Negro Education* contesting the racist theories and revealing the inaccuracies and flawed methodology of the pseudo-scientists attest to this fact. From the *Journal*'s beginnings in the early 1930s, African-American scientists and educators combatted many of the racial/racist myths that then abounded in dominant discourse.[9] They clearly illustrated the fallacy in the "selective migration" myth of the ultra-hereditarians. If southern-born Black children raised and schooled in northern states had higher I.Q. levels than Black children schooled in southern states, it was not, as the ultra-hereditarians maintained, because the migrant parents were "inherently superior" to the African-Americans who had remained south. Rather, it was due to the more favourable schooling conditions available in some northern schools (see McAlpin 1932). In addition, contributors to the *Journal of Negro Education* also combatted the myth that light-skinned Blacks were more intelligent than dark-skinned Blacks (see Peterson 1934; Thompson 1934; St. Clair Price 1934; Jenkins 1936). They also revealed the a priori assumptions of scientists (see St. Clair Price 1934), identified the biases in supposedly "objective" tests (see Peterson 1934; Freeman 1934) and noted the effect of rapport between examiners and subjects in I.Q. testing (see Canady 1936).

But such tests, proposed and supported by the dominant group, were used to defend policies of segregation (in the U.S.), to limit and deny entrance to immigrants and refugees, and to continue the testing and sorting of all children, thus granting opportunities to some while denying opportunities for others. It was in this climate that Toronto Board of Education Trustee Edith Groves, regarding her "Visit to Special Auxiliary Classes in American Cities," stated:

> Thirty per cent are Jewish; 30 per cent are Italian; 12.5 per cent are Negroes; 17 per cent are Slavic, leaving only about 10 per cent who are children of white American parents. It seems to me that these figures are sufficient to suggest to Canada that she guard well her ports of entry. (see Appendix to Toronto Board of Education Minutes 1919: 755)

Six years later, in 1925, Groves would put forth a motion that "the attention of the proper Federal authorities be called to the need for exercising greater vigilance at ports of entry respecting the mental standards of infant and adult immigrants" (Toronto Board of Education Minutes 1925: 205). The motion was seconded by Trustee Edmunds and was carried. The fact that trustees presumed a right to influence federal immigration authorities reveals the power that some individuals/groups could wield to the detriment of "others." At that time, dominant ideas about race were such that even non-Anglo whites were racialized.

Unfortunately, contemporary manifestations of biological racism still exist in the work of authors such as Charles Murray and Richard Herrnstein. As did their predecessors, contemporary racists produce their work under the guise of "objectivity," while their political motives are abundantly clear. For example, Gould (1994) notes that in the preface to their book, *The Bell Curve*, Murray and Herrnstein stated that "this book is about differences in intellectual capacity among people and groups and what those differences mean for America's future." He also critiques the authors' assumption that there is a single general measure of mental ability (i.e., the "g"/general factor) which "is measured reasonably well by a variety of standardized tests, best of all by I.Q. tests designed for that purpose" (as quoted in Gould 1994: 143). While Murray and Herrnstein admitted that there was only one of the three major schools of psychometric interpretation that supported their view of "g" and I.Q., they based their entire book on this theory. Using one way of measuring intelligence when we/they are aware of multiple intelligences without discussing the limitations of their theory is intentionally misleading (see Gould 1994: 143, 144). There is an error in using I.Q. tests when we know them to be culturally biased. Statistical bias may be analyzed in the *The Bell Curve* but cultural bias is not (Gould 1994: 145). Since the book's publication the biases/slants and critical academic omissions have been much criticized as racially based, yet Murray has responded by denying that race is an important factor in the book, a denial which in and of itself is necessarily questioned and critiqued by Gould (1994: 141).

New Meanings and Readings of Race

Contemporary readings of race usher in alternative/new meanings and social practices. Such readings mark a radical (but not total) shift from biology and science, that is, scientific racism. Today it is widely held that the idea of race and the practice of racism denote a conflation of class, religious and broad-based cultural and political concerns and definitions. There have emerged new social meanings of race that inform and interpret the practice of cultural racism. The new culturalized and politicized meanings of race also speak to particular ways communal differences come to be expressed (see Anthias and Yuval-Davis 1992). The complex politics of social and communal differences converge with material and economic concerns.

"Cultural racism" (Fanon 1967), as the new racism, is characterized by the re-emergence of culture in debates about races, a politicized understanding of culture, cultural production and the politics of identity. A particular focus is on the analysis of cultural processes and forms and the examination of racialized discourses and practices in the arts, media, literature and other cultural spaces and forms. As Solomos and Back (1995: 414) point out, cultural racism is about how different racisms are manifested today in definitions of citizenship, nationhood and nationalism without an overt or necessary recourse to biological inferiority. Such definitions, constructed and propagated through nationalist discourse, "organize" and institute the boundaries which currently exist; boundaries which, far from simply imposing a definition of who is or is not Canadian, imply "whose humanity *is* or *is not* greater." Such new readings of race bring to the fore questions of identity and identifications and the associated privileges of race. The wearing of *hijab* in Canadian schools, for example, or turbans in the RCMP comes to be seen by the dominant group as a challenge to what mainstream society through nationalist discourse has constructed as the "Canadian identity."

The Importance of Race Identity

Crucial to contemporary thinking and academic engagement about the race concept are questions of identity and representation. In contemporary critical race discourse, attention is drawn to the study of race as an examination of the connections between identity and practice. Race has become a study of identity and identifications, that is, questions about who we are and what we do. New forms of political identities continually use race and racial consciousness to develop and implement their progressive politics of change. These political movements mobilize around particular forms of identity (e.g., class, gender, race and sexual orientation) [see also Anthias 1992, Gilroy 1987, cited in Solomos and Back 1995: 413]. In speaking about the importance of race identity for effective political practice, the focus is on the practical use of an essence, not its mere theoretical invocation (see Spivak 1993). In other words, the politics of race identification requires some awareness and acceptance of the "risk of essence" [in this case a racial "essence"] or the "unavoidable usefulness of something that is dangerous" (Spivak 1993: 5). In more practical terms what this means is that we must be aware of the possibilities of the notion of race (like identity) and its limitation for engaging in the politics of educational and social change.

Martin (1995: 6) has argued that identity derives its meaning from what it is not, that is, from the "other." In other words, to paraphrase Stuart Hall (1991), identity is a split, dialectic and dialogic relation between the "self" and the "other." Identity implies both uniqueness (selfhood) and sameness (relations with/to others). To acquire an identity, one must be perceived to be identical to, or identify with, someone else and, at the same time, exhibit some uniqueness.

While racial identity implies being a member of a racial group, racialized identity includes becoming an active member of a racial identity group. There are important facets to the racialization of identity. We make an important distinction between *racial identity* (to have a given racial identity) and a *racialized identity* (the act of becoming or assuming an identity) [see Ibrahim 1996; Dei 1997]. Both forms of identity are important for the discussion. The invocation of a racial identity is tied to the social construction of race. To espouse a racial identity implies a uniqueness as well as a sameness with others. A recognition of the complex, dynamic and fluid nature of racial identity implies that in different historical contexts individuals and groups are racialized as different and subject to differential and discriminatory/unequal treatment. Race (like gender and class identities) is fundamental for engaging in society. Race identity influences the social and political practices in which we choose to engage. Racialized identity can emerge from a collective identification. At the collective level, there is a psychological dimension to racial identity, as in a sense of shared emotions, feelings and experiences that come with lived and received histories. Racial and racialized identities, understood in the social constructionist sense, are rooted in the material, ideological, political and historical processes and conditions of society.

There are two key questions for a discussion concerning the politics of racial and racialized identities: how do individuals and groups use identities and identifications to engage in political practice; and, how do we seek to represent ourselves as we undertake political practice for social change (see Dei and James 1998)? Answering these questions depends on the recognition of *four* interrelated concerns having to do with interrogating identity: First we have the politics of one's subjective position. That is, whatever we seek to do is a political decision that reflects desires, politics and emotional and material interests. However, an assertion of the relevance of positionality does not mean its essentialisation. Second, the specificities of the situation and contexts in which one is engaging in a specific political act are important, that is, an awareness of the context and the practice implied by the context. The situation and context influence the political act in as much as the subject influences the context of his or her political action. Third is a recognition that the contextual basis of knowledge is *practice* and *experience*. This means that, as we seek the "epistemic privilege" of personal knowledge, it ought to be understood that experience itself is in need of theorizing (see also Butler and Scott 1992; Dei 1996). A (re)theorization of experience requires a linkage to broader macro-structural forces and constraints and an exercise in self-criticality, political/personal implication and self-reflexivity. The practices of self-criticality and self-reflexivity also imply that as we seek to question the authority of the subject and reflect on the value of subjective knowledge for political action, we do so in a manner that does not paralyze the subject as a knower (see Spivak 1993). Last is an awareness of the extent of power relations and asymmetries embedded in multiple identities, that is, identities are sites of power differences. Discourses about difference are produced from sites of power, influence and control. Thus, some discourses about difference are privileged while others are seen as oppositional. This is quite evident and pervasive, for example, in Euro-American schools. The move towards anti-racist pedagogy within the schools, despite existing anti-racism policies, has not taken place. The policies are there but curriculum, school structures and educators have not shifted from the multicultural paradigm (see Rezai-Rashti 1995: 11; James 1995: 32–33). In addition, some mainstream educators view other pedagogic discourses, such as critical pedagogy, as more "acceptable" while they hold a different view of Afrocentric knowledge and Afrocentric schools. As well, when the issue of race is raised in classrooms and other educational settings the discussion often moves away from race. Again, this is not to deny the multiple identities we hold, nor to deny the effects of heterosexism, sexism, classism and ability. However, it is a common phenomenon that many students wish to avoid the questions of race, racism and race privilege, and that, purposely or not, some students shift the discussions to a more "comfortable" topic.

White as Racialized Identity

When race is discussed, an aspect/dimension least raised is whiteness and white privilege. An examination of the everyday, common-sense knowledge and practice of racism reveals the ascription of race to "others" but not to the dominant group. For example, sometimes white is racialized or ethnicized for privilege. Many times, however, white is deracialized and rendered invisible in the eyes of dominant groups. Within multiple sites and locations, a certain kind of whiteness is produced in relation to its referential "other" (see also Nestel 1996). Whiteness does not only represent itself "as a universal marker for being civilized" (Giroux 1994: 75), but also as being "raceless" (Fordham 1988).

McIntosh (1990), Roman (1993), Frankenberg (1993a), Sleeter (1994), Thomas (1994), Giroux (1997), Delgado and Stefancic (1997), among many others, speak of the necessity of comprehending whiteness as a serious intellectual project. Frankenberg (1993a: 242) stresses that interrogating whiteness is a first step in anti-racism practice when one is positioned dominantly in relations of domination. Solomos and Back (1995), while suggesting the interrogation of whiteness as a form of identity and political discourse, caution against the danger of "reifying whiteness and reinforcing a unitary idea of race" (p. 418). They call for locating any discussion of whiteness in "a particular empirical and historical context (Solomos and Back 1995: 418). In addition, as Frankenberg (1993b) has demonstrated, "social geographies of race" have varying effects on ways in which whites conceptualize themselves and each other, as well as those around them. Class will also intersect with race to construct selective memory. For example, when asked who lived in the neighbourhood or household growing up, a white, middle-class woman from the Southern U.S. had memories of a

Black family living in the neighbourhood, but did not recall the Black woman domestic worker who taught her to walk until the question of employment arose (Frankenberg 1993b: 60). White working-class women living in "quasi inte-grated" settings, indicated a greater awareness of their whiteness and different conceptualizations of people of colour (Frankenberg 1993b: 72, 74). Often, however, white people who are aware of racial oppression seem to be less aware of race privilege. Whites tend to conceptualize race, racism and racist social structures as external to them, not as elements that shape them and their reality (Frankenberg 1993b: 52).

For the purpose of our discussion, an important learning objective is the intellectual and political recognition of whiteness and how white subjectivities are racialized for preferential treatment. There is a valid intellectual challenge to rupture the equating of whiteness with "normal" and "pure" which allows the dominant group to easily assume the "mantle of invisibility" (hooks 1992).[10] Preferential treatment accorded to whites was/is also constructed differently along gender and class lines. This included the construction of white femininity which consisted of more than privilege. It was and is about the "exalting" of white women and conversely the debasement of women and men of colour. This would lead Sojourner Truth, in 1852, to state in front of a hostile audience of white women and men, "ain't I a woman" (hooks 1981). Of course, there has always been resistance to the dominant culture's racist images/portrayals of Black womanhood. The work of organizations such as the Negro Women's Club, the Canadian Negro Women's Association, the Eureka Club, as well as the UNIA speak to this.[11]

During the colonial regimes, white feminists portrayed Hindu women "as victims of barbaric cultural customs from which they needed help to escape" (Ware 1993: 129) and French photographers/painters (among other Europeans) portrayed African and Arab women as sexualized, cloistered or both. These racist photographs/paintings were also used as postcards, serving as an intru-sive mechanism to "open up" the "colonized" society to the colonizers (see Allola 1986).

The construction of white femininity was also such that white (Anglo) women during the nineteenth century were actively engaged in trying to restrict immigration, invoking the racist argument of the need to protect white woman-hood from men of colour. For example, when African-Americans from Okla-homa began settling in the Prairies, the Imperial Order of the Daughters of the Empire sent a petition to Ottawa warning that white women would become prey of Black men (see Troper 1972: 281). In this case, racially constructed notions of white femininity were used along with racially constructed notions about Black men.

As well, white women suffragettes often appropriated abolitionist dis-course to further their own cause. Using the analogy of enslavement, they either equated their "plight" to that of enslaved Africans, or stated that enslaved

African women enjoyed better conditions than did white women. "No female slave is obliged ... to resign her privileges ... of forming acquaintance, friendship ... with any individuals of her fellow slaves" (Ware 1993: 103–4).

In the nineteenth century, white male physicians and gynecologists attempted to prevent white women from intellectual pursuits, based on the ridiculous argument that it would weaken their reproductive organs and thus cause them to fail as "mothers of the Anglo-Saxon race" (see Smith-Rosenberg and Rosenberg 1972: 351). Admittedly, this attempt at control of women's lives is indeed degrading. However, there is still evident the "exaltation" of white Anglo women because they, according to white supremacist beliefs, could produce a "superior race." While gynecologists were concerned that white, middle-class women should stay at home to rest, their laundry and domestic work was left to Black and immigrant women. Similarly today, many white middle-class women have been able to work outside the home only because Black, Filipino (and some southern European) women work raising their children and cleaning their homes, under social conditions whereby adequate affordable childcare is not available for their own children.

In addition, intrusion on the reproductive rights of women of colour has also occurred. Indeed, racism has been such that whites have always attempted to control the reproductive rights of women of colour: forcing enslaved African women to have many children (hooks 1981: 39); preventing Black women domestics immigrating to Canada from bringing their families with them; the sterilizing of and testing of reproductive technologies on "Third World" women.[12]

Race and Immigration

In public discourse and official policy, nowhere is race so central as in immigration matters. The mythology assigning purity to whiteness and "carnality/sin" to Blackness would create in the white imagination a fear of a Black [or Asian] presence. This of course would lead to, among other deeds, restrictions on immigration (see Simmons 1998). The construction of whiteness during the nineteenth century created these restrictions along a racial hierarchy of Nordic, Alpine, Mediterranean, with people of colour either last or totally excluded from the list of prospective immigrants. Although historically some white groups were racialized, there was still a hierarchy of privilege based on skin colour.

Notions about race determined "who got in" and when. Thus, anti-semitic sentiment would allow the Canadian government to send Jews seeking asylum in Canada back to Europe where many would face their death (see Abella and Troper 1991: 64). Myths about racial groups were summoned to keep out those whose racially constructed "visibility" subverted/challenged white norms. As an example, the supposed inability of Blacks to adjust to the Canadian climate was used to deny them entrance to the country during the early 1900s. Conversely, some Caribbean Blacks were allowed entrance to work in Sydney,

Nova Scotia's steel plant's coke ovens because, in addition to labour concerns, it was presumed that they would withstand the hot coke ovens better than whites (see Calliste 1993/94: 135). Assimilationist arguments were also used to restrict the immigration of Indians:

> The native of India is not a person suited to this country … accustomed as many of them are to the conditions of a tropical climate, and possessing manners and customs so unlike our own people. (Mackenzie King's report on Indian immigration in 1908, in Bolaria and Li 1988: 171)

At times, economic interests allowed for non-white immigrants to enter Canada as a source of cheap labour. For example, the Chinese were brought into Canada to work on the construction of the Canadian Pacific Railway "when it was next to impossible to secure white labour" (Woodsworth 1972: 142). When labour on the railroad was no longer needed and the Chinese began to move into other areas of employment, the Canadian government imposed a series of head taxes against them (Li and Bolaria 1983: 5), and the Chinese Immigration Act of 1923 virtually excluded all Chinese from entering the country for twenty-four years (Bolaria and Li 1988: 107). As well, head taxes were imposed against South Asians (Bolaria and Li 1988: 170; Li & Bolaria 1983: 5) and a "gentleman's agreement" between Canada and Japan helped to limit the immigration of Japanese (Li and Bolaria 1983: 5; Bolaria and Li 1988: 134). The continuous journey stipulation of 1908 also kept out South Asians (Bolaria and Li 1988: 170).

In addition, numerous works (Henry et al. 1985; Das Gupta 1996; Brand 1991; Silvera 1989; Calliste 1993) have pointed to the racist/sexist stratifications regarding employment. In Canada, many Black men could only gain employment with the railroads, and these job opportunities were almost exclusively as sleeping car porters until about the 1960s (Calliste 1987: 1). Work for Black women was racialized as well. The fact that most African-Canadian women could only gain employment (or gain entry into the country) as domestics has been well documented (see Brand 1985, 1991; Silvera 1989). Roles ascribed to Black women and men did not change much from the 1700s to the 1900s. In 1763, General James Murray, first British Governor of Quebec, had requested that enslaved Africans be brought to Canada: "[W]ithout servants, nothing can be done, … and Canadians will work for nobody but themselves. Black slaves are certainly the only people to be depended upon" (Hill 1981: 7). A similar statement was made in 1911, when a white employer wrote:

> The fact is that housework has become almost impossible with regard to the whites…. There remain for us a small number [of whites] … who spoil everything…. The importation of the creoles is a benefit and

the government should favour their importation. (in Calliste 1993/94: 141–42)

Racist, sexist and classist factors came into play in the case of Chinese immigrating to Canada during the late nineteenth and early twentieth centuries. Chinese men came as unfree wage labourers or as merchants (see Satzewich 1989: 311). Racism from the white working and ruling classes was such that Chinese men were forced out of wage labour or limited to domestic service (see Satzewich 1989; Sugiman 1992: 20). With limited work opportunities, Chinese-Canadians had no choice but to start their own businesses, opportunities for such often being limited to restaurants and laundries. Even then, discriminatory laws were devised by whites, one being the city of Hamilton's by-law 73 prohibiting the establishment of laundries in areas where they already existed (see Chan 1983: 70). And Chinese women, along with Portuguese, Greek, South Asian and African-Canadian women were employed in garment factories under horrible working conditions (Chan 1983: 153). Through their fight against anti-Chinese laws and practices, Chinese-Canadian women and men were successful in winning reunification of families, enfranchisement for Chinese-Canadians, as well as improving working conditions (see Sugiman 1992: 16, 21).

Along with creating restrictions in immigration and employment, the elevation of whiteness (and corresponding debasement of Blackness) also produced a proliferation of racist popular culture. Thus, African-Canadians would find themselves in 1915 fighting to ban the racist film "Birth of a Nation" from coming to Canadian cities. The film, as described in the African-Torontonian newspaper the *Canadian Observer*, was an attempt "to degrade [Black] people, create race hatred, and cast a stigma upon the women of the Race" [1915, Sept. 18: 4]. African-Canadians were successful in banning the film in Windsor; in Toronto, they were successful in convincing Premier Hearst to issue instructions to the official censor to eliminate the most "objectionable" scenes in the film (see *Canadian Observer* 1915 [Dec. 11, Sept. 25]).

In addition, the politics of the Tarzan stories provide an interesting study of the white imagination in popular culture. As Newsinger (1986) demonstrates, Edgar Rice Burroughs, who wrote the Tarzan stories from 1911 to the 1940s, used them to comment on political events and to uphold the British empire and colonialism. Playing to the myths of the hereditarians, Tarzan's "domination" of the "jungle" was attributed to heredity and "superior breeding." The stories promoted racist violence and upheld the mythology of white superiority along with white femininity. Thus, whites could be reassured to distinguish their "humanity" from that of the "other."

Through the racist lens of the white eye, white popular culture has historically (and currently) been a tool to promote racist/sexist discourse and stereotypes. As an example, Canadian artist Benjamin West could present the image

of the "Noble Savage" contemplating "The Death of Wolfe," when in fact, no
Aboriginal was present at James Wolfe's death. This portrait, touted as "authentic," has been reproduced in school textbooks (see Francis 1993: 13–14) where
the image of a white commander (read *superior*) is centre, with that of the
"faithful savage" looking on. Similarly, Canadian photographer Edward Curtis
staged photographs depicting the "vanishing Indian," providing props (wigs,
clothing) for his models and doctoring photographs (which were also reproduced and sold as postcards) to convey *his* image of First Nations' people
(Francis 1993: 40–41).

Conclusion

Society is experienced in multidimensional ways. Racial categories constantly
shift and change. It is important therefore that political and academic practice
not reify and continue to reinforce oppressions through a bounded race concept
and racial types. All social boundaries (like social categories) need to be
challenged. As Lui (1996) points out, "marginality or otherness are required for
boundaries to have meaning" (p. 17). Resisting the closed structures of racial
categories will require that we go the "untravelled path to find common
ground" or in search of the [un]known.

At the same time it is perilous to imagine that some day and somehow the
race concept will cease to have meaning. Race is not a stable, unproblematic,
homogeneous category or entity. Today the notion of race is invoked in many
ways to reflect diverse political, ideological and historical interests. The race
concept will continue to have analytical and explanatory relevance in society.
Race has been a powerful lens for reading and interpreting society.

The term, race, has far-reaching implications in terms of how we deal with
new political cultures, social relations and conflict. At the heart of understanding new meanings of race are questions of individual and collective social
identities and the power and privileged relations embedded in our constructions
and negotiations over material and symbolic resources of society. While historical meanings of race continually shift beyond biological explanations, the
understanding of race and the practice of racism today are primarily anchored
in interpretations of culture, politics, language and religion which have emerged
to offer alternative readings of race and the processes of racialization. We
continue to work with race not because there is some unanimity in its meaning,
but rather the designation of race has powerful social effects in everyday
practices.

Similarly, as already pointed out, operating with a discursive orientation
that posits the saliency of race does not imply a denial of other trajectories of
social difference, nor a negation of the lived reality of the "simultaneity of
oppressions" (although this has been a fault, for example, of the courts; see
Duclos 1992). In addition, an analysis of the race concept in various historical
and political contexts is not to be viewed as an end in itself. An examination of

methods of resistance as well as ways in which people define themselves in various situations can lead to a greater understanding of the various manifestations of the race concept. Such an understanding can only be effective when it moves us to ever more powerful ways to resist/fight racism and racist practices, as well as other oppressive constructs.

Notes

1. While taking the position that these concepts are interrelated, we list them for clarification. We take the view that ideas are located within the person and may not be generated from a material base. "Social" refers to the relationships between and among people/s; "political" refers to choices made based on relationships of power; and "material" refers to the material consequences of these discursive practices.

2. In the context of this essay, *we* is used to refer to all who read this paper and share in the politics of anti-racism change.

3. In the context of this book, African and Black are used interchangeably to refer to people of African descent and those who identify as such.

4. The term "bature" was originally used for the first Europeans and Arabs encountered but over the years has developed to refer to anyone who is light-skinned. The term is now also used to refer to East Asians (Adebayo, personal communication, Sept. 15, 1996).

5. Such racist ideology was used to affect policies around schooling, immigration, employment, as well as everyday personal freedom. The Canadian pass laws regarding First Nations people existed well into the 1930s and 1940s and served as an example to the then government of South Africa. The violent experience of residential schooling perpetrated on First Nations people is well-known. As well, white trustees and townspeople did much to prevent African Canadian children from attending schools; this included, among other things, physical and emotional violence and the gerrymandering of school districts. African Canadians resisted through petitions, court action, community-based education and the establishment of their own schools.

6. In 1884, potlatching became prohibited under amendments to the Indian Act of 1880 (see La Violette 1973: 43).

7. See Gould 1981: 45. Similarly today, individuals working within the multicultural paradigm stress an interest in "celebrating differences," when this not only fails to address power relations in society but also degrades to the "us" and "them" scenario, where "they" are seen as "exotic," "other," "outside the norm" and thus ab-normal, less than.

8. While some may argue that the histories of polygenesis and I.Q. testing are not linked, they did contribute to creating or reinforcing a mythological hierarchy of races, which intentionally or not, reinforced hierarchies of rewards and punishments.

9. Although some mainstream scientists had come to recognize the fallacy in their previous assumptions (see Thompson 1934: 494 re. C.C. Brigham), many were still operating under racist a priori assumptions during the 1920s and 1930s (see St. Clair Price 1934 for a contemporary discussion on this). *The Journal of Negro Education*, founded in 1932, devoted numerous articles to the question of intelligence testing, providing data which dismantled myths and acting as a counter-

hegemonic source of information regarding this and other educational, economic and political issues.

10. Although, as we have seen, in the case of service workers such as domestics and railroad porters, they too become invisible, or rather, insignificant, in the white mind.

11. These are only a few of the organizations that were quite active in the early 1900s to about the 1950s and onwards. African/Black women's organizations have of course existed before and after this date (for earlier organizations and activism, see Bristow et al. 1994).

12. In the early 1990s, at a screening of the film, "La Operacion," Canadian women of colour stated that Black and First Nations women have rarely had problems finding some doctor to perform an abortion; it was almost encouraged.

Chapter Two

Your Place or Mine?
Transnational Feminist Collaboration
Sherene Razack

> The most frightening thing about imperialism, its long-term toxic effect, what secures it, what cements it, is the benevolent self-representation of the imperialist as saviour. (Spivak 1992: 781)

Recently, I, along with several other feminists of Caribbean origin located in the North, attempted to determine how a feminist research collaboration with our sisters in the Caribbean region could function to our mutual benefit. We chose to begin this discussion at the Annual Caribbean Studies Conference, held in 1996 in Puerto Rico. The setting is not incidental to how I experienced the event. Suffused with a longing to "go home," to feel at home, enjoying being with scholars who still danced, I was aware, nonetheless, of the see-saw of belonging and not belonging, of the confusion of understanding myself to be a Canadian feminist scholar as well as a Caribbean one, and of a range of difficulties inherent in either label. This chapter grew out of my attempt to thread my way through the politics of location.

What are the differences between a Caribbean feminist scholar located in the North and one located in the South? In this chapter, I want to pay attention to geography and to argue for a place-based feminism. That is to say, before we can enter into useful transnational feminist research collaborations, we will need to be conscious about how globalization scripts us, women of colour, in highly specific ways, regulating our bodies differently in the North than in the South. I propose to explore here only the regulation of women of colour feminist academics in the North. While I cannot say how such a critical understanding of my subject position would have affected the collaborative project, at the very least, it would have enabled me to be clearer about how I am/ not the same as my sisters in the South. Our differences, I maintain, are as important as our similarities. A mapping of them enables us to assess "the conditions of possibility" for each of our feminisms (Grewal 1996: 11).

I will begin by briefly discussing the meaning of transnational feminism. I note that what this means for me is that I must consider how I am implicated in the flow of ideas, labour and capital that marks the financialization of the globe. I then consider how these flows "script" me as a native informant in the Western academy, leaving me only a very small space in which to negotiate responsible scholarship. Feminist native informants occupy a specific space in the West as well and I discuss this in order to determine what an oppositional space might look like within teaching and scholarship. Moving from this general discussion to an example, I then explore what accountable feminist research practice in the North might look like in my own research. Finally I conclude that being aware of my subject position means tracing the hierarchies in which I am both subordinated and privileged. Since this is necessarily a geographically and transnationally inspired analysis, it simply means that I would bring to the table of future feminist collaborations a more careful discussion of what is and is not oppositional in feminist practice, given our geographic locations.

I cannot pursue here a comprehensive exploration of a racialized subject position such as my own (Indo-Trinidadian). Such inquiries demand an attention that I cannot offer in this research. Others have explored the various narratives that script South Asians in the United States (Grewal 1994; Dhaliwal 1994; Paur 1994; Ahmad 1992, 1994) and Indo-Caribbeans in Trinidad and in Canada (Espinet 1989, 1992, 1994). While I would urge pursuing the specificities these authors identify, as well as others, for example, academic knowledge production, Aboriginal (Crosby 1991) and African-American women (Ducille 1994), here I limit myself to exploring the general subject position of racialized immigrant women in universities in the North. I suggest below that differences within this group are often suppressed by an academy interested only in a homogenized, authentic Third World subject. The imperial politics of saving the colonized is key to the production of Authentic Third World Women. Further, those of us designated as Third World women also suppress differences among ourselves, partly in resistance, partly in accommodation. In exploring the constraints of this subject position, I want to argue for a heightened self-consciousness about the connection between place, identity and knowledge production.

Transnational Feminism

Transnational feminist practice is becoming a fashionable concept, slowly replacing the more imperial-sounding global feminism. Transnational signals first of all that locations are linked to each other in ways that demand that we as feminists pay attention to flows of capital, labour, cultural and knowledge production between nations and regions (Grewal and Kaplan 1994: Introduction). Flows can be quite abstract, however, and we don't easily trace what is happening to specific bodies caught in the drift. Gayatri Spivak conveys some of the bodies, sites and events on my mind when I think transnationally. She describes transnationalism as: "Eurocentric migration, labour export both male and female, border crossings, the seeking of political asylum, and the haunting in-place uprooting of 'comfort women' in Asia and Africa" (Spivak 1996a: 245). This movement of bodies links spaces—the border, the places of prostitution, the asylum hearing, and bodies—the migrant, the prostitute, the immigrant and the refugee. If we pursue, as Said recommended, how one social space authorizes another (Said 1993: xvii), for example, how the asylum hearing simultaneously structures the First and the Third Worlds—the former as the clean, ordered spaces of the saviours of refugees, the latter as the disordered, chaotic space of the refugees—we realize that transnational flows also structure relations among women. Racialized women become bodies to be saved by white women, although saving happens differently in each geographical location, an argument I will turn to in the central part of the chapter.

When I seek to examine my own academic subject position, and specifically here as an example, my research into women's claims for asylum, I will thus ask how I am implicated in this complex web of hegemonic relations. At the very least, a transnational approach makes it obvious that my own scholarly subject position is not so simply theorized either as one of a privileged scholar from the North, or a marginalized scholar of colour originally from the South. So much depends on the context in which I do my work, the context in which it is received, and the regulatory practices of scholarly production in both regions. In short, so much depends on the flows of capital, labour, culture and knowledge and thus on geography.

Northern Women Scholars of Colour as Native Informants

There is an important difference in material privilege between an intellectual based in the North and one based in the South.[1] On a seemingly mundane but crucial level, those of us in the North enjoy considerable access to a wide range of intellectuals, to books and to computers. The information flows these enable feed our own production and we can circulate our ideas both in the North and in the South more quickly as a result. Those of us originally from the South but based in the North can play a unique role in the exercising of this overall material privilege and the domination that it buys. We can be used, for example, as Gayatri Spivak points out, as stand-ins for the South. Our class and regional advantages notwithstanding, we can go to conferences like the UN Conference on Women at Beijing and represent "women of colour," completely eliding the differences between us and poor women of colour in the North and in the South. Ultimately, we can end up being complicitous with an agenda to show global national unity: here we all are solving our problems together (Spivak 1996b). In this role, we undermine, for instance, Southern feminists who wish to underscore the economic and social devastation the North continues to wreak on the South.

Location in the North is often assumed to be a white subject position and I want to focus here on when it is not, beginning with Spivak's point about stand-ins for the South. As she put it:

> In the untrammelled financialization of the globe which is the New International Order, women marked by origins in the developing nations yet integrated or integrating into the US or EEC civil structure

are a useful item. Gramsci uncannily predicted in his jail cell that the US would use its minorities this way. And remember Clarice Lispector's story, "The smallest woman in the world," where the pregnant pigmy woman is the male anthropologist's most authentic object of reverence? (Spivak 1996a: 262)

What I want to suggest is that, both more generally and in the realm of feminism, racialized immigrant women scholars in the North are regulated differently from our sisters in academies in the South. We are sometimes a "useful item" in globalization, playing a small part in maintaining the hegemony of Western states. In paying attention to this specificity as it emerged in the context of my research on asylum claims, I will argue that those of us immigrant women of colour in the academy in the North who work from a feminist basis find that our status depends on being able to be native informants. We are obliged to facilitate the imperial feminist politics to which Spivak alludes in my opening quote. Our role is frequently to help the First World engage in a politics of saving the women of the Third World and we decline at our peril. Caught up in the compelling discourse of saving women, we do an imperial dance. We can become the academy's most authentic object of reverence, an icon that redeems the First World, or its uncooperative native, a reviled scholar guilty of that most wretched of native sins—ingratitude. It is within these constraints that we negotiate our feminist research collaborations and strive for responsible scholarship.

Let me then clarify the term native informant as it might be applied to academic immigrant women of colour in the North. To do this, I must go a little backwards into my own academic history to the many scholars who helped me to name what I will henceforth call *our* (that is, racialized immigrant women in the academy's) native informant dilemma. In my early reading of "the toxic effect of imperialism," I encountered an article written by Julie Stevens and delivered at a conference in January 1986. Stevens, anticipating later critiques of experience as a category of scholarly inquiry (Mohanty 1991; Scott 1993), explored how knowledge of non-Western women is produced in academic work. She concluded that Western feminism "saves itself from appearing imperialistic by celebrating cultural specificity or 'difference' in the lives of non-Western women" (Stevens 1986: 100). In such scripts of cultural difference, Western women scholars present themselves as saviours, ignorant of the realities of non-Western women, but able and willing to facilitate the retrieval of their voices for the sake of global feminism. Such non-Western subjects are then depicted romantically as real women who have resisted patriarchy. Of course, Real Non-Western Women are invested with the characteristics that Western women scholars think they ought to have. A particular favourite is the tribal woman whose voice of resistance has been so lovingly retrieved for the West. This narrative tradition continues in some Western feminist political movements, for example the natural childbirth movement, where non-Western women are thought to be the true embodiment of natural womanhood, the native able to give birth squatting, and in this so unlike her Western sister. Apart from erasing from view any women of non-Western origin *in* the West, this representation keeps the binary Native/non-Native firmly in place and it reserves for Western white women the role of being the only ones to truly appreciate what the natives have to offer—birth in a squatting position (Nestel 1995).

What, then, can be the role of women from the South who are not tribal women to be saved, but are instead sisters in Northern feminist organizations or colleagues in Northern academies? At least one strong option is the role of feminist native informant. That is, we are most valued for our special capacity to assist with the retrieval of non-Western voices. Jenny Sharpe reminds us that unlike "the critic who specializes in a single period or genre of English literature, the 'Third World expert' is expected to know the heterogeneous cultures of the entire non-Western world—an assumption that ignores the relative autonomy of regional histories and cultural traditions" (Sharpe 1994: 20).

In *Woman, Native, Other*, Trinh T. Minh-ha sheds light on the academy's relentless call for the authentic ethnic voice and its corresponding demand for native informants. Trinh describes the familiar position of the Third World woman in the Northern academy:

> Now, I am not only given the permission to open up and talk, I am also encouraged to express my difference. My audience expects it and demands it; otherwise people would feel as if they have been cheated: We did not come to hear a Third World member speak about the First (?) World. We came to listen to that voice of difference likely to bring us *what we can't have* and to divert us from the monotony of sameness. (Trinh 1989: 88)

Only an authentic native will do, of course, as Trinh reminds us:

> the *unspoilt* African, Asian or Native American, who remains more pre-occupied with her/his image of the *real* native—the *truly differ-ent*—than with the issues of hegemony, racism, feminism and social change (which s/he lightly touches on in conformance to the reigning fashion of liberal discourse. [Here,] inauthenticity is condemned as a *loss* of *origins* and a whitening (or faking) of non-Western values. (Trinh 1989: 88–89)

Obviously, not all of us have standing as unspoilt natives. Skin colour and country of origin can sometimes make a difference, depending on the specific racist narratives that are in circulation. For instance, in the Canadian context of Toronto, I speculate that Caribbean Black women who cannot offer, or refuse, access to more fashionable parts of the Third World are not often hired into tenured positions.[2] Light brown women like myself, usually Asian (but very infrequently Indo-Caribbean), are less threatening in that vital first encounter of the interview. If we are especially careful to talk about diversity, and less about race, and to confine our scholarship to the South and not to North/South imperial relations, we can sometimes disarm the critics long enough to get hired. In Trinh's words, we can sometimes succeed in being the voice of difference they long to hear. Possibly the same is true of continental African women. The Black candidate without exotic appeal has, I would speculate, less lead time to make this impression and is, in any event, burdened with the "disfigured images" of mammies, matriarchs and whores (Morton 1991).

The Authentic Native Informant is permitted no specificities, no complexities with regard to class, histories or sexualities. If I attempted to present myself as an Indo-Caribbean, straight, educated working-class woman of Muslim origin, who but a small few would be able to thread their way past the stereotypes propping up many, if not most, of these labels in the popular and scholarly imagination? And who would care? The difficulty of attempting a more complex naming was brought home to me one day during a faculty discussion of a candidate's suitability for a position. A colleague admiringly praised the candidate for having the courage to write against Islam, his imagination fed by the highly publicized cases of Taslima Nasreen and Salman Rushdie. He did not consider that what would be courage in Bangladesh or Iran is, in the Western academy, grist for the mill of orientalism, a system of representations of the Islamic world as barbaric that has very specific material effects (Said 1979a). I hasten to add that candidates are *read* in these ways, their best intentions notwithstanding. However, there is a powerful pull towards the category of unspecified Third World woman. If we, potential native informants, revealed what Mary John has described as "the imbrications of one's history within History," there is a chance we will not get the job (John 1989: 50).

Undifferentiated Third World Others not only have few specificities, but we are not expected to teach about them. It would be difficult for my students to learn to read identities such as mine without the analytical tools to understand multiple locations. The transnational analysis that would help, the analysis of migration and capital flows, nationalisms, the production of ethnicities in late capitalism, the politics of nation-states, the operation of North American imperialism and its impact on knowledge production, etc., can only be taught when there ceases to be an imperial demand for exotic voices of difference. That is, what the teaching of transnational analytical frameworks powerfully disrupts is the idea that the Third World or racial minorities in the First World can be known, mastered and saved. Exploring, for instance, the debt crisis or the resultant race-ing and gendering of the labour market both in the North and the

South (see, for example, Brah 1994), students come up against their own complicity, a position that conflicts with the imperial one of needing to feel that one has done one's best for those who are culturally different.

Saving Women or Being Saved

Under the conditions of imperial knowledge production, it is undeniably difficult not to be a native informant by trying to fill one of the few designated spots (Third World expert, development scholar, etc.). Few alternative options present themselves for racialized immigrant women scholars seeking to enter the academy or to gain tenure. The options are also scant in women's studies. The dominant Western feminist project remains one in which white Western women often gain their entry into the category *citizen* through their role of taking care of their less fortunate sisters of colour. This brand of feminism has old historical roots. Antoinette Burton and Vron Ware have written of the white woman's burden in India in the nineteenth-century (Burton 1992; Ware 1992). Scholars such as Jenny Sharpe convincingly argue that the new European nineteenth century female subjectivity that we see in novels such as *Jane Eyre* is a subjectivity grounded in the moral and racial superiority of Britain as colonizer. After Jane first left Rochester and went to another town, the only real option open to her was a proposal of marriage that would have her leave England and go to the colonies as a missionary wife. There were not many other avenues for making herself anew domestically (Chow 1993: 11; Sharpe 1994: 50). In the end, she decided against the alternative and returned to Rochester. In *Home and Harem,* Inderpal Grewal also reveals this dynamic at work. Grewal traces how "universalist feminist discourses that have seen themselves only in relation to men have, in fact, been articulated in relation to other women" (Grewal 1996: 11). Suggesting that imperialism was in fact constitutive of white English women's relations with men, Grewal shows "how English feminists use the image of what they saw as victimized 'sisters' in India, for instance, in order to position themselves as English citizens when the notion of the 'citizen' was itself gendered" (Grewel 1996: 11).

Just as white women in the nineteenth century facilitated imperialism through the assumption of the role of saviour of less fortunate women, so too white women in the twentieth century, in the academy and in the female professions, can also gain a "toehold on respectability" (Fellows and Razack 1998), that is, the possibility of a public role, through the same hierarchical relations and the politics of saving. Tikka Jan Wilson describes this for the Australian context, first in colonialism and later in the development of the welfare state. Pointing out that white Australian women were deeply implicated in the disruption of Aboriginal families through child removals and other aspects of state and church intervention, she notes that they would later gain employment in the developing social welfare sector (Wilson 1996: 14). Detailing the scholarly research on this issue, Wilson reminds us of the multiple ways in which "imperialism produced a situation in which many white women of various classes, and in various ways were significant agents of the assimilation process" (Wilson 1996: 12). They were the matrons, assistants and teachers at special institutions for Aboriginal children, the welfare officers, the primary employers of Aboriginal domestic servants and the supervisors of the few Aboriginal women who could get jobs as cleaners and laundresses in hospitals (Wilson 1996: 13).

In the Canadian context, a similar development has ensued. Public life, in the form of employment opportunities available to white women has been an option in many of the same sectors to which Wilson refers. White women are overwhelmingly today's social workers and teachers, for example, and the little research there is reveals how these female professions remain saturated with imperial longing to save, civilize or educate unfortunate others (Jeffery 1994; Robertson 1994; Phillips 1995). In the academy, while white women are still locked out of the male preserves of the sciences, and most of the humanities, philosophy, political science and history, they have made some inroads into psychology, sociology and education. At least one opening has come through women's studies where early work revolved around the definition of gender without race, except in the study of oppressed Third World women. This situation has mostly changed, but in Canada, at least, it has not meant the hiring of women of colour (or critical white women for that matter) who teach from an anti-imperialist or a transnational perspective.

In sketching this picture of white women's complicity with imperialism then and now, I want to stress that the very structure of imperialism left white women very few alternatives for participating in public life. Marginalized themselves, they are able to establish their citizenship in an imperial nation in few ways other than as the caretakers of more marginalized women. It is precisely this combination of privilege and penalty that structures women in hierarchical relation to each other, and which we see in the production of racialized women as native informants in the academy. We, too, are enjoined to establish ourselves, in different ways, on the backs of other women.

One central way in which we, as aspiring native informants, become complicitous with the academy's requirement for an unspecified native, is our silence on the differences among ourselves. Some scholars have described this silence as it operates with respect to class. Taking her own example as an Indian national producing knowledge in a Western academy, Mary John noted that it is possible that middle- and upper-class Indian women make one of the smoothest transitions to the Northern academy, equipped as they are with an Indian education that already privileges the West and its epistemological frames. Asking "What happens after we come West?" she notes that such Indian women intellectuals sometimes experience a privileged intellectual space into which, however, "cracks of marginality" soon appear as racism erodes class privilege (John 1989: 60). Those of us scripted as undifferentiated Third World Others legitimately fear, however, that we will be dismissed if we begin to discuss class privilege. I know that I have shied away from discussing *both* my origins as a working-class, Indo-Caribbean woman and my recent elevation to the middle class. Confessing the former identity, I often experience the drop in status that comes from being a "kitchen Indian" from Trinidad, a "watered down, not good grade A Indian" who does not speak an Asian language and who is not sufficiently authentic (Mootoo 1993: 45). Alternatively, if I note my current middle-class status, I experience a quick dismissal as someone who does not really *know* about poor women. In either case, knowing is connected to being and to authenticity.

Significantly, although each group of women (white, Fake Indians, Real Indians, Real Africans, etc.) is powerfully drawn into imperial knowledge production in a variety of ways, our very presence in the academy is, in different ways, inevitably subversive. That women and minorities are bodies that do not belong in the hallowed halls of academe is underlined repeatedly through racial and sexual harassment in universities, and the powerful backlash against the hiring and promotion of Aboriginal and minority women.

While I believe that refusing to be native informants, and struggling to avoid saving and being saved, is what we must do, I would like to think more strategically than I have done before about what it means in practice to disrupt the hierarchies in which we are caught. To do so, I shall explore a specific part of my research on women's claims for asylum and sketch, as a beginning, the transnational approach that underpins a scholarly position with more integrity than the ones I have so far been describing.

Asylum Claims in the Basis of Gender Persecution: A Case Example

In examining the asylum claims of women fleeing spousal violence (Razack 1995), that is, those making the relatively new claim of gender-based persecution, I encountered in case after case a focus in the hearings (and in the legal literature) on the "barbaric" customs of non-Western cultures, for example, female genital mutilation (FGM). Importantly, a focus on FGM takes away attention from other forms of violence against women, and it masks how the North creates and sustains the conditions in the Third World that increase domestic violence against women, and inhibit women's means of defending themselves. I am thinking here of the North's role in devastating the economies of the South.

Asylum from gender persecution has been granted only when a culture can be inferiorized, although this in itself does not guarantee entry. We would do well here to recall that colonizers often articulated their superiority to colonized populations in gendered terms—we treat our women better (Sharpe 1994: 119). The violence perpetrated by an individual man and the social and economic constraints on the claimant's specific capacity to resist, a more stable and just basis to adjudicate such claims (but one in which the North's economic role might show up), is never considered. For example, as I discussed elsewhere (see Razack 1995 for a full discussion and documentation of the following cases) in the widely reported case of Khadra Farah, a Somali woman whose husband was extremely violent both towards her and the children, female genital mutilation (FGM) became the focus of the case effectively eclipsing spousal violence. Farah testified that her husband was a powerful man who had on his side Somali law in which fathers gain custody of the children in the event of divorce. Her husband had already successfully abducted her son. Farah claimed that were she and her daughter to be returned to Somalia, her daughter would be subjected to FGM, as she herself had been at the age of eight. FGM helped, I would suggest, to transform the situation of a man oppressing a woman to the point of persecution from an ordinary case into an extraordinary one. Note here the way patriarchal assumptions are directly sustained by racist ones: ordinary sexual violence is permissible, even routine; extraordinary violence, the point at which we agree to cry "stop," and grant asylum, is violence inflicted by the natives upon their women.

My work on asylum claims, and its imperial structure, became deeply personal when I encountered descriptions of women like myself (and not like myself); that is, Indo-Trinidadian women, whose flight from violent abusive men was inevitably framed as a flight from a dysfunctional culture in which men were unusually violent, and women unusually passive (see, for example, Savi's and Indra's case in Razack 1995) I could not counter, as I longed to do, that the men of my culture were not more violent towards women than were Canadian men. Wanting neither to condone the violence nor demonize the culture, I was caught, as so many Aboriginal women and women of colour have been, between a rock and a hard place (Razack 1994). In any event, I was not a credible enough Third World informant, having specialized in Canadian studies and having been too long off the boat, both of which "white" me and mark me as inauthentic.

What then are my options in reporting this research? My difficulties are manifest when I consider the dominant feminist tools of analysis on which I could draw. When gender-based harm is understood only in terms of what men do to women, and the list of wrongs centres around sexual violence, my only feminist role is an imperial one—except that on this score I cannot speak with the cultural authority of a white feminist. Hence, I *must* be a kind of native informant, if domestic violence done to the bodies of women with skins and cultures like mine are to come into view. That is, from my privileged cultural insider position, I can say with confidence that sexual violence *does* routinely occur in my culture and hope that, for the sake of the asylum seeker, I have not whited myself so much as to be disbelieved. A native informant ceases to be a native informant when she fails to tell the academy (and other elite institutions, such as legal fora) what it wants to hear. My knowledge claims can be easily dismissed as fake, inauthentic and non-feminist (see the examples given by Homa Hoodfar in Fellows and Razack 1994: 1070).

Northern feminists of colour are in the classic double bind. We need to protest vigorously against FGM, or against specific Islamic regimes guilty of crimes against women, or against violent Indian men, but in doing so we fit snugly into a racist agenda. This constraint may not occur in the same way for our sister scholars in the South itself, where other difficulties attend such struggles. For us in the North, the furor over FGM, Islam and asylum claims of women fleeing barbaric cultures function as a kind of internal policing of borders. It is intended to remind us of who is civilized and who is not. Further, Northern feminists are not likely to give up their preoccupation with FGM because such a move would endanger their own precarious hold on the academy as citizens engaging in a proper defence of the social and moral order—an affirmation, as it were, of the meaning of whiteness.

Towards Integrity

Can those of us wanting to resist being taken up as Third World informants choose between the story of sexism and the story of racism? Can we abstain from naming the violence and its multiple sources? If the answer is no, what language would we use to communicate such complexities and how would we be heard? Grewal suggests that in her teaching she assists her students to make transnational linkages, for example, about fundamentalism, by encouraging them to examine religious formations in the United States and elsewhere (1996: 19). I endorse this comparative approach but often find that it is less than persuasive given the stranglehold that orientalist images have both in the popular and scholarly imagination. My students simply do not believe that there is anything so barbaric in Christian-Anglo culture as the wearing of the veil or FGM, and neither does the Immigration and Refugee Board. Clearly this is also the case among many white North American feminists as well as some North American feminists of colour (Grewal 1996: 12), who have jumped into the fray to save immigrant women from FGM with an alacrity that testifies to the way FGM, as the great signifier of Third World barbarism, confirms First World superiority. Comparatively less energy is forthcoming on issues such as Third World debt, immigration head taxes or the police shootings of Black youth.

How then do we racialized immigrant women actually speak and write of these issues in the North? Clearly, we will have to pay close attention to our specific reception in the academy, to the import our words have and to the strength of the imperial feminist politics that surround us. As hard as it may be, in some cases, this may mean we stop speaking and writing about FGM or barbaric Islamic regimes for awhile, until we can better prepare the ground for a more critical and nuanced reading of these issues. This, of course, is easier said than done in the context of asylum claims.

I endorse a methodology that begins with an increased vigilance about transnational flows as they shape the lives of the women we speak of (and always for) and as they shape ourselves. It is a methodology that pays attention to specificity. Imperialism demands that we understand women either as victims or agents, as saviours or as saved, but not as complicated subjects acting within several hegemonic systems. Our task is therefore to materialize women from the South, or racialized women in the North for that matter, *and ourselves*, as real women but not in the way of authentic militant tribals, for example, or as women beaten down by barbaric or culturally dysfunctional regimes, religions and cultures. Instead, we focus on how women are embedded in several hegemonic systems.

An important point of entry is to examine hierarchical relations among women. For instance, in noting that feminists of the First World gain their status and their careers from saving women of the Third World, we are recognizing how the status of one group of women *relies on* the subordination of another group of women, and how both groups are produced in the capitalist, imperial and patriarchal politics of the academy to have differently limited options. In further differentiating, as I have here, the unique supporting role in imperialism available to racialized immigrant women, we can map the different ways in which hegemonic systems produce subjects.

To accept the position of native informant and to fail to note the difference in social space (John 1989) between my own position as an academic in the North and other immigrants/migrants/asylum seekers is to be complicitous with elites who gain from the idea of an undifferentiated Third World Other who can be known and managed. Analytical frameworks that begin with hierarchical relations among women are not of course new, either among white feminists or feminists of colour. The ways in which women are differently implicated in the processes of capital accumulation, for example, were explored a decade ago by Maria Mies in *Patriarchy and Accumulation on a World Scale* (1986). Mies pointed out then that women are "both divided and connected by commodity relations" and she saw that an understanding of patriarchy as limited to what men do to women masks hierarchical divisions based on class that sustains patriarchy in the first place (Mies 1986: 3). Relatively inattentive to race and to the micro-sites at which hierarchical relations are lived, Mies' concern with capital accumulation nevertheless introduces the idea of hierarchies among women, an opening taken up more recently by other white feminists scholars, notably Cynthia Enloe (1989; 1993), Anne McClintock (1995) and Ann Stoler (1995) and by numerous scholars of colour (Collins 1990; Grewal and Kaplan 1994). Although they each pay varying degrees of attention to how women oppress women, such scholars have produced historical work on what Black feminist Patricia Hill Collins first called "the matrix of domination" (1990: 229). Collins noted that the matrix of domination contains few pure victims or oppressors and that "each individual derives varying amounts of penalty and privilege from the multiple systems of oppression which frame everyone's lives" (1990: 229).

If we are to have any hope of moving beyond complicity to responsibility, it lies in a micro tracing of the interlocking systems in which we are embedded. An example of such work can be found in those feminist scholars who have considered the issue of reproduction as a transnational, stratified system; that is, as a system in which the reproductive futures of one group of women requires devaluing the futures of another group of women (Ginsburg and Rapp 1995: 3). Shellee Colen, who developed the concept of stratified reproduction explains it this way:

> By *stratified reproduction* I mean that physical and social reproductive tasks are accomplished differentially according to inequalities that are based on hierarchies of class, race, ethnicity, gender, place in a global economy, and migration status and that are structured by social, economic and political forces.... The hiring of West Indian childcare labor in the United States, which linked New York City and the English-speaking Caribbean in the 1970s and 1980s, opened a window on a transnational system of stratified reproduction in which global processes are evident in local, intimate, daily events, and in which stratification itself is reproduced, as childcare occurs across class lines, kin lines, and oceans. (Colen 1995: 78)

I quote Colen at length to illustrate the features of this transnational approach that incorporates interlocking systems and the notion of complicity. We could not understand West Indian childcare workers without understanding their white female employers. Further, both groups of women are produced in a global economy that relies on race, class and gender subordination. Gender, sexual, class and racial norms all combine in site-specific ways to both produce and sustain the positions of various women. Without heterosexuality, for example, one cannot imagine childcare being organized as the exclusive responsibility of women. The debt crisis and its antecedents in colonialism have left Caribbean women with no choice but to seek work in the countries of the bankers. North American women negotiate their own reproductive futures in a context of inadequate childcare options or flex-time. Colen takes her work beyond the macro level, to how these relations are lived by both groups of women. When middle-class women as employers of Black domestic workers discipline themselves to ignore the fact that their domestic workers are also mothers, when they internalize middle-class norms of childrearing and gender roles for professional women that requires the economic and social arrangements Colen describes, and when racial discourses handily sustain the idea that a Black domestic worker is not the same kind of mother, we see the many levels at which hegemonic systems make subjects.

Middle-class or economically advantaged women in the North complicitous in these arrangements cannot then champion a feminist politics that begins with migration flows and economic processes without first recognizing our complicity. This is why a central aspect of a transnational feminist approach is its attention to complicity. How embedded are we in the arrangements we describe? Ginsburg and Rapp recommend that we begin to trace this by focusing on the "processes through which hierarchies are made to appear inevitable" (Ginsburg and Rapp 1995: 3). What stories do we tell ourselves that explain why domestic workers come from the South? In tracing these patterns, we will find ourselves as dominant and subordinate. Significantly, as Ginsburg and Rapp remind us, there are then no straightforward oppositional positions. There is only a combination of accommodation and opposition (1995: 11). When the tracing of multiple hegemonic systems leaves us with a heavy sense of futility, understanding that there is accommodation and opposition perhaps enables us to see a ray of hope. For it is in working out (but not becoming resigned to) the multiple roles we have that we can better calculate when a specific political response is likely to be effective or not. Questions of strategy are better answered when we begin to unpack multiple systems. To return to Colen's example, it is not oppositional to refuse to hire Caribbean women as domestic workers, for this would do little to interrupt the macroeconomic processes underpinning the hierarchy between women that is evident here. Moreover, for obvious reasons, this option is not one Caribbean women are likely to support. Instead, those of us positioned to hire domestic workers have to work on several levels at once—paying fair wages, fighting for better conditions of immigration, for forgiving Third World debt, etc. Most of all, interrogating hierarchical relations should at least make clear how our own privileges are intertwined with our penalties, and how both are structured on the backs of other women; in engaging in struggle to change this situation, we do so first of all to save ourselves.

Applying this methodology to my research on asylum claims, I would need to track what produces Southern women as refugees and those of us in the North as their saviours—both the imperial kind and the native informant kind. I would need to examine when, and to what extent, my own role as a feminist scholar reproduces these hierarchies rather than disrupts them. In so doing, I must be clear how paying attention to the specificities (the histories, flows, nationalisms, etc.) is paying attention to myself. This is not because I am the same as a refugee woman, but because we are each constrained, differently and unequally, by the same systems. The forces that compel me to speak in certain ways, and to be heard by others, sometimes speaking for, sometimes speaking about, the Third World, are the same ones that demand that asylum seekers present themselves as victims to be saved by generous Westerners. If it is clear that I cannot simply walk away because the oppressive forces in their lives shape my own, it is equally evident that I cannot make my career by unproblematically pleading our cases as women oppressed in patriarchy, or under imperialism, or under capitalism. Just as refugee women are not straight-forwardly victims or agents, so too I, as a feminist scholar, cannot position myself in either of these categories. I will have to find a way to explore interlocking systems as they structure women in hierarchical relation to each other. And I will have to explore this in terms of my own subject position as knowledge producer. I have tried to do so in this chapter through an examination of the production of racialized immigrant women as native informants and accomplices in the imperial enterprise.

This chapter began with my wish to arrive at the table of transnational feminist collaboration with a better understanding of my own subject position as a feminist scholar of colour originally from the South but located in the North. If I were to be at that table today, I would see my goal as the practice of what I referred to at the beginning of the chapter as place-based feminism. My nostalgia, homesickness and urge to connect notwithstanding, I would have to begin with what I share and don't share with my feminist sisters in the South. I might share a country of origin and a culture, and in a general way, I share the subordination of being racialized in a white supremacist world. But the micro-processes of this racial positioning are different, depending on class, colour, sexuality, physical and mental ability, and geographic location. In this article, I have mainly addressed the latter. I conclude that to be of the North is often, though not always, to enjoy a greater access to resources (information technology, books, access to other scholars, better material conditions). Within this material base, to be in the belly of the beast, as the North is sometimes described, means that feminists of colour can only have credibility as native informants who will help the North to reconfirm its own superiority as saviours of less-developed peoples. We can only resist this complicitous role through a critical understanding of how we are positioned in transnational flows of ideas, labour and capital. The discussion between feminists of colour in the North and those of the South must begin with the processes of globalization in this new international world order. It will not be enough to gravely discuss the increasing economic hardships that drive the people of the South northwards, or the increasingly harsh disciplining of migrant bodies in the North. We will need to examine how we, as racialized feminist activists and knowledge producers, are implicated in these flows differently from our sisters in the South. My aim has been to provide a basis for this collaborative discussion.

Notes

1. My thanks to Honor Ford Smith for always insisting on this point in conversations.
2. I cannot document this, but at the end of 1997, neither York University nor the University of Toronto had more than one or two African women as tenured faculty.

Chapter Three

"The Hindu Woman's Question"
Canadian Nation Building and the Social Construction of Gender for South Asian–Canadian Women
Enakshi Dua

Recently, a central issue in anti-racist theory has been to identify the links between the projects of nation-building, discourses of race and the institutional manifestations of racism.[1] In this context, Balibar (1991) and Miles (1989) have argued that the social construction of the nation-state is central to understanding the institutional forms of systemic discrimination in society. As these theorists point out, there are two dimensions by which there exists a potential for an articulation between nationalism and racism. The first concerns the processes by which a sense of the "imagined community" is generated and reconstructed within the nation-state. The second concerns the processes by which the state permits and organizes the recruitment of labour from outside the nation-state in order to affect its central role as the guarantor of the reproduction of the capitalist mode of production. As Miles (1989) demonstrates, it is the contradiction between these two dimensions that can give rise to institutional forms of racism, particularly in allocating migrants from colonized countries to unequal sites in class formations.

In Canada, recent research has pointed to the interrelationship between Canadian nation-building and the discourse of race. Researchers such as Ward (1978), Roy (1989), McLaren (1990) and Valverde (1991) have shown that Canadian nation-building and its concomitant moral order were tied to the discourse of racial purity. The social construction of Canadian nationalism was premised on the notion that certain races were suited or unsuited for citizenship. Thus, Canadian nation-building had a clearly racial and ethnic discourse, as it favoured Anglo-Saxons both in terms of skin colour and social organization.

Furthermore, recent feminist research has shown that Canadian nation-building and its attendant discourse of racial purity has had a significant impact on the social organization of sexual and gender relations for Anglo-Saxon women. As Valverde (1991, 1992) and Iacovetta (1998) demonstrate, the discourse of racial purity was intimately tied to the discourse of social purity, which regulated morality, sexuality, gender and family relations for Anglo-Saxon and other European women. These works suggest that nation-building with its associated racial politics played an important role in shaping sexual and gender relations in Canada. In particular, Canadian nation-building was tied to the social construction of Anglo-Saxon women as "mothers of the race."

However, missing in these bodies of work is the impact of Canadian nation-building and its discourses of racial and sexual purity on the social construction of sexuality, gender and family relations for Asian-Canadian women. In this chapter, beginning from the premise that experiences with gender are not universal, but vary according to class, race and ethnicity, I begin to explore the specific ways in which gender has historically been constructed for South Asian–Canadian women. The presentation is based on a larger research project that investigates a public debate that took place between 1910 and 1915 concerning whether women from South Asia should be allowed to migrate to Canada, a controversy popularly referred to as the "Hindu Woman's Question." Virtually all sectors of Canadian society took part in this debate. During this period, members of the Canadian public, politicians, newspapers, women's groups and religious organizations all debated whether or not "Hindu women"[2] should be allowed to enter Canada. The issue also captured international attention—from the British government, the colonial government in India and anti-colonial activists in India. The debate has been recorded in a variety of Canadian, British and Indian sources.

This chapter is an initial exploration of the ways in which late nineteenth-century and early twentieth-century Canadian nation-building and its concomitant racial politics discursively constructed notions of what constituted gender for South Asian–Canadian women. The presentation is based on reports concerning the "Hindu Woman's Question" in *The Victoria Daily Colonist* (Victoria). The *Daily Colonist* was chosen for the first stage of research, as British Columbian newspapers offered the most detailed coverage of the controversy around Asian migration.

The focus of this essay will examine the debates on the "Hindu Woman's Question" to determine how Canadians discursively constructed the category of "Hindu woman." In order to analyze the development of this discourse, I will employ Billig's (1987) use of rhetorical analysis. Billig has pointed to the importance of not only understanding metaphors and language, but of understanding the construction of arguments. As he suggests, to understand a political text, it is necessary to understand its argumentative context. Thus, I will pay attention to the ways in which both sides in the debate (those in favour and those opposed to South Asian women's migration to Canada) put forward their positions and how these positions are juxtaposed either implicitly or explicitly against counter-arguments. As we shall see, while "Canadians" were divided on this question, through debating the advantages and disadvantages of allowing women from South Asia to enter Canada, both sides formed a racialized and gendered understanding of the category of "South Asian–Canadian woman." Thus, the "Hindu Woman's Question" illuminates the ways in which South Asian–Canadian women have been racialized and gendered within the Canadian nation-state.

Canadian Nation-Building and Asian Migration: 1850–1920

Asian migration to Canada was shaped by the contradictory demands of capitalist expansion and nation-building. Migration from China began around 1850 (Bolaria and Li 1988), followed by migration from Japan and South Asia. This was an important period in Canadian history, as a nation-state began to emerge out of a colonial formation. It was a period of capitalist expansion in agriculture and industry. The growth in commodity production led to an increased demand for labour.

The entry of Asian migrants was clearly linked to the demand for cheap wage labour. It is in this period that the Canadian economy would make an uneven transition from a staples economy dominated by the fur trade and fisheries to a peripheral capitalist economy dominated by agriculture and industrial production. As Laxer (1973, 1989) and Naylor (1975) have shown, the focus of the Canadian state's economic policy in this period was a system of high tariffs designed to ensure the survival of industrial capitalism in central Canada. The tariff policy was supported by immigration and transportation policies devised to settle the West with a white settler class involved in the production of agricultural commodities for world markets. Crucial to the state's economic policy was the construction of the railways, in order to transport labour power and consolidate a national market in Canada. Together, these forces created a demand for labour.

As Canadian governments experienced difficulty attracting enough British and European migrants, they began to allow limited migration from Asia. Thus, in the second half of the nineteenth century more than 50,000 men from Asia would be admitted to Canada. However, from the very beginning these men were defined as "temporary" workers rather than potential citizens of Canada. Throughout these years, successive governments strictly regulated the entry of Chinese, South Asian and Japanese men according to labour market needs. At the same time, the state enforced differential residency and citizenship status for Asian immigrants[3] (Bolaria and Li 1988; Raj 1980).

This differential residency and citizenship status was located in the post-colonial project of Canadian nation-building. As a white settler nation, the Canadian nationalist project was based on two dimensions: first, the marginalization of indigenous peoples in relation to the new nation-state, an historical process that was consolidated through the Indian Act (Bourgeault 1988; Dickenson and Wotherspoon 1992; Ng 1993; Stasiulus and Jhappan 1995); second, Canadian nation-builders faced the challenge of creating a sense of identity—an "imagined community"—among the new arrivals. As Balibar (1991) and Miles (1989) have pointed out, nation-building and the construction of an imagined community have often been based on the construction of racial and linguistic differences. In Canada, the creation of an imagined community hinged on the notion that Canada was, in the words of John A. Macdonald, "a white man's country" (Government of Canada, House of Commons Debates,

June 19, 1869: 887). This notion of Canada as a white man's country succeeded in simultaneously marginalizing indigenous peoples from the nation-state and unifying European newcomers to Canada. Thus, while capitalist expansion created a demand for wage labour, the contradictory forces of Canadian nation-building meant that the incorporation of wage labour was racialized in important ways.

This discourse of Canada as a "white man's country" would define the relationship of Asian migrants to the newly emerging nation-state. As Valverde (1991), Roy (1989), Ward (1978) and Warburton (1992) demonstrate, the notion of an imagined community was also premised on a racist discourse of Chinese, Japanese and South Asian peoples.[4] According to this discourse, Asian people were incapable of assimilating into "Canadian" society. As the *Victoria Daily Colonist* argued in an editorial:

> [The] objection to the Asiatic is that he does not and cannot assimilate with the white race.... More centuries than anyone of us can say have erected barriers between the two great divisions of the human race, and they cannot be pulled down with impunity. (*Victoria Daily Colonist,* March 9, 1912)

Moreover, as the basis for the imagined community in Canada was whiteness, Asian migrants were seen as a threat to the very process of nation-building. Thus, another editorial claimed:

> Under most conditions it will be difficult to blend the various races now here into a wholesome Canadian citizenship. To admit the Oriental, especially before a political and ethical reserve is built up in Canada, would make the task of Canadian citizenship almost a hopeless problem. (*Victoria Daily Colonist,* February 20, 1912)

As the discourse of racial purity became tied to notions of citizenship and nation, the Canadian government justified its policy of restricting the entry of Asians and maintaining their differential status. This meant that, despite pro-settlement policies and a shortage of wage labour, Asian men were defined as temporary workers. Immigration laws and other legislation implemented this temporary status. Asian men were unable to vote, were denied naturalization and were legally prohibited from owning certain kinds of property. Moreover, while all other migrants to Canada were allowed and encouraged to sponsor the immigration of their families, Asian men were forbidden to sponsor spouses and children. This restriction was enforced through a variety of regulations that differed according to nationality—ranging from head taxes, to the "continuous journey" stipulation, to outright prohibitions (Bolaria and Li 1988). But while different measures were employed to regulate the migration of women from

China, Japan and South Asia,[5] in all three cases these measures operated to restrict female migration. Thus by 1912 there were no more than 2,000 Asian women in Canada (Bolaria and Li 1988).

By the turn of the century, Chinese, Japanese and South Asian men began to challenge the restrictions on the migration of their spouses. In the case of the South Asian community, the issue became a matter of public debate when two men initiated a court case that challenged the restrictions imposed on the immigration of their spouses.[6] In 1911, Bhag Singh and Balwant Singh, residents of Canada returning from a trip to India, left Calcutta with their wives and children. Despite trying in Calcutta, Rangoon and Hong Kong, they were unable to secure passage to Vancouver. They were able to purchase tickets from Hong Kong to Seattle, but were denied entry into Canada through the United States. Finally, in 1912, after embarking from Hong Kong to Canada, they arrived in Vancouver. Since the men previously had been landed, they were allowed to enter Canada. However, the women and children were detained and ordered deported (Johnston 1989). At this point the two men, with the assistance of the South Asian community, filed a court case—challenging the restrictions on the entry of their spouses.

"The Hindu Woman's Question" quickly became a subject of heated public debate. "Canadians" were divided over whether South Asian women should be allowed to migrate to Canada. Members from virtually all sectors of Canadian society would participate in the debate[7]—members of the public, politicians, women's organizations, trade unions and religious groups. Moreover, the debate drew national and international attention as it captured the interest of eastern (including Quebec) and western Canada, as well as England and India.

One of the most interesting and salient aspects of this debate is that the question of South Asian women migrating into Canada was limited to the entry of the spouses of Asian men already residing in the country. This premise reflected and reinforced existing immigration policies. While single women from certain European countries were allowed to enter as independents and in some periods were encouraged to do so (Van Kirk 1981; Roberts 1979),[8] single Asian women or those Asian women with spouses elsewhere were prohibited from entering Canada. It is important to note that the South Asian community failed to address these barriers, as South Asian men focussed their challenge solely on the legislative prohibitions against the entry of their spouses—not on the prohibitions against the entry of all South Asian women. Thus, the gendering of South Asian women in Canada was limited to that of a spouse. It was in their role as wives of South Asian men that South Asian women were seen as either dangerous or desirable to Canadian society.

Racial Dominance and South Asian Women:
Linking Gender, Communities and Nation-Building

The overwhelming majority of groups and individuals recorded as speaking on this matter were opposed to the admittance of South Asian women. According to these writers and speakers, "The Hindu Woman Question" was one of the most serious questions to confront Canadian society. As one observer stated:

> The question of admitting Hindu women is one of the gravest which has confronted the Province for some time and I hope that the Government will not take a step which will be a matter of regret possibly for all time. (*The Victoria Daily Colonist,* February 20, 1912)

According to these individuals and groups, allowing South Asian women entry into Canada threatened not only the entire process of Canadian nation-building, but the process of empire-building. Thus Martin Burrell, federal minister for agriculture, stated in a speech to the Canadian Club in Toronto:

> The question of Hindu women immigration is not only a great question with us in British Columbia; it is the dominant question of the whole empire. It is a question of ultimate dominance between the Far East and the West, of the final supremacy of the yellow or the white. (*Victoria Daily Colonist,* March 4, 1912)

According to these speakers and writers, the question of whether South Asian women should be allowed in Canada was centrally tied to the racial politics of the nation-state, as the issue became a matter of the economic and social dominance of the "white race." The question that arises is: why was the migration of South Asian women more threatening than the migration of South Asian men? What was it about South Asian women's racialized gender that threatened to tip the balance in the contest for "ultimate dominance between the Far East and the West"? How was it that the migration of Asian women was connected not just to Canadian nation-building but also to the British Empire? In answering these questions, we see a layered interaction between race and gender.

In the ensuing debate, the primary reason that South Asian women were seen as a threat was in their perceived relationship to South Asian men. Several recorded speakers argued that the presence of South Asian women would encourage increased migration from India and other parts of Asia. For example, Frank Andrews, in a public meeting in Victoria, argued:

> Let the wives in, and in a few years no one could tell the results. Either Japan or China, if emigration was unrestricted, would flood the country [and would lead to] a gigantic problem such as the United States

has to face in their Southern States. (*The Victoria Daily Colonist,* February 10, 1912)

Another speaker, ex-British army officer Major C.B. Simonds, at the same meeting argued that:

> The admittance of the wives of Hindus into this Province must be prohibited at any price … if British Columbia allows Hindu women to come their presence will create a sociological problem which will be well nigh impossible of solution. If they are allowed in, the immigration of them will be impossible to control or stop. I question if any government would be able to solve the problem. *(Victoria Daily Colonist,* February 20, 1912)

The Canadian government shared the view that easing immigration restrictions for South Asian women would increase the migration of South Asian men. According to *The Victoria Daily Colonist,* F.C. Blair, who was appointed as a special commissioner to investigate the subject of immigration of Hindu women into Canada, in his report to the federal government held the same position:

> It is understood that the Report is adverse to opening the door to the Hindu people, and states that the admission of the wives of men now in Canada will be a step in the direction of reopening the whole issue. The contentions of Sundar Singh and his associates are not upheld. (*Victoria Daily Colonist,* February 29, 1912)

It is clear that these writers and speakers felt that increased migration from Asia would challenge the basis for the "imagined community" in Canada, and they elaborated on how the entry of South Asian women presented a challenge for Canadian nation-building. Several writers and speakers argued that the danger of South Asian migration was that it would lead to the establishment of ethnic communities. The editors of *The Victoria Daily Colonist* on March 9, 1912, predicted that "[i]f they were permitted to come in limited numbers they would set up communities distinct from white communities." As the imagining of the Canadian nation was based on the rhetoric of Canada as a "white man's country," the emergence of ethnic communities was not only undesirable, but furthermore undermined the racial basis on which Canadian nation-building was founded.

Significantly, these Canadians regarded the arrival of South Asian women within the nation-state as the catalyst that would promote the emergence of ethnic communities. These speakers and writers assumed that such communities were not simply the result of male migration but were the consequence of female South Asian migration. For example, in a debate in the Victoria local of the National Council of Women, Mrs. Andrews is reported to have argued

> that the admission of their wives would mean a Hindu colony in British Columbia. The danger that this province, unless measures were taken to prevent it, would become the home not of British people but of Oriental was pointed out. (*Victoria Daily Colonist,* January 23, 1912)

In other words, according to the majority of Canadians, the entry of South Asian women was particularly problematic in that *as women* these migrants would facilitate the emergence of ethnic communities.

women

Importantly, it is in establishing the connection between South Asian women and South Asian communities that the gender dimensions of the debate begin to crystallize. In this discourse we can see how the gender of South Asian women (and indeed other Canadian women) becomes linked to their communities. First, the entry of South Asian women was feared because it would lead to South Asian men maintaining a permanent residence in Canada. Second, it was assumed that it was the presence and the labour of women that led to the creation and maintenance of communities (and nations). Notably, the gendering of South Asian women as creators of ethnic communities paralleled the gendering of Anglo-Saxon women as reproducers of the nation. However, while the work of Anglo-Saxon women in reproducing the Canadian nation was to be valued, South Asian women were seen as a menace to that same nation—threatening to spawn the kinds of communities that would imperil the nation-building project.

creators of ethnic communities / reproducers of the nation

Writers and speakers went on to explain why it was that the presence of South Asian women would facilitate the emergence of ethnic communities. First, they suggested that the presence of the women would lead to alternative ways of organizing social and family life. Major Simonds asserted in an article that:

> The question will arise, are the wives and families to come here under the Indian social laws ... as they are exercised among various sects, or are they to come under our system? ... Polygamy is a part of the sociological conditions of the Hindu, so the question comes up as to whether all or only one or two wives of each person is to be admitted ... with the advent of family life among the Indians here how are the laws to be administered among them? Are they to have native leaders and the joint magistrate system, or will the matter be left in the hands of the police? These are all questions to be considered before Hindu women are to be allowed to come to British Columbia. (*Victoria Daily Colonist,* February 9, 1912)

Indian social laws / Polygamy

Similarly, H. Hall argued at a public meeting in Vancouver that allowing Hindu women to enter into Canada

> would be promoting polygamy in their midst. Besides they had no
> right to split up Hindu family life and leave one wife in India and bring
> another here. There was no morality in that. (*The Victoria Daily
> Colonist,* February 10, 1912)

In making the argument that South Asian women facilitated the emergence
of ethnic communities by introducing alternative ways of organizing family
life, these writers further racialized and gendered South Asian women. Significantly, underlying this argument was the acknowledgement that the social basis
for Canadian nation-building was indeed racialized—that Canadian nation-
building was premised on a racialized definition of a moral and social order,
one that was defined as "Anglo-Saxon." In addition, this discourse gendered
South Asian women; underlying this reasoning was the assumption that it was
women who were responsible for maintaining social and cultural mores, that it
was women who were the bearers of tradition. According to the majority of
Canadians in this period, it was as bearers of South Asian social mores that
South Asian women posed a greater threat to Canadian society than South
Asian men.

Along with the fear of a cultural challenge to Anglo-Saxon "traditions"
was the fear of the sexuality of South Asian women, particularly of their
fertility. Underlying the fear of being overrun by "Asiatics" was the fear of the
supposedly unrestricted fertility of South Asian women. Thus, an editorial in
The Victoria Daily Colonist claimed that:

> If they were permitted to come in unlimited numbers, they would in a
> short time so occupy the land that the white population would be a
> minority. If British Columbia is not kept "white," Canada will become
> Asiatic. (*Victoria Daily Colonist,* March 9, 1912)

Furthermore, some writers and speakers objected to the acceptance of
South Asian women on the grounds that the products of their much-discussed
fertility—their children—could not be assimilated into Canadian society. As
Frank Andrews argued in a public meeting in Victoria:

> White peoples' children, of whatever race, could be put through the
> schools, and made into Canadians; not so with the Hindus or other
> Asiatics. (*Victoria Daily Colonist,* February 10, 1912)

Similarly, Charles Tisdall, a member of British Columbia's legislature and one
of the more rabid advocates of Asian exclusion, stated in a speech to the
legislature:

Quite recently a Hindu delegation approached the Government with a request to be allowed to bring in their wives and children. The experience of other parts of the Empire have not been satisfactory in this respect.... These and other Asiatic races can never assimilate with us, and I think the government should ... do all in its power to protect us from them. (*Victoria Daily Colonist,* January 11, 1912)

To summarize, newspaper reports on the "Hindu Woman's Question" in the *Daily Colonist* suggest that the majority of Canadians opposed the entry of South Asian women into Canada. According to those people who spoke and wrote about the question, the entry of South Asian women threatened the very process of nation-building. For these Canadians, the threat South Asian women posed was located in their gender as well as their race. The most striking feature of this debate was that it was limited to those South Asian women who were spouses or children of South Asian men residing in Canada. The question was not whether South Asian women should be allowed to migrate, but whether the wives and daughters of South Asian men who were residents of Canada should be allowed to migrate. (I will return to this point.) South Asian women were seen as a threat to Canadian society because their presence would facilitate the permanent settlement of South Asian men, and thus the emergence of South Asian communities. In the context of the imagined community—the white man's country—the presence of such communities was defined as a threat to the nation-state.

South Asian Women, Patriarchy and Morality: "So That a Man Could be Seen at His Best"

Not all members of Canadian society opposed the entry of South Asian women. Some writers and speakers spoke out in favour of allowing South Asian women to enter Canada. While these individuals were definitely a minority, they formed a vocal minority. A clear pattern can be identified among those who supported a less restrictive policy. Those favouring the admittance of South Asian women were often members of women's groups (especially the Imperial Order of the Daughters of the Empire [IODE] and the Ottawa office of the National Council of Women), adherents of certain religious organizations, and residents of eastern Canada, especially Ontario and Quebec. But what is most notable here is that, despite their position, these speakers and writers shared a common world view with those who opposed the entry of South Asian women.

The support of many of these speakers and writers came from their concern over the international dimensions of the debate. Nationalists in India had begun to use the prohibitions against South Asian women entering Canada as an example of the unfairness inherent in the Commonwealth system and the unjustness of British Rule in India[9] (Huttenback 1976; Johnston 1989). Indeed, Indian nationalists helped to organize the legal challenge and provided some funding for it (Johnston 1989). The British government, fearful of the possible repercussions, in turn pressured the Borden government to resolve the matter before it became a major international issue.

Some in Canada were sympathetic to the concerns of the British, and called on the federal government to allow South Asian men to bring their wives into Canada. President Falconer of the University of Toronto argued that South Asian men should be allowed to sponsor their spouses, pointing out that "imperial interests were concerned, and that their exclusion might create trouble in India" (*Victoria Daily Colonist,* January 9, 1912). Similarly, in a debate at the Vancouver local of the National Council of Women, Miss Crease argued that

> this question is an imperial one, and [she] hoped that in their deliberation Council women would bear in mind the advice of Earl Grey to keep one hand on tradition and both eyes on the stars. (*Victoria Daily Colonist,* January 23, 1912)

Others protested "against denying to Hindu fellow subjects a privilege granted to Chinese and Japanese foreigners," pointing out "that Hindu women were excluded because of the regulation of a continuous journey." These writers and speakers pointed out that because the continuous journey stipulation was mainly oriented towards prohibiting migration from South Asia it was discriminatory. Thus the National Council of Women moved a resolution

> which deplored the fact that the exclusion of the wives of Sikhs in Canada should be based on a legal quibble and that discrimination should be made against the Sikhs, apart from [the] Oriental. (*Victoria Daily Colonist,* January 23, 1912)

Finally, a few writers argued that, as citizens of the British empire, South Asian men and their spouses should be allowed to enter Canada and deserved special consideration. At a public meeting in Vancouver, Mr. Boggs objected to "the exclusion of fellow subjects of the Empire" (*Victoria Daily Colonist,* February 10, 1912).

While raising these issues, the pro side put forward one major argument in favour of allowing the wives of South Asian men entry. Importantly, the assumptions underlying this argument further racialized and gendered South Asian women in the Canadian context. The pro side argued that South Asian women should be allowed to enter Canada on the grounds of morality and fairness—however, this fairness was referenced to South Asian men. This side argued that "morality" dictated that South Asian men be allowed to live with their wives. Thus, in a debate in the Vancouver local of the National Council of Women, Mrs. Hannington argued that it was not a question whether Hindu immigration should be allowed. The men are here. They are British subjects. The attachment of Sikhs to their wives and children is well known. Christianity and morality alike forbade that they should be allowed to live in the Province without homes. (*Victoria Daily Colonist,* January 23, 1912)

Similarly, Falconer argued "on the grounds of common humanity, the East Indians should be allowed to bring their wives into the country" (*Victoria Daily Colonist,* February 10, 1912).

In making the argument that the standards of morality and fairness should be applied to South Asian men, the speakers and writers attempted to "de-demonize" South Asian men. Thus, some writers argued that:

The Sikhs were not idolaters nor polygamists. Each man the husband of one wife. They treated their women well and as agricultural labourers filled a useful place in the community. (*Victoria Daily Colonist,* January 23, 1912)

Similarly, Mrs. Gordon argued:

The Hindu was desirable as a citizen; he was as industrious and law abiding.... Why should there be any discrimination between British subjects? ... They should remember no man was common or unclean. (*Victoria Daily Colonist,* February 10, 1912)

Interestingly, these arguments shared a number of similarities with the earlier arguments that opposed the entry of South Asian women. Notably, these speakers also limit the debate to the matter of South Asian women who were spouses of men already residing in Canada. The intent to limit the issue was clear when the Imperial Order of the Daughters of the Empire requested that the federal government "allow the men of India already in Canada and able to maintain them the right to bring their wives and families" (*The Victoria Daily Colonist,* January 23, 1912). None of those advocating that South Asian women be allowed to enter Canada were arguing that *any* South Asian women be able to enter the country; rather, they were arguing only that men residing in Canada be allowed to have their wives with them.

The motivation for arguing that South Asian men deserved the right to have "families" was not simply based on notions of fairness, but was premised on the racial and gender politics underlying nation-building. Underlying the argument that South Asian men deserved the right to have families was the fear of the sexuality of South Asian men—particularly the fear of sexual relations between South Asian men and white women.

Several of the speakers and writers who were advocating the entry of South

Asian women were doing so only because they were opposed to all-male migration. For example, the National Council of Women called on the federal government to "end the present state of affairs by either allowing Sikh women to enter Canada or by sending Sikh men back" (*Victoria Daily Colonist,* May 29, 1912). Several churches took the same position, with the Ministerial Association of Winnipeg declaring that:

> Speaking of the Sikhs in British Columbia, who are separated from their wives … the Government owes it to these people to either let their wives come or to buy them out and let them get away home. (*Victoria Daily Colonist,* April 9, 1912)

Thus, while for most Canadians the sexuality of South Asian women represented a danger to the racialized nation; ironically, South Asian men posed the same hazard for the pro force. The white man's nation required racial purity. In this context, South Asian women were desirable in that they represented a barrier between South Asian male workers and the racialized nation.

Second, the argument that South Asian men deserved the right to have families was also based on a desire to ensure that the social and moral order underlying the Canadian nation was maintained. As can be seen above, a recurring theme in the discourse was that "the moral order" dictated that South Asian men be allowed to live with their wives and families. As Mr. Boggs argued, it "was not just or moral, having admitted Hindus to bar their wives and families" (*Victoria Daily Colonist,* February 10, 1912).

The desire to ensure that South Asian men were included in the moral order underlying the project of nation-building was quite complex. As I suggested, in part it was based on the desire to ensure that a racialized nation was reproduced. However, it was also based on fear that South Asian men would undermine the gender politics of nation-building. Recently, several theorists have noted that in the racial politics of nineteenth-century nationalisms, the family was defined as a central institution (Balibar 1991, McClintock 1995, Stoler 1995). In Canada, Valverde's (1991) work also suggests that the racialized project of nation-building led to regulating familial and gender relations such that heterosexual, nuclear and patriarchal relations were imposed. In this context, South Asian men not only undermined the project of nation-building through their race, but also through their status as single men. Without the presence of their wives and children, South Asian men threatened the centrality of patriarchal relations in Canadian society.

Therefore, the efforts on the part of some Canadians to allow South Asian women to enter Canada can be seen as an attempt to maintain the gender politics of nation-building by ensuring that South Asian men also participated in patriarchal relations. The emerging discourse repeatedly referenced the entry of South Asian women into Canada in terms of the rights of South Asian men—

as opposed to the rights of South Asian women. As Reverend Dean Doull argued in a public meeting in Vancouver, the question of Hindu women entering British Columbia was

> an imperial question and they owed it to their fellow subjects of the empire to consider their welfare. It was even more than that: it was a question between man and man, and of the rights of their brother man. (*Victoria Daily Colonist,* February 10, 1912)

Significantly, the desire to ensure that South Asian men were able to participate in familial relations also ensured that these relations were patriarchal and heterosexual. While we have seen that others were worried that the entry of South Asian women could promote polygamous familial relations, those in favour of the entry of South Asian women took the view that these familial relations were quite compatible with "Canadian" notions of family. For example, at a public meeting in Vancouver, Mrs. Gordon pointed out that "a man to be seen at his best must be surrounded by his wife and family" (*Victoria Daily Colonist,* February 10, 1912). As this speaker implied, the crucial issue in maintaining the social order of Canadian nation-building was not so much ensuring that familial and gender relations were organized through the nuclear family, but rather that familial relations were organized through heterosexuality and patriarchy. As this side argued, the entry of South Asian women into a racialized nation ensured that the centrality of patriarchal relations was not undermined.

According to the minority of Canadians who sided with the South Asians in this debate, imperial concerns and "morality" dictated that South Asian women be allowed into Canada. However, like those who argued against the entry of South Asian women, the desirability of South Asian women was located in their gender as well as their race. The South Asian women were desirable only as spouses for South Asian men. As spouses, these women would act as a barrier to relations between the South Asian men and white women. For these Canadians the prospect of "ethnic communities" was reassuring, as the presence of such communities would safeguard the racialized project of Canadian nation-building. Secondly, South Asian women allowed South Asian men to participate in the gender relations that underlaid a racialized nation.

"The Hindu Woman's Question": Canadian Nation-Building and the Social Construction of Gender for South Asian–Canadian Women

My preliminary investigation into the "Hindu Woman's Question" suggests that this debate provides a unique opportunity to explore not only the links between Canadian nation-building and the racialization of gender for South Asian–Canadian women, but moreover to further our understanding of the interconnections between late nineteenth- and early twentieth-century Canadian nation-building and the discourses of race and gender. Like nineteenth-century nationalisms in other metropolitan and settler nations, nation-building in Canada was constituted on a discourse of race and gender. As this chapter suggests, the discourse of Canada as a "white man's country" was intimately tied to racializing gender for both Anglo-Saxon and South Asian–Canadian women.

Importantly, in Canada the imagining of the nation was racialized. In the context of colonial conquest, nation-builders defined Canada as "a white man's nation." This discourse of nation made not only First Nations people invisible within the nation-state, but defined the relationship that Asian migrants would have with the emerging Canadian nation-state, economy and society. An imagined community based on whiteness meant that, unlike European migrants, Asians in the Canadian national economy threatened the very process of nation-building. As a result, a racial discourse emerged of Asians as incapable of "assimilating" into Canadian society, and the Canadian state moved to legally define Asian migrants as temporary workers to Canada. Thus while Asian migrants were important to economic expansion in this period, the racialized discourse of Canadian nation-building defined them as outsiders to the nation-state.

Not only was the discourse of the nation racialized, it was also gendered. In effect, the construction of Canada as a "white *man's* country" gendered the entire nation, as it required the reproduction of a white population. This had significant implications for both Anglo-Saxon women and for women of colour. As Valverde's (1991, 1992) work suggests, the racialized project of nation-building both constructed Anglo-Saxon women as "mothers of the race" and led to the regulation of the sexual and gender relations of Anglo-Saxon women.

Significantly, this discourse constructed gender and familial relations for South Asian women that were remarkably similar to those devised for Anglo-Saxon women. While Anglo-Saxon women were constructed to be "mothers of the nation," South Asian–Canadian women were constructed as mothers of ethnic communities. Underlying this construction was the gendering of women as responsible for maintaining culture and tradition in a community or in a nation. Thus, while Anglo-Saxon women biologically and socially reproduced the nation, South Asian women biologically and socially reproduced "communities." Depending on one's point of view, these communities were either the ruin of the nation-building project, the "white man's country," or with their internal supports and containment morally saved the project.

Further Study

As this chapter has been based on the coverage of the "Hindu Woman's Question" in one regional newspaper, we need to be careful not to generalize the discursive construction of South Asian women in the *Victoria Daily Colonist* to all those who were involved in the debate. This essay does raise the importance of a detailed investigation of the racial and gender politics that premised Canadian nation-building. Several questions remain. For example, to what extent are there regional differences in the discursive construction of South Asian women? What role did Quebec play in shaping the racial politics of Anglo-Saxon nationalism? In what ways did the conquest of First Nations people shape the rhetoric of Canada as "a white man's nation"? What influence did imperial policies and the imperatives of empire building have on the racial politics of Canadian nationalism? How did each of these forces shape gender relations in this period?

In addition, this chapter raises the importance of investigating the relationships between Anglo-Saxon women and women of colour in this period. My exploration of the "Hindu Woman's Question" suggests that women's groups, especially the National Council of Women and the IODE, played an important role in racializing gender for South Asian women in Canada. Both groups constructed South Asian women as barriers to prevent South Asian males from becoming sexually involved with white women, and both promoted patriarchal relations among South Asian migrants. This raises the question of whether middle-class Anglo-Saxon women shared a commitment to a racialized nation and to what extent they shared a commitment to a gendered nation. How did this rhetoric reinforce notions of the superiority of white femininity in Canada? To what extent did this rhetoric allow Anglo-Saxon women to become gendered representatives of the white nation?

Finally, the "Hindu Woman's Question" begs the question of how Canadian nation-building racialized gender for Chinese- and Japanese-Canadian women. While Chinese and Japanese migrants were also defined as outsiders to the nation-state and immigration policies also restricted the entry of Chinese and Japanese females, we know little of how gender was socially constructed for these groups of women.

This chapter begins to explore the importance of the Canadian nation-state and its concomitant discourses of race and gender for understanding the institutional forms of systemic racism against South Asian women in Canada. The most significant aspect of the racialized project of nation-building is that the potential of South Asian–Canadian women to contribute to the public space of either production or social reproduction has been defined as dangerous. The exclusion of South Asians from the Canadian imaginary community has meant that rather than desiring South Asian women as workers or as "reproducers of the nation," these women have been imagined as desirable only as spouses for South Asian men. Importantly, the legacy of this discourse has continued to shape the structural relationship South Asian women have with Canadian society. The policies of the Canadian state—especially on matters of immigration and multiculturalism—reconstruct South Asian women as spouses to male migrants and thus continue to marginalize South Asian women in their relationship to the Canadian economy and society.

Notes

1. Following Miles' (1989: 73–77) distinction between race and racialization, I will use the concept of racialization to refer to "those instances where social relations between people have been structured by the significance of human biological characteristics in such a way as to define and construct differentiated collectivities" (Miles 1989: 75).

2. While the public discourse labelled South Asian women as Hindu, it is important to note that the majority of South Asian women who entered Canada were Sikh. For the purposes of this chapter, I will use the term South Asian–Canadian women to refer to the Sikh and Hindu women who migrated to Canada.

3. The kinds of restrictions on Asian migration varied in different periods. While in periods of acute labour shortage, Asian indentured male workers were actively recruited by middlemen; in periods of labour surplus or unrest, restrictions were placed on Asian migration. Asian migrants also faced a series of discriminatory regulations that defined their status as temporary workers. For example, Asian workers were required to carry identification, were unable to vote or to own certain kinds of property and were prohibited from entering into certain occupations; in addition, Asian workers and their children were unable to apply for naturalization. See Bolaria and Li (1988), Sharma (1982), Ramcharan (1982), Law Union of Ontario (1981) and Women's Book Committee, Chinese Canadian National Council (1992) for more detailed discussion of immigration policies in this period.

4. While Valverde (1991), Roy (1989), Ward (1979) and Warburton (1992) all demonstrate that the notion of an imagined community was also premised on a racist discourse of Chinese, Japanese and South Asian peoples, they offer very different explanations concerning the origins of this discourse. For example, Ward (1979) relies on psychological and cultural explanations, while Roy attributes anti-Asian sentiment to economic tensions and class formation. The most persuasive explanation is offered by Valverde (1991), who places the discourse of racism in the context of nation-building and the regulation of a moral order.

5. Notably, the measures used to restrict migration from China, South Asia and Japan varied. In the case of migration from China, the government of Canada restricted migration through a variety of regulations, such as head taxes, as well as outright prohibitions. In the case of migration from Japan, the Canadian government entered into a "gentlemen's agreement" with the government of Japan, in which the Japanese government restricted the number of emigrants to Canada. In the case of migration from India, the government of Canada enacted the "continuous journey" stipulation. These provisions stipulated that only persons who came directly from their country of origin could enter Canada. As the only steamship that provided a continuous journey from India was owned by Canadian Pacific Railways, immigration officials directed the CPR to not sell tickets to "Indians." The use of different rules and regulations for different countries did not reflect different attitudes towards migrants from these countries, but rather the different geo-political relations between governments. In the case of India, because of her status within the Empire, overtly racist policies were seen as threatening colonial rule in the subcontinent. Thus, the continuous journey regulation was used as an indirect method of restricting migration. See Bolaria and Li (1988a, 1988b) and Raj (1980) for a more detailed discussion.

6. It is important to note that South Asian men focused their challenge on the

legislative prohibitions against the entry of their spouses—not on the prohibitions against the migration of Asian women.

7.   Notably, First Nations were among the few groups in Canada who appear to have remained silent on the issue. This reflects the degree to which the First Nations had been marginalized from mainstream Canadian society in this period.

8.   In certain periods, single European women (especially those from Britain) were encouraged to migrate to Canada. As Van Kirk (1981, 1985) shows, in the early nineteenth century the entry of British women was seen as an integral part in creating a "white" settler colony, particularly as it allowed colonial authorities to regulate sexual relations between colonial men and First Nations and Metis women. Moreover, as Roberts (1979) argues, in the early twentieth century the migration of single women from Britain was seen as a solution to the problem of unemployment in Britain, as well as contributing to the development of a "white" settlement in Canada. However, it is important to note that despite the importance of single white women for racializing the Canadian nation-state, these women, especially if they were working class, were also defined as dangerous to the moral order. As Valverde (1991) shows, in the late nineteenth century the fear that single working-class women would not regulate their sexuality within the confines of the moral order led these females to be defined as a social problem. Importantly, in order to resolve the tensions between creating a white nation and regulating morality, rather than prohibiting the migration of single British women, the Canadian state instituted several policies designed to "Canadianize" them.

9.   The movement of labour from India across the Commonwealth had been contested by Indian nationalists. Colonial and Commonwealth policies had restricted the free movement of Indians, despite India's status within the Empire and the rhetoric of equality for all residents of the Empire. See Huttenback (1976), Gangulee (1947), Kondapi (1951) and Tinker (1976) for an more elaborate discussion of Asian migration within the Empire.

Chapter Four

The Case of Émilie Ouimet
News Discourse on Hijab and the Construction of Québécois National Identity
Helle-Mai Lenk

La faiblesse des mythes nationalistes réside dans le fait qu'ils ne peuvent tolérer failles ou déviances. C'est parce qu'ils se présentent comme des *systèmes totaux* qu'ils sont vulnérables à l'opération d'un révélateur stratégiquement bien placé. Ils sont promptement alarmés par des choix et des actes indépendants qui sont pourtant à la portée de tout le monde. (Nadia Khouri 1992: 120)

Introduction
On September 7, 1994, the first day of the school year, a Montreal high school student was sent home for wearing an Islamic headscarf, or *hijab*, allegedly in contravention of the school's dress code. This incident unleashed a considerable debate in the Quebec media and the society at large, culminating in a report tabled by the Quebec Human Rights Commission.[1] In this chapter, I will be examining the degree and range of controversy leading up to this report. For my analysis, I have collected all news reports, editorials, opinion articles and letters to the editor that appeared in three Montreal dailies: the French-language *La Presse* and *Le Devoir* and the English-language *Gazette,* as well as the Toronto-based national newspaper, the *Globe and Mail*, over a three-month period immediately following the initial incident. My contention is to show how race and racism become articulated within these news discourses surrounding *hijab* and how these articulations in turn attend to different political projects relating to nationalism.[2]

The approach that I use is perhaps closest to what is known as discourse analysis, as practiced most prolifically in the area of press analysis by Teun van Dijk. Van Dijk's research has consistently shown that the mass media play a crucial role in the reproduction of racism by perpetuating stereotypes and prejudice about minority groups. By mapping, annotating and analyzing the development of certain aspects of the *hijab* story, I aim to lay bare inconsistencies between the apparent content of these discourses which stress tolerance, equality and pluralism, values that most Canadians and Quebeckers feel are inherent to their national identity, and the often racist undercurrents that inform their articulation. What do I hope to achieve by all this? If these discourses require a demystificational hermeneutic, it is not only so that we can become less their dupes, but also so that we can recognize and further an alternative way of speaking, one that might actually make good on claims to the "moral duties of respect, of tolerance, of solidarity towards one another" (Gouvernement du Québec 1995). However, as Michel Foucault's whole project has demonstrated, even to imagine certain transformations of a system of knowledge and discourse, one must first expose the rules of its functioning. I, therefore, see my task also as an attempt to demonstrate the potential of a form of "insurgent" educational practice; the analytical tools exemplified here can and need to be learned, taught and popularized (Meijer 1993). For it is only when we become aware how textual power is wielded, how it rhetorically persuades and seduces, how it produces "common sense," that we can begin to "challenge the dominant ethnic consensus [and] write within an explicitly anti-racist perspective" (van Dijk 1991: 22).

In this endeavour, however, it is not my interest to brand particular journalists or specific newspapers as "racist." Rather, the point that needs to be emphasized is that "racism is a structural and ideological property of white group dominance and therefore characterizes the Press as a whole" (van Dijk 1991: 22). Indeed, an attendant project might look at precisely the ways in which the press works together to forge the idea of "white" superiority, of a European or Western perspective. Étienne Balibar has described how the British and French colonial powers played "their" natives off one another and prided themselves,

> in competition with one another, on their particular humaneness, by projecting the image of racism onto the colonial practices of their rivals. French colonization proclaimed itself "assimilatory," while British colonization saw itself as "respectful of cultures." The other White is also the bad White. (1991: 43)

The legacy of this colonial racism is regularly reenacted in the anglophone and francophone press in Canada. When, for example, the *Globe and Mail* runs an article on its front page entitled "Educators outside Quebec mystified by *hijab* ban" (Nasrulla 1994), the implication is that such things can happen only in Quebec and are representative of the peculiar shortsightedness of Quebec society. Similarly, *Le Devoir* dissimulates the rise in anti-Semitic incidents in Montreal under the headline "Quatre fois moins d'actes antisémites à Montréal qu'à Toronto" (Vear 1993). By under-reporting racist occurrences closer to their home constituencies, these newspapers divert their readers rather than implicating them in the events described. The social order at home remains unsullied, intact. The groups on whose behalf these concerns are being expressed are reduced to the status of pawns in a contest of asserting "white" sovereignty or, as Balibar quips, which "White nation is spiritually 'the whitest'" (Balibar 1991: 43).

Some Quantitative Results

I will start my analysis with a few figures about the frequency and distribution of the *hijab* coverage in the press.[3] Media attention peaked immediately. Of the forty-three articles published by the four newspapers during the three months, no fewer than twenty-two appeared in September. The number of articles dropped to fourteen in October and seven in November. *La Presse* and *Le Devoir* published fifteen and seventeen articles respectively in three months, whereas the *Gazette* published nine and the *Globe and Mail* only two.[4] This uneven apportioning of coverage suggests a lack of consensus between the French and English press about the newsworthiness of the *hijab* issue. That *La Presse* and *Le Devoir* each published almost twice as many articles as the *Gazette* may, at least partly, be explained by the fact that the initial incident occurred in a French-language school in the east end of Montreal, a largely French-speaking area.

Van Dijk, however, claims that the "distribution of media attention is one of the first hints about a typical press 'panic'" (1988a: 220). Therefore, I will argue that the vigourous debate that this incident provoked in the French media was also no doubt fueled by the critical historical juncture through which francophone Quebec society is now passing. The fall of 1994 was a particularly tumultuous time. On September 12, five days after the Émilie Ouimet incident, the provincial elections were narrowly won by the Parti Québécois. As the prospect of an independent Quebec became more of a possibility, media discussion centred increasingly around what is known as "le projet de société."[5] In other words, what kind of society does Quebec—the "new" Quebec—want to become? Less prominent but no less partisan were the school board elections held on November 20. In this case, candidates were necessarily divided according to whether or not they supported the deconfessionalization of schools—that is, the replacing of Catholic and Protestant school boards with linguistic ones. As I will show in the following analyses, these key political events figured prominently in the debate surrounding *hijab*.

Unfortunately, it is not possible to study in detail all forty-three articles. I have, therefore, restricted my investigation to two particular areas. In the first instance, I examine what are known as "proper news articles"—that is, those descriptions of news events that are sometimes deemed to be strictly factual or value-free. However, I show that "[i]mplicit opinions can be expressed or signaled even in the most factual news report" (van Dijk 1988a: 124). My corpus consists of the articles that "broke" the Émilie Ouimet story in each of the newspapers. I argue that subsequent reaction was largely fed by these initial accounts, the ways they defined the situation and the prejudices and stereotypes they promulgated. In the second instance, I look at the acknowledged site of opinion-making in newspapers, editorials and more specifically those of the French-language press. I show how the particular argumentative strategies employed serve to determine the limits of what is sayable, to erase the political determinants of the press and to produce a consensual position supportive of established power relations.

The Case of Émilie Ouimet: A Brief Chronology

To understand the analysis reported below, I will give a brief chronological account of the main events related to the Émilie Ouimet story as they appeared in the press:

- September 7, 1994: Twelve-year-old Émilie Ouimet is sent home from Louis-Riel Secondary School in Montreal for wearing an Islamic head-scarf, allegedly in contravention of the school's dress code.
- September 12, 1994: Émilie Ouimet is admitted to Lucien-Pagé Secondary School where wearing *hijab* is permitted.
- September 13, 1994: The parents' committee at Louis-Riel Secondary School refuse to put the issue of the school dress code on the agenda of their monthly meeting.
- September 19, 1994: Lorraine Pagé, the President of the *Centrale de l'enseignement du Québec* (CEQ), comes out in favour of religious and cultural diversity in Quebec schools, including the wearing of *hijab*.
- October 25, 1994: Bernard Landry, the Minister of Immigration and Cultural Communities, encourages public discussion on the *hijab* issue and implies that the government may have to intervene.
- November 22, 1994: The St. Jean Baptiste Society unveils a document outlining its views on the conditions of citizenship in a sovereign Quebec. François Lemieux, its president, states that wearing *hijab* is not compatible with Quebec society.

News Stories: "Just the Facts"

La Presse broke the Émilie Ouimet story and printed it as a feature article (Appendix 1)[6] by its ethnic affairs reporter on the front page of the September 9 edition, two days after the event. The following day, September 10, both the *Gazette* (#19) and the *Globe and Mail* (#22) ran shorter, signed articles on their inside pages citing *La Presse* as their source. *La Presse* also continued coverage with a second article (#2). *Le Devoir* did not take up the story until September 15, more than a week after the initial event (and three days after the provincial elections), and then in a very summary fashion with an unsigned article (#11) on an inside page. The smallest of the four newspapers, *Le Devoir*'s reticence can partly be explained by its size as well as by the omnipresence of the elections to which it, as the newspaper of the Quebec political elite, devoted extensive coverage. More notably, however, in an editorial on September 7 (Bissonnette 1994), the day Émilie Ouimet was asked to leave Louis-Riel Secondary School, *Le Devoir* had endorsed the Parti Québécois in the upcoming elections, elections that it was favoured to win. In all likelihood, *Le Devoir* did not consider it politically propitious to introduce a potentially contentious issue into the campaign, hence its decision to delay coverage until after the elections.[7]

 An informal comparison between the articles in *La Presse*, the *Gazette* and the *Globe* reveals important differences in discourse rules and news values even if, as I indicated above, both English papers were dependent on information from *La Presse* for at least part of their coverage. A quick perusal of the content indicates that, on the whole, *La Presse* focussed on the main events (approximately 80 percent of content),[8] albeit, as I will demonstrate below, from a decidedly elite perspective. In the *Gazette* and the *Globe*, although the information about the main event was based on the *La Presse* report, it was presented less prominently (from 30–40 percent of content) and the correspondents provided more political analysis and evaluation. In the *Gazette*, for example, approximately 35 percent of the article was taken up by discussion of Bill 107, the law designed to bring about non-denominational schooling and its role in the *hijab* debate. Most significantly, the *Gazette* entered the fray with an implicit attack on the government's position: "Parti Québécois chief Jacques Parizeau has said that a promised commission on the future of Quebec education won't touch on the role of religion" (#19). The French newspapers only broached the subject of Bill 107 in later opinion articles (#8, #14) and taking their cue from the government, which did not intervene in the *hijab* debate until more than six weeks after the initial incident, remained silent on its broader socio-political implications.

Analysis of News Stories

A discursive analysis of news reports can, of course, be undertaken at many levels. My study of news stories emphasizes news schemata. In the following sections, I analyze the use of two structural news characteristics, headlines and quotations, in the reports of *La Presse,* the *Gazette* and the *Globe and Mail.*

Headlines

As van Dijk has often pointed out, headlines have special relevance in news discourse (1988b, 1991: 50–70). In my analysis of the initial reactions to the Émilie Ouimet story, I concentrate on the ideological implications of headlines—that is, the socio-political position from which the news events are defined:

> Since [headlines] express the most important information about a news event, they may bias the understanding process: they summarize what, according to the journalist [or the editor], is the most important aspect, and such a summary necessarily implies an opinion or a specific perspective on the events. (van Dijk 1991: 51)

A cursory glance at the headlines of the three newspapers that chose to report on the initial incident concerning Émilie Ouimet reveals how each formulation has defined the situation differently:

- Élève expulsée de son école parce qu'elle portait le foulard islamique (*La Presse*, Sept. 9)
- Montreal principal denounced for ousting teen in Islamic garb (the *Globe and Mail*, Sept. 10)
- *Hijab* ban at Louis Riel fuels debate about religious expression in schools (*Gazette*, Sept. 10)

In its headline, *La Presse* places the victim first in the sentence, thereby dissimulating the identity of the perpetrator of the action, the principal. In the text, however, Émilie Ouimet—the "élève expulsée"—is not interviewed; in fact, as we shall see, the principal of the school is the most oft-quoted personage and it is largely his perspective that informs the article. The *Globe and Mail*, on the other hand, chooses to inculpate the principal. He is identified near the beginning of the headline and burdened with two negative predicates; not only is he being "denounced" but he also bears the responsibility of "ousting." In addition, the fact that he is from "Montreal" figures prominently.[9] The *Gazette* alone displays a broader preoccupation. By choosing the nominalization "*hijab* ban," it deflects attention away from individual blame and focusses instead on the social consequences of this incident. It acknowledges that we are in no way dealing with an exceptional occurrence, but rather a form of structural discrimination that requires the input of society as a whole, hence a "debate about religious expression."

Quotations

According to van Dijk, one of the most important functions of quotations in news reports is to "allow the insertion of subjective interpretations, explanations, or opinions about current news events, without breaking the ideological rule that requires the separation of facts from opinions" (1991: 152). Therefore, one can say that those people or groups whose descriptions, interpretations and opinions are routinely embedded in news accounts are probably also those whose ideology most closely resembles that of the reporter or newspaper in question. Not all sources are equally credible. When *La Presse* reporter François Berger, for example, seeks out information about the Émilie Ouimet story, he finds it not in the person of Émilie herself, whose credibility he effectively diminishes by frequent use of the epithets "jeune" and "petite."[10] Rather he quotes at length Émilie's principal, the very person responsible for removing her from the school, but nonetheless a figure of greater authority because of his position, age and gender and therefore a seemingly more reliable source.

The only instance when François Berger does quote anyone on Émilie's "turf," it is her mother in the second *La Presse* article. However, Mme Ouimet's words come after her person has already been rendered suspect in the previous day's article. There, she is wrongly identified as a recent Muslim convert, and it is implied that she has imposed this predicament on her hapless daughter: "La mére d'Émilie, Mme Henriette Ouimet, nouvellement convertie à la religion musulmane, avait envoyé sa fille à l'école en *mouhajjaba* (femme musulmane portant le voile)." Not only do the *Gazette* and the *Globe* both pick up this erroneous piece of information and include it in their initial coverage, but the latter chooses to elaborate on the fictions: "Émilie Ouimet's parents [!] refuse to allow her to return to the Louis-Riel school because they obey the *sharia*." In the second *La Presse* article, the information is corrected: Mme. Ouimet is not Muslim but respects the choice her daughter has made following the example of her aunt and her cousin. Not surprisingly, unlike *La Presse*, neither the *Gazette* nor the *Globe* take the trouble to communicate these precisions to their readers. It is easier to reinforce a stereotype—that is, to continue to demonize Islam (as a coercive religion)—than attempt to unravel the complexities of an incident for which prevailing explanations do not work.

La Presse nonetheless does make a semblance of seeking out the opinion of Mme. Ouimet. Her very real concerns about the taunting her daughter received on the first day of school ("Are you afraid of being raped?") are included in the second day's article. Van Dijk, however, has observed that, in cases of discrimination or racism, when negative actions of elite groups are involved, the opinions of the victims, if heard at all, are usually "followed by 'independent' (that is, white) sources that soften or deny these accusations" (1991: 154). Thus, although the journalist François Berger does seek out the opinion of Mme. Ouimet, her concerns are undercut by the accompanying remarks, a reiteration of the principal's views from the previous day's article:

> Mme. Henriette Ouimet, la mère d'Émilie, dit hier à *La Presse* que sa fille s'était fait apostropher, à la rentrée des classes mercredi, par des jeunes qui lui auraient demandé: <<As-tu peur de te faire violer?>> La tenue islamique risque de <<marginaliser>> l'élève, a expliqué pour sa part le directeur de l'école Louis-Riel, M. Normand Doré. (#2)

What Berger is saying here is that, in effect, the principal's analysis of the situation has proved correct. The situation that he feared—that is, the marginalization of Émilie—has indeed occurred and, according to him, Émilie has only herself to blame. Van Dijk claims "the move of reversing the blame by attributing it to the opponent [is] part of a well-used strategy of 'blaming the victim'" (1991: 192). By asserting that Émilie herself has acted in such a way that prejudice or unfair treatment is justified, the principal deflects attention away from the aggressive behaviour of his students, and renders unproblematic his own inaction in that regard. François Berger, by choosing to highlight the principal's views, is thus able to insert, at a crucial point in his text, what he obviously considers a relevant opinion statement without, however, being held responsible for its content. Meanwhile, the underlying beliefs and ideologies that promoted the discriminatory actions of both the principal and the students remain unexamined and unchallenged.[11]

In both the *Gazette* and the *Globe*, minority opinions are more prominently engaged. In my informal content analysis, I found that whereas *La Presse* devoted little more than 8 percent coverage to dissenting views, critical reactions from ethnic, human rights and anti-racist groups comprised 32 percent of the content in the *Gazette and* 27 percent in the *Globe*. In both *La Presse* and the *Gazette*, negative reactions to Émilie Ouimet's expulsion are voiced by the group S.O.S. Racisme and the Canadian Jewish Congress, both of whom issue news releases. Only the *Globe* deems it important to consult a Muslim. Nonetheless, Abdul Amer, spokesperson for the Muslim Community of Quebec, gets less coverage in the *Globe* than the representative of the Canadian Jewish Congress, who also has the prestige of being quoted directly. In none of the papers do we hear a Muslim woman's reaction to the Émilie Ouimet incident, only the *Gazette* gives general coverage to their views on *hijab*. It runs two news articles that are completely informed by the opinions of two community leaders, Fatima Houda-Pepin and Mayada Mourabet Hakim, and an academic, Homa Hoodfar (#34, #41)

In the entire three-month *La Presse* coverage, not one article is authored by an ethnic minority speaker. This discrepancy reaches its ultimate absurdity when it asks a well-known columnist, Nathalie Petrowski, to don *hijab* for one week and travel the streets of Montreal "pour voir la réaction des gens sur [s]on passage." One wonders if it wouldn't have been more pertinent to ask a Muslim woman about *her* daily reality in Montreal but, as van Dijk observes, minorities are seldom considered reliable sources on issues, such as prejudice and discrimination, that might put whites in a bad light (1991: 159). Not surprisingly, Petrowski's series of articles, which runs on three consecutive days in March 1955, are replete with racist innuendo about Muslims and Arabs. In the final installment of her series, she summarizes her findings on "la réaction des gens" in the following manner: "À l'indifférence ou à la gêne des Québécois qui me prennent pour une cousine proche de Mère Teresa, les musulmans opposent un regard plein de convoitise." Clearly, in Petrowski's reasoning, "les Québécois" and "les musulmans" fall in opposite camps. Is it not possible for a "musulman" to be a "Québécois"? Who then is a "Québécois"? These are precisely the questions around which the Émilie Ouimet story turns.

To return to that incident then, we have seen how, as van Dijk has so perceptively observed, "the social hierarchy seems to be reproduced in the rhetorical hierarchy of credibility and reliability" (van Dijk 1988c: 87). Émilie Ouimet is not interviewed, her mother's words are undermined, and Nathalie Petrowski becomes the Muslim woman surrogate. The voices of women and children are as under-valued in the textual economy of these news reports as they are in public life—and this, even when they are white! Indeed, as I will argue in more detail in my conclusion, Émilie Ouimet is perceived as a transgressor precisely because she is "white but not quite" (Bhabha 1994). She is, in Ann Stoler's words, the "enemy within" who has transgressed the "interior frontiers" of the nation (Stoler 1995: 52). The ultimate aberration is not the *hijab*-wearing Muslim woman; rather it is Émilie Ouimet's betrayal of her Québécois identity. To this effect, in several of the news articles, an explicit comparison is made between the recalcitrant Émilie Ouimet and other Arab Muslim students who, unlike her, have changed their mode of dress and have learned to perform the dominant identity: "M. Doré a dit avoir reçu, la semaine dernière, la visite d'une mère d'origine arabe, portant le *hijab*, qui a compris et accepté les règles vestimentaires de l'école. Sa fille est arrivée à l'école sans le voile" (#1). (See also #6.) We can well ask: who is Émilie Ouimet then? She is neither "Nous" or "les Autres" but rather a shattering of that distinction. As Nadia Khouri has pointed out, it is precisely those events and acts that reveal or deconstruct "les oppositions binaires: Nord/Sud, Noir/Blanc, Métropole/Colonies, Civilisés/Primitifs, Tribu/État, Europe/Afrique, Moderne/Archaïque, Majorité/Minorité" (Khouri 1992: 109) that are ultimately the most destabilizing of a political order. That is why, as I will demonstrate in the following section dealing with editorials, Émilie Ouimet is perceived as a threat to the social body, one that Petrowski's "Québécois" nation at least must defend itself against.

Editorials

Of the four newspapers under study, three editorialized on the issue of the veil during the period under study, *La Presse* and *Le Devoir* with one article each (#6 and #29, respectively) and the *Gazette* with two (#20, #43). Here the differences between the two French newspapers and the *Gazette* are striking, not only in the opinions elicited but also the argumentative strategies employed. Not surprisingly, considering the viewpoint implicit in its news stories, the *Gazette* in its first editorial categorically denounces the actions of the Louis-Riel principal as "quite wrong." Appealing to classic liberal notions of rights and responsibilities, it states its position on the issue of *hijab* with a rhetorical question: "Why should any public or quasi-public institution—in a society that recognizes religious freedom as fundamental—not make reasonable accommodation for observant members of religious minorities?" In the second editorial, which appears on November 24 largely in reaction to the St. Jean Baptiste Society document (see chronology), the *Gazette* once again criticizes the government for its inaction on issues of religious tolerance, a theme which has run through most *Gazette* reports (#19, #34, #42). In another article in the same day's issue, the *Gazette* quotes Sheema Khan, a *hijab*-wearing Montrealer, who says an increasing number of Muslim women are facing harassment at school and work, a fact that she attributes to the uncaring attitude of the government:

She traces the backlash to an incident in September, when a 13-year-old girl was sent home for wearing the *hijab* to school. The provincial election campaign was at its height at the time. Khan said it didn't strike her until later that neither Parizeau nor Liberal leader Daniel Johnson took a stand to defend the girl's religious freedoms, as protected in the Quebec and Canadian charters of human rights. "That was dangerous, and that allowed it to mushroom." (#42)

In each of the three *Gazette* articles, the Émilie Ouimet controversy is seen as a struggle over people's rights to religious expression. Islam is therefore invoked as the primary explanatory force behind the current popularity of *hijab*. In recent years, however, the predominance of the religious paradigm as an interpretive tool for discussions of Muslim women has been criticized for promoting an ahistorical, static conception of women:

> The overall effect of this paradigm is to deprive women of self-presence, of being. Because women are subsumed under religion presented in fundamental terms, they are inevitably seen as evolving in nonhistorical time. They have virtually no history. Any analysis of change is therefore foreclosed. (Lazreg 1988: 86)

The religious paradigm, when applied to the controversy generated by the Émilie Ouimet incident, precludes any attempt at understanding why at this particular historical juncture *hijab* has emerged as a significant factor in Islamic women's lives. According to Shahnaz Khan, Muslims in Canada experience isolation and exclusion from the dominant society:

> Our marginalization was most clearly expressed during the Gulf war, when the media promoted (and continues to promote) negative stereotypes of Arabs/Muslims. Notwithstanding the spiritual aspects of Islam, for this minority in Canada, asserting Muslim identity appears to have become an integral part of maintaining a presence. Canadian Muslims want the past to generate strength and dignity with which to face discrimination and exclusion from mainstream life in Canada. (Khan 1993: 53)

By focusing on Canada's liberal traditions and insisting on a rights-based solution to the controversy, the *Gazette* is able not only to gain political points at the expense of the Parti Québécois government, thereby confirming the self-satisfied biases of its mainly anglophone readership, but also to effectively remove itself and them from the less savoury aspects of Canadian life—that is, the racism and sexism which is an inherent, structural property of Canadian society as a whole, the *hijab* controversy being but one manifestation.

In the French newspapers, on the other hand, although the *hijab* debate provokes some discussion of school reform, its implications for Quebec society as a whole are left untouched. Typically, Agnès Gruda concludes her editorial in *La Presse* with the following solution: "Ce n'est que dans une école vraiment laïque que l'on pourra en toute cohérence interdire tout apparat religieux, quel qu'il soit." This, of course, begs the question: If school is the place where societal values are learned, is it not also a reflection of that society? If wearing *hijab* is to be forbidden in schools, is it not to be expected that this will also be the case in society at large? These are precisely the kinds of issues that are not addressed.

Even more evasive is editorial-writer François Brousseau in *Le Devoir*. The reader can search in vain to find the newspaper's opinion about the *hijab* debate in Quebec, for its editorial deals solely with the controversy in France! Perhaps this is not so surprising considering the content of *Le Devoir*'s news stories during the three months surveyed (of the eight proper news articles that *Le Devoir* published on *hijab*, only three dealt with the situation in Quebec, the remainder being about France).[12] That France figures prominently in Quebec media discourse can, of course, be explained by the historical, linguistic and cultural ties between the two societies.[13] Moreover, France's long tradition of secular schooling[14] is undoubtedly a point of interest amongst Quebeckers grappling with Bill 107. Nonetheless, given the greater numbers and the extremely different history of the Muslim population in France,[15] one can seriously question whether comparisons are apt. Although the editorial in *La Presse* is also structured as a comparison of the situations in France and Quebec, it seems that Agnès Gruda is somewhat conscious of the bad fit. She concedes that "le débat ne se pose pas exactement dans les mêmes termes ici et dans l'Hexagone [France]." Nonetheless, she perseveres. Having admitted that while in France there are more than a thousand Muslim women who wear *hijab* to school, and in Quebec at the most multiethnic school only 15, she continues:

> [C]e qui est clair, c'est que la vague des tchadors [en France], née d'une toute petite goutte, a pris les proportions d'un psychodrame. Le Québec n'est pas immunisé contre un tel effet multiplicateur. (6)

Other than fearmongering, it is difficult to find any other purpose behind this kind of slippery slope reasoning. Devoid of facts or historical background, the article constructs Islam as the imputed evil, ready to take over the world. While Gruda favours the medical metaphor ("psychodrame," "immunisé"), or Islam as spreading disease, Brousseau at *Le Devoir* frames his diatribe in military terms: "des intolérants se réclament de la liberté et du pluralisme pour avancer leurs pions," "des petits commandos épris de <<liberté>> vont, d'une école à l'autre." His predilection for the military image is justified as a defense of France against Islam: "La France est aux portes du Maghreb. Des attentats contre les Français ont eu lieu, ayant pour origine les milieux islamistes algériens."[16]

Brousseau, however, leaves the history of France's own aggressions in North Africa untouched. In this respect, his conclusion merits a closer look, if only for the transparency of its argumentative moves and rhetorical operations, and the consequent ideological knowledge produced.

> Les sociétés modernes ont tous besoin de diversité, de tolérance devant le multiple et le différent. Mais elles ont tout autant besoin de cohésion et de références partagées. À cette fin, l'école est un instrument essentiel. Car la face négative du multiple—on le sait, on l'a vu et on le verra—s'appelle libanisation, balkanisation, yougoslavisation. (29)

In the first sentence, Brousseau tries to convey the impression that he is for tolerance and diversity. In a society where the official norms dictate that racism is immoral or illegal, one major strategy in discourse about minorities is positive self-presentation (van Dijk 1991: 187–88). However, these disclaimers are necessarily always followed by a restrictive "but." And so Brousseau qualifies his magnanimity by appeals to cohesion and shared references. His memory for "shared references," however, is selective; while invoking the spectre of Algerian Islamic hordes, for example, apparently best forgotten are 130 years of French colonial rule in that country, a period of untold ruthlessness and subjugation but apparently unrelated in Brousseau's mind to Algeria's present deplorable state.[17]

In the final sentence of his editorial, Brousseau spells out the dire consequences of giving way to pluralism. He is aided in his assertions by a self-conscious patterning of language. Any reader will most certainly feel the effects—even fall under the sway—of Brousseau's rhetoric, but a critical response requires an awareness of how the process works. The forceful repetitions of phrases ("on le sait, on l'a vu et on le verra") and syllables ("libanisation, balkanisation, yougoslavisation") no doubt heighten the emotional impact of Brousseau's warning. However, another, albeit unintentional, effect is their pounding sameness, a not untimely reminder of the consequences of a pluralism thwarted.

Conclusion

In my introduction to this paper, I remarked on the disproportionate amount of attention the *hijab* issue attracted in the French press. This analysis has shown that also qualitatively the coverage afforded by English and French newspapers differed significantly. Not only did they both implicitly and explicitly, in news stories and editorials, take opposing stances on *hijab*, but the consistent refusal of the French press to broaden the context of the debate and engage the issue of *hijab* at the level of socio-political concerns is, I think, evidence of a lurking, unacknowledged malaise. It is to this point that I would now like to briefly turn. The Ouimet family gets racialized, even though they are white, so-called "Québécois de souche," because they have decided to adopt cultural values and behaviour that are perceived by some to be antithetical to what constitutes the Québécois nation. They are victims of what David Goldberg, among others, has referred to as "the new racism," or race coded as culture (Goldberg 1993: 73). This obsessive circling by the Quebec media around the Émilie Ouimet story is, I think, not exhausted by the fact that she wears a *hijab*. There is something else more vital going on—and it is marked by the evasive silence around her "whiteness." What we are confronted with here is not unlike the submerged fear that haunted the colonial enterprise: the danger of "going native," of individual and hence racial degeneration.[18] Patrick Brantlinger has identified the arche-typal event as Stanley's discovery of Livingstone, white man meeting white man in the depths of the African jungle:

> [T]he famous scene of "Dr. Livingstone, I presume?" suggests a narcissistic doubling, a repetition or mirroring. The solipsistic repression of whatever is nonself or alien characterizes all forms of cultural and political domination. (Brantlinger 1985: 215)

In analogous fashion, the *hijab*-wearing Muslim is revealed to be none other than a Québécoise "pure laine." *Mais quelle laine?* Who in Quebec today can guarantee that their genetic make-up owes nothing to the 1,132 Africans brought to New France and Lower Canada between 1686 and 1806 (Trudel 1960: 89)? And even the most nationalist-minded of Quebec historians will attest that "marriage between Indians and whites has always been more common among the French Canadians than among the English" (Rioux 1978: 23–24). We can add to this all the other ethnic and racial groups which are integral components of Quebec society and history. In other words, what Émilie Ouimet has so graphically revealed is the deep ambivalence of the laundered categories in which the Québécois national identity has been traditionally inscribed. Is it possible to be Québécois(e)—and also Other? "[T]o exist is to be called into being in relation to an otherness," says Homi Bhabha (1994: 44). But what happens when that Otherness turns out also to be the Self or, as Bhabha observes, "the threat of cultural difference is no longer a problem of 'other people' [and] becomes a question of the otherness of the people-as-one" (1994:150)? At precisely the moment when the Québécois national project is once again fully underway, a project that is dependent on the articulation of a distinct histori-cally-centred Québécois identity, the Émilie Ouimet incident serves to high-light the fragility of that notion. A national project of a state can seldom be seen as equally representative of the interests of all who live within its physical boundaries (Anthias and Yuval-Davis 1992: 32). Those who are unable to share in the narrative of the nation, its origins, its uniqueness, its mission or, as with the Algerians in France and the indigenous peoples of Quebec, those who conjure up the wrong stories are not included. It remains to be seen how these emerging counter-narratives from the nation's margins are taken up in Quebec, if at all.[19] If the issue of *hijab*, however, is at all representative, it is unlikely that the national press will be the locus of a paradoxical discourse.

Notes

1. See Commission des droits de la personne du Québec (1995). According to a recent report in *La Presse*, because of budgetary cutbacks as well as internal problems, the Commission has been hearing and ruling on an increasingly reduced caseload over the last few years. Therefore, the very fact that the Commission chose to rule on this issue is indicative of its importance (Berger 1995: A4).

2. Since the European colonial presence in the Middle East and North Africa, Muslim women and their wearing of *hijab* have often been vital sites of struggle in debates on nationalism and culture. See, for example, Ahmed (1992), Hoodfar (1993) and Lazreg (1994).

3. The following is a breakdown of the forty-three articles on *hijab* by newspaper and type. *Le Devoir* published seventeen articles, twelve about Quebec and five about France. Eight were information-type articles published by *La Presse*, twelve were about Quebec and three about France. Nine articles were information-type, four were opinion pieces and there was one editorial and one letter to the editor. The *Gazette* published nine articles, all on Quebec. There were five information-type articles, two editorials, one opinion piece and one letter. The *Globe and Mail* published two information-type articles on Quebec.

4. The *Globe and Mail*'s paltry output is not altogether indicative of a lack of interest. In the subsequent three-month period (Dec. 1994–Feb. 1995), nine articles on the *hijab* issue were published.

5. Reference to Quebec's "projet de société" was first made in 1977 in the Charte de la langue française (loi 101) (Gouvernement du Québec 1977: 34). The latest envisagement of Quebec's social project can be found in the document entitled "Déclaration de souveraineté" made public by then-premier Jacques Parizeau on September 6, 1995.

6. All references indicated by a number sign (#) and a number refer to the forty-three core articles retrieved from the four newspapers during the three-month period under study.

7. Curiously enough, after the elections, *Le Devoir* ran two opinion pieces reproving the lack of discussion on issues of immigration and citizenship during the campaign. See Tremblay (1994) and Laïdoui (1994) for opposing viewpoints.

8. The percentages were arrived at informally (by counting the number of paragraphs devoted to each theme) and thus are only meant to be comparative.

9. Two other non-Quebec newspapers also chose to run the *hijab* story on September 10. Interestingly enough, unlike the *Globe and Mail*, neither the *Calgary Herald* ("Girl sent home for wearing Islamic dress") nor the *Vancouver Sun* ("Muslim pupil sent home for wearing traditional head covering") felt the location of the story warranted prominent display in the headlines. The *Globe and Mail*, as I noted in my introduction, has taken a particularly self-righteous stance around the issue of *hijab* and Quebec.

10. In the *Gazette*, Émilie is qualified as a "13-year-old." The *Globe* describes her as a "teen" or "teen-ager."

11. *La Presse* is the only one of the four newspapers that had its ethnic affairs reporter cover the Émilie Ouimet story. It is also the paper that reported it most consistently. Nonetheless, one cannot accuse François Berger of oversensitivity to the ethnic viewpoint. Reporting on the parents' meeting at Louis-Riel school, he explains that "l'expulsion de la jeune musulmane Émilie Ouimet a *provoqué un ramdam* [my emphasis]" (#4). Here, in a seemingly banal turn of phrase, he perpetuates the contempt for Ramadan, Islam's holiest month, as first articulated by the French colonizers in Algeria. According to Gallimard's *Trésor de la langue française. Dictionnaire de la langue du XIXe et du XXe siècle (1789–1960),* the expression "provoquer un ramdam" was introduced into French from the Arabic around 1890 by French soldiers in the Algerian army:

> "[L]e sens du mot en français vient du fait que l'aspect le plus caractéristique du ramadan, aux yeux de nombreux non-musulmans, soit l'intense et bruyante activité nocturne qui suit les journées de jeûne durant ce mois." According to *Le Robert. Dictionnaire historique de la langue française,* it later also entered "dans l'argot des prostituées (1918) pour 'amour physique.'"

For an analysis of another ethnic slur that reveals a parallel history of sexism, racism, imperialism and war, see David Roediger's "Gook: The Short History of an Americanism" (1994: 117–20).

12. Of the thirty-six articles surveyed from Quebec newspapers, including the *Gazette*, in only one case (#13) is reference made to policies in place in other parts of Canada. Specifically, in *Le Devoir,* Lorraine Pagé (see chronology) castigates Quebec for being "la seule province canadienne à ne pas avoir de politique en matière interculturelle," this with one child in five in Montreal schools having been born outside Canada. On the other hand, as Yuki Shiose and Louise Fontaine point out, it is not in the interests of the nationalist agenda of Quebec's élites to make explicit comparisons with other Canadian provinces: "Les élites (intellectuals, universitaires, technocrates, dirigeants politiques) ont systématiquement promu l'idée d'une différence radicale entre le Québec et les autres provinces du Canada pour légitimer leur demande d'une espace étatique autonome par rapport au gouvernement fédérale" (Shiose and Fontaine 1995: 105).

13. Another more incisive take on the filial relationship of Quebec to France might situate it in the context of what Edward Said has described as the colonizer's "power to narrate, or to block other narratives from emerging or forming" (Said 1994: xiii). To illustrate his point, Said quotes a passage from Frantz Fanon's *The Wretched of the Earth.* Although referring to the colonial context in Algeria, Fanon's words could be construed as equally revelatory of Quebec as a settler society whose story must be told from European parameters: "The settler makes history and is conscious of making it. And because he constantly refers to the history of his mother country, he clearly indicates that he himself is the extension of that mother country. Thus the history that he writes is not the history of the country which he plunders but the history of his own nation in regard to all that she skins off, all that she violates and starves" (1961: 51). In other words, the Québécois nation-state is given a pedigree; its integrity (otherwise threatened by the violence

of its founding moments and its continued exclusions) is stabilized by extending its heritage through space and time to include France. By mapping its history onto the territory of the "mother country," the "imagined community" which is Quebec is able to transcend the disruptive aspects of its existence and to more closely approximate "homogeneous empty time" (Anderson 1983: 26) or "immemorial spatial memory" (Alonso 1994: 387), the preferred chronotopes of the nation.

14. A school which was "publique, laïc et obligatoire" was created in France in 1881–82 (Boyzon-Fradet and Boulot 1991: 237).

15. Muslims may form the second largest religious group in France but "[c]ontrairement aux juifs et aux protestants, les quatre millions de musulmans de France ne jouissent pas d'un réseau d'écoles confessionnelles subventionnées par l'État (dites conventionnées).… La seule école musulmane qui obtient aujourd'hui une aide du gouvernement français est à 10 000 km de Paris … à l'île de la Réunion" (#12). In Quebec, on the other hand, there are 80,000 Muslims (Houda-Pepin 1993). In 1991, government subsidies granted to private elementary and secondary institutions, including Muslim schools, accounted for approximately 52 percent of their total funding (Commission 1995: 45).

16. A pernicious manipulation of the depiction of events in Algeria and France and their superimposition on the Quebec landscape are not the exclusive preserve of the Quebec "mainstream" press. See Richard Martineau's "Leçons d'Alger" in the alternative weekly *Voir* (1995). See also Bélanger and Émond (1996) and Geadah (1996). For a trenchant critique of this tendency, see Tahon (1996).

17. For a less sanguine view of the French role in Algeria, see Ruedy (1992).

18. See, for example, the controversy surrounding the 1989 National Film Board/Radio Canada co-production *Disparaître*: "Il véhicule la menace pour les femmes du retour à la natalité, sinon l'immigration, devenue trop visible, risque de mener à la disparition de la société québécoise et de la race 'pure laine'" (Recourt and Alcindor 1990: 32). Or, contemporaneous with the Émilie Ouimet incident, the alarmist headline of a *La Presse* article decrying the influx of children of non-French/non-British origin in Quebec schools: "Les Québécois: la nouvelle minorité visible. Dans les écoles de Montréal, la proportion des allophones ne cesse d'augmenter" (Berger 1994). The implications here are twofold. First, as in Petrowski's articles, it is understood that "Québécois" and "allophones" form mutually exclusive groups. Second, not only are the "Québécois" in danger of becoming a minority (or of being "swamped by immigrants," to use Margaret Thatcher's infamous phrase), they will be *"visible,"* that is, their supposedly white faces will be outnumbered by those of "allophones," who are assumed to be dark-skinned.

19. See, for example, Vincent (1992) for a media analysis of the Oka crisis or, as she calls it, "Crise québécoise." See also Legault (1994) on the still active suppression of information concerning the events of October 1970.

Appendix
Articles on *Hijab*
September 1994

La Presse
#1 Élève expulsée de son école parce qu'elle portait le foulard islamique (Berger, François). 9 sept.: A1
#2 L'élève au voile islamique ira dans une autre école: La mère d'Emilie Ouimet a demandé son admission à la polyvalente Lucien-Pagé (Berger, François). 10 sept.: A3
#3 La France interdit le foulard islamique dans les écoles. 11 sept.: A7
#4 Port du *hijab*: les parents de l'école Louis-Riel seront consultés (Berger, François). 15 sept.: A3
#5 Les directeurs d'écoles conviés à étudier le port du *hijab* (Berger, François). 17 sept.: A3
#6 L'école à voile (Gruda, Agnès). 19 sept.: B2 [Éditorial]
#7 Les Québécois sont divisés sur le port du voile islamique (Berger, François). 25 sept.: B12
#8 Il serait naïf de considérer le hidjab comme un simple symbole religieux (Baril, Daniel). 28 sept.: B3 [Opinion]
#9 Des principes fondamentaux sont en jeu dans le débat sur le foulard islamique (Gaudet, Jules Édouard). 28 sept.: B3 [Opinion]
#10 Lorraine Pagé et la tolérance du sexisme ordinaire (Côté, J.). 30 sept.: B2 [Lettre]

Le Devoir
#11 Voile islamique: Les parents évacuent la question. 15 sept.: A2
#12 La France voilée: Le foulard islamique alimente encore le débat sur la laïcité de l'école (Rioux, Christian). 19 sept.: A1
#13 Le port du hidjab dans les écoles: La CEQ souhaite l'adoption d'une politique d'éducation interculturelle (Montpetit, Caroline). 20 sept.: A3
#14 Gérer des normes (Baillargeon, Normand). 20 sept.: B1 [Opinion]
#15 Hidjab et crucifix (Bourgault, Pierre). 20 sept.: A6 [Opinion]
#16 France: Le foulard islamique est interdit dans les écoles. 21 sept.: A6
#17 Pas d'élèves voilées (Gomez, Daniel). 28 sept.: A8 [Lettre]
#18 Lever le voile sur le hidjab: Où finit la tolérance et où commence la discrimination sur le port du voile islamique au Québec? (Geadah, Yolande). 28 sept.: A7 [Opinion]

The Montreal Gazette
#19 *Hijab* ban at Louis Riel fuels debate about religious expression in schools (Wells, Paul). Sept. 10: A13
#20 Religious observance merits respect. Sept. 10: B4 [Editorial]
#21 Ethnic diversity being denied (Gold, Jennifer). Sept. 27: B2 [Letter]

The Globe and Mail
#22 Montreal principal denounced for ousting teen in Islamic garb (Picard, André). Sept. 10: A4

October 1994

La Presse

#23 Québec envisage d'intervenir sur le port du voile islamique (Berger, François). 26 oct.: A16

#24 Un lycée de Lille expulse huit autres étudiantes portant le voile islamique. 26 oct.: A16

#25 La France <<laïque>> déclare la guerre au voile islamique (Robitaille, Louis B.). 30 oct.: A2

Le Devoir

#26 Le foulard islamique (Gingras, Adrien). 3 oct.: A8 [Lettre]

#27 La controverse sur le voile islamique en France: Des musulmans font de la résistance. Journée de désobéissance au règlement Bayrou. 3 oct.: A6

#28 L'affaire du foulard en France: La vie d'un lycée est perturbée. 6 oct.: A5

#29 Les islamistes et l'école laïque (Brousseau, François). 6 oct.: A6 [Éditorial]

#30 La tête dans le sable pour le voile islamique: Peut-on mettre sur un pied d'égalité le hidjab, la kippa, le turban et même la croix chrétienne au cou? (Vaillancourt, Yves). 12 oct.: A9 [Opinion]

#31 Les intégrismes religieux: Un appel au dépassement de l'homme (Racicot, Luc). 12 oct.: A9 [Opinion]

#32 Hidjab et soumission (Bernatchez, Suzanne). 20 oct.: A6 [Lettre]

#33 Landry veut un débat sur les symboles religieux à l'école (Paré, Isabelle). 26 oct.: A1

The Montreal Gazette

#34 Forcing *hijab* on teachers unacceptable: Houda-Pepin (Bellemare, André). Oct. 24: A3

#35 Quebec won't support *hijab*s in public schools, Landry says (Block, Irwin). Oct. 26: A6

The Globe and Mail

#36 Time to debate headgear issue, minister says. Oct. 26: A4

November 1994

La Presse

#37 Le foulard islamique (1) (Gagnon, Lysiane). 5 nov.:. B3 [Série]

#38 Le foulard islamique (2) (Gagnon, Lysiane), 12 nov.: B3 [Série]

Le Devoir

#39 La France et l'islam: 2-Le choix de Rahima: À l'ère de Madonna et de Claudia Schiffer, elle a choisi de porter le voile (Rioux, Christian). 8 nov.: A1 [Série]

The Montreal Gazette

#40 *Hijab* incompatible with Quebec society, nationalist group says (Norris, Alexander). Nov. 23: A4

#41 Lemieux blasted for remarks attacking *hijab*s (Norris, Alexander). Nov. 24:. A3

#42 "Not compatible": minorities feel excluded when values are attacked (Curran, Peggy). Nov. 24: A3 [Opinion]

#43 *Hijab*ophobia in Quebec? Nov. 24: B2 [Editorial]

Chapter Five

Challenges Confronting African Immigrant[1] Women in the Canadian Workforce[2]

Patience Elabor-Idemudia

The Plight of New African Immigrants

Today, more Blacks from Africa and the Caribbean, with women constituting a large part of the numbers, are coming into Canada as family members under the family reunification program, as refugees fleeing regional ethnic conflicts and, to some extent, as independent immigrants with education and skills. Their experiences are different but parallel to those of earlier Blacks who came in as slaves fleeing death from the United States, and as freed slaves who were used as indentured workers in agricultural production. They find themselves confronted with unequal access to employment, limited chances for social mobility, marginalized and with inadequate opportunity to integrate into the Canadian Mosaic[3] which in itself is stratified and unequal.

Most of the independent-class immigrants, consisting mostly of highly educated women, have only been able to find work (if at all) at low-status jobs in homes and institutions, doing what is generally considered to be "Black women's work."[4] These women, in addition to suffering from the inequality faced by most women such as low wages, part-time employment, lack of job security, occupational and industrial segregation in women's job ghettos, sexist discrimination, sexual harassment and high unemployment, are confronted by racism, class exploitation and structural discrimination (Boyd 1984). They face discrimination in employment, as well as in the areas of education, housing and immigration, all of which serve to perpetuate inequality.

The family class of immigrants consists of women and children who migrate to Canada as wives and dependents. The women in this category are assumed to have financial guarantees and therefore are not expected to work outside their homes. Their primary responsibility is seen to be with child care and housework (Estable 1989). This, in effect, reproduces traditional gender ideology with regard to the sexual division of labour. The sponsorship agreement of up to ten years puts these women into a dependency relationship with their male principal applicants. Their dependent status is maintained and perpetuated by various institutional processes which have negative implications. For example, the inability of these new African/Black immigrant women to (1) access certain federal social services, (2) voice their experiences in family abuse situations, or (3) access services and programs depending on how provincial and municipal regulations are interpreted in relation to the sponsorship agreement (Lee 1990) have an impact on their quality of life. Moreover, government-subsidized programs such as English/French as a Second Language (ESL/FSL) courses offered by Employment Immigration Canada (EIC) are not easily accessible to the women since they are seen as "not destined for the labour force." Estable and Meyer (1989) see such policies as affecting immigrant women adversely, since about 43 percent of them in 1986 did not know either official language. Community organizations representing immigrant women agree that the Employment Centre's practices place women in a double bind since they have limited access to language training and language upgrading, and are often limited by their childrearing roles from participating even in existing skill retraining programs or in adult education programs. Without these skills, they cannot find wage work. Additionally, the inadequacies of the child care system, the inadequate awareness of the legal rights of workers, and the obligations of the employers all serve to compound the limitations under which sponsored immigrant women may engage in waged work and integrate into the Canadian way of life.

What is obvious here is that sponsored immigrant women are vulnerable to the goodwill of the male principal applicant's confirmation that the sponsorship agreement is intact. This can be said to be due to a combination of patriarchal logic with the principles of racial and ethnic exclusivity embedded in immigration and citizenship laws that are particularly devastating to women who are often not perceived as adults in their own right. Such immigration policies establish the parameters for the "legitimate" entry, settlement and access to social services and paid work of immigrant women. In doing so, they severely limit the women's access and entitlement to the fruits of liberal democratic, feminist and class struggles (Boyd 1989; Anthias and Yuval-Davis 1993). In order to ascertain and/or substantiate some of the challenges identified in the literature and highlighted so far, a case study of problems confronted by African immigrant women in Toronto is presented in the next section of this chapter.

A Case Study of African Immigrant Women
Background Information
It is important to note that although the immigrant women in this study are all Africans, they do not constitute a homogenous group. They differ from one another in language, cultural heritage and style of dress, as well as religious affiliation, political ideology and social class (Moodley 1983). Other factors such as their reasons for immigration, the social climate and immigration policies at the time of their arrival in Canada, as well as their immigration status and their economic situation affect their life experiences in Canada (Horna 1990). For this reason, it is problematic to characterize all immigrant women as a homogenous group. However, once in Canada, these lines of distinction tend

to disappear because of their similar experience of being treated as "outsiders."

The subjects of this study consist of 100 women from continental Africa who have lived in Toronto for at least three to five years. They include women who have come to Canada as students, housewives, economic and political refugees and migrant workers. They represent at least 15 countries in Africa identified as Uganda, Kenya, Tanzania, Nigeria, Ghana, Liberia, Sierra Leone, Zaire, Zimbabwe, South Africa, Malawi, Sudan, Ethiopia, Somalia and Zambia. Their ages range from twenty-seven to sixty-five, and sixty-eight of them identified themselves as married. They all speak some English, sixty of them can read and write the English language, they all have primary and some secondary level of education, with twenty-five of them having some post-secondary education. Twenty of the 100 women had lived in an European country before proceeding to Canada.

As continental African migration to Canada is recent, limited research has been done on this group's integration into the Canadian society (Kazosi 1988, 1992; Neuwirth 1989; Moussa 1993). Although studies relating to labour market integration of other women of colour and immigrants exist, few studies have focussed exclusively on African immigrant women's relationship with the Canadian labour force prior to this study. However, related existing studies serve to generate useful information (Boyd 1986; Brand 1993; Iacovetta 1986; Leah 1991; Ng 1988; Ng and Estable 1987). Such research findings on immigrant women show a bi-modal pattern of employment with over-representation of immigrant women in the manufacturing and service sectors in comparison to Canadian-born women (Boyd 1986). Findings from a general survey to assess "employment, education and training barriers" of immigrant women in Toronto indicate "the largest area of employment was in service occupations followed by industrial jobs" (COSTI 1991).

Objectives of the Study

In order to test the bi-modal pattern of immigrant women's employment, the specific case of African women's relationship with the Canada labour force was examined. The objectives of the study were:

- to document the current employment patterns of African women relative to those of other women
- to analyze African immigrant women's educational and socio-economic background
- to identify barriers to African women's employment and describe the employment needs and concerns of African immigrant women in Toronto
- to analyze current resource allocation models used for allocating employment programme resources, and to evaluate agencies' cost-effectiveness in meeting African women's employment needs.

The research was guided by the following questions:

1. What are the barriers that have confronted African women in their efforts to become gainfully employed?
2. What perceptions about and attitudes toward the barriers African women encounter, due to race, class and gender discrimination, do agency personnel and employers have?
3. What assumptions do agency personnel/employers and the women themselves make about the relative merits of gender roles and women's waged work as (African) family members?
4. What employment services do agency personnel/employers view as most suited to meeting African women's needs and why?

Methodology
To better meet the objectives of the study, both quantitative and qualitative research methods of data collection were used. The research necessitated cooperation with individuals of three different social constituencies—immigrant women, immigration personnel and their agents, and employers. The duration of the field research was four months. The project followed five stages:

1. information gathering involving a review of current literature and organizations working with African immigrant women;
2. focus group meeting of African women that served as a brainstorming session for the development of questionnaires;
3. the design of the questionnaires;
4. administration of the questionnaires to a snowball-selected 100 African women; and
5. personal in-depth interviews with ten African women.

The selection process involved using one person as a link to the next. A list of names for initial contact was obtained from the telephone book, agencies working with immigrants (e.g., Canadian-African Centre for Training (CANACT), African Research and Training and Education Centre (ARTEC), Immigrant Women's Centre, Centre for Francophone Africans, Ontario Coalition of Agencies Serving Immigrants (OCASI), etc.) and from government-funded immigrant-aid community organizations. The people first contacted were then asked to pass on the word to others with whom they were in contact. The rationale for using the snowball method was that members of the communities were accessible to other members. Names suggested were followed through with phone calls and personal visits.

In addition, contacts were made with personnel of the Immigration and Employment office in Toronto to collect information and be more informed about the process of immigration. Documents produced by the office on the process of emigrating to Canada were collected and examined in order to collect information on the services available to immigrants. Contacts were also made with non-governmental agencies that provide services to immigrants in Toronto. After all the interviews and contacts, the research findings were collated and documented for analysis.

The adopted quantitative research method involved the administration of field survey questionnaires to a 100 snowball pre-selected African immigrant women for the purpose of collecting information about them and their experiences in Canada. The questionnaires were designed with sixty items focussed on the respondents' socio-economic background (e.g., marital status, educational background, income), actual employment and employment needs, aspirations, stress management behaviour and survival strategies used to cope with stress. Efforts were made to have as representative as possible a sample reflecting age, marital status, region/country/ethnic group of origin, entry status and education (professionals, degree holders, technicians). This was accomplished by pre-setting quotas to be met in each of the variables and ensuring that the respondents met with such quotas before being selected for the interviews. Telephone, face-to-face and mail interviews were conducted. A three-tier envelop method was used to ensure confidentiality.

The qualitative research aspect involved holding in-depth interviews with ten immigrant women. Open-ended questions were administered and the process required the hiring of translators from the immigrant community to translate the questionnaires to ethnic languages. The use of tape recorders was eliminated because the women did not want their voices taped. When asked why, the respondents expressed concerns and fear that the information might be used against them. Despite assurances from the researchers to the contrary, they still did not feel comfortable and threatened to withdraw from the interviews if tapes were used. Interviews were held with personnel of ethnocultural agencies catering to the needs of immigrant women and immigration officials. A participant observation method was used to gather information on how government and non-government agency personnel adapt to factors in the wider environment which are largely beyond their control, such as policy guidelines and funding constraints in their efforts to deliver effective client services.

Results
Findings and Analysis of Information from Immigration Documents
Information gathered from immigration documents collected during a visit to the office showed that, prior to 1952, Canadian Immigration policies and practices involved the racialization of potential immigrants through a nationality preference system which favoured European immigrants over non-Europeans. Emphasis was placed on white immigrants because they were considered to be of "superior stock," more desirable and more assimilable than immigrants

of colour (Fleras and Elliot 1996: 290). Non-Europeans were deemed undesirable and policies were put in place to prevent their immigration to Canada. For example, Section 38(c) of the Immigration Act of 1910 was amended in 1919 to create a class of immigrants considered to be "undesirable" for admission to Canada. Included in this category were

> those belonging to nationalities unlikely to assimilate because of their peculiar customs, habits, mode of life, methods of holding property and because of their probable inability to become readily assimilated or assume the duties and responsibilities of Canadian citizenship within reasonable time after their entry. This was seen as something that would consequently prevent the building of a united nation of people of similar customs and ideals. (Manpower and Immigration 1974: 9–10)

Accordingly, potential migrants were racialized and ranked in categories, with "preferred" immigrants being drawn from Great Britain, the United States, France and, to a lesser extent, Northern and Western Europe. The federal government subsequently extended its preferential policies to include other "white" immigrants, including Ukrainians, Italians, Poles and Hutterites who were previously classified as "non-preferred." This was due to the failure of its efforts to produce the large numbers of "preferred immigrants" required to settle Canada's western prairie land (Henry et al. 1995: 72).

Post-World War II economics in Canada were characterized by industrialization and rapid technological expansion which created a need for new labour sources. Canada responded by dropping its restrictive and overtly discriminatory immigration policies in order to create an immigrant labour force to fulfill its need. This move occurred under the 1967 Immigration Regulations, which also introduced the "points system," whereby immigrants (regardless of origin or colour of skin) were awarded points based on job training, experience, skills, education and knowledge of English or French. In addition, immigrants were selected on the basis of whether there was demand in the Canadian market for their occupations.

In 1971, the Canadian government adopted a multiculturalism policy and its ultimate purpose was to integrate Canada's many cultural groups and to achieve "unity in diversity." The policy was intended to support and promote cultural differences which would supposedly strengthen Canadian identity. In 1988, parliament created the Canadian Multiculturalism Act which further advocated the eradication of racial discrimination, which was already outlined in the Canadian Charter of Rights and Freedoms in 1985. The question remains whether or not the Act has been actively promoting racial equality beyond delegitimating racial discrimination.

A new immigration proposal and Citizenship Act was set forth by the

Canadian government in the fall of 1994 and adopted in 1997. Changes suggested by the new proposal include:

1. a reduction in overall immigration levels from 230,000 to 190,000;
2. attracting "economic" immigrants through the business-class category;
3. adopting a moratorium on immigrant investment funds and the possible need for bonds or financial guarantees for sponsoring families;
4. shifting of costs of settlement from the taxpayer to the immigrants;
5. a crackdown on abusers of health and social welfare systems (that is, the immigrants who "abuse" the system);
6. the separation of parents and grandparents into a category different from the family-class category;
7. knowledge of English or French as critical; and
8. a separate refugee program. (CEIC 1994)

Despite existing multicultural ideology emphasizing equal opportunity and tolerance, Canada still reflects an immigration policy rooted in racial and class biases. This latest immigration proposal has special implications for race, class and gender and can be said to constitute a renewed racialization and sexualization of immigrants. In essence, the new strategy is more concerned with economic/material gains rather than humanitarian concerns. Its emphasis on admitting those immigrants who possess the appropriate skills and wealth desired by Canada, and its goal of maintaining a certain type of "social fabric" is not only discriminatory but exclusionary. Numerous people who face persecution in other countries and who might seek asylum in Canada are poor and may not meet the language requirement. By adding a language requirement and proposing a guaranteed financial bond, Canada is able to limit the entry of immigrants from non-white countries and increase immigration from white European countries. By stressing a "preferred" type of immigrant, Canada is able to reduce the overall number of immigrants admitted under the family-class category and as refugees. Its déjà vu all over again.

Findings of the Survey
Employment Patterns
The work status of the 100 respondents in the study was found to consist of fifty-eight women who were gainfully employed—mostly in service sector jobs. Of those fifty-eight employed, thirty-eight were working for pay on a full-time basis and twenty on a part-time basis. Of the forty-two women who were unemployed, twenty-eight were actively seeking jobs while fourteen were not working for pay or seeking jobs (see Table 1). Forty of the fifty-eight women in the paid labour force said that they put in twenty hours or more work per week. Thirty-five of the fifty-eight reported their hourly pay to be $6.50 per hour when $7.25 per hour was the minimum wage in Ontario. This disparity is

significant because it reflects inequality in wages for work of similar value. Twenty gainfully employed women reported hourly wages equal to the minimum wage while three reported incomes higher than the minimum wage. When average annual income ($8,500) was examined, the data suggested that immigrant women were not adequately paid. The nature of employed women's jobs included cleaning, childcare, homemaking, caring for the elderly, dishwashing, restaurant work, making beds in hotels, hairdressing and sewing in garment industries. These are traditional female jobs in the service sector, but they are ghettoised, marginalized and are notorious for their poor working conditions and inadequate benefits.

Table 1: Work Status (N=100) and Working Conditions (N=58)				
Employment Status	Working Conditions	Number	Percent	
Full-time		38	38	
	Adequate (N=40)			
Part-time		20	2	
	Inadequate (N=18)			
Unemployed (Actively Looking)		28	28	
Unemployed (Not Looking)		14	14	
Total		100	100	58
Source: Field Survey 1994.				

Most of the women could find jobs only in the marginal labour market where they are subject to exploitation because of their non-unionized position. They are concentrated in the low-paying, low-status, labour-intensive jobs in the manufacturing and service industries, repeating the past history of female immigrants of colour. They often find it difficult to get out of these job ghettoes because of their lack of Canadian work experience and limited proficiency in English. Added to this is the non-recognition by employers of their education, training and experience acquired before coming to Canada. This is rather ironic considering that, since the 1960s, Canadian immigration policy has sought to recruit "Third World" immigrants with high levels of education, as well as professional and technical skills, while labour demand and family reunification policies also brought in many less-skilled and less-educated family members of primary male immigrants. However, there has been no concomitant creation of an adequate labour market, nor any significant attempt to address the issue of access and the numerous barriers to the trades and professions that the highly trained and educated racialized immigrants confront when looking for jobs for which they are qualified. This racist practice has only served to further foster racism in the current situation of state-sponsored capital restructuring (including the free trade agreement with the United States), which has heightened assaults on the labour market.

Concerning the question of working conditions, forty of the fifty-eight working women reported that their working conditions were adequate. Adequate conditions were said to include a good working relationship with the supervisor, a good workplace atmosphere and access to the allotted time for breaks. Eighteen women said that their working conditions were inadequate. Inadequate working conditions consisted of long hours, job insecurity, understaffing and overwork. On the whole, there appeared to be more dissatisfaction with working conditions than the quantitative data suggests. It was later revealed during the in-depth interviews that the women were unwilling to provide details about their working conditions because of concerns for their job security.

The trends observed in the findings recorded above support the dual labour market theory which posits that a primary and a secondary sector exist in the labour force, which consists largely of white males occupying the primary sector characterized by stable employment, strong trade union organization and representation, relatively high pay and good working conditions. The secondary sector, on the other hand, is characterized by predominantly female or visible-minority labour with instability of employment, low trade-union organization and poor conditions of work (Anthias et al. 1993). Black migrants or women are, indeed, employed more often in unskilled and semi-skilled jobs in particular occupations and industries, many involving low pay and minimal job security. For this group of immigrant women in Canada, the fact of their race and gender coupled with the stereotypic ideology and stigma endemic to their social construction as "immigrants" and/or "women of colour," assumes their limited knowledge or lack of formal education (Ng 1988). They are stigmatized as a people who speak English—if at all—with an accent and who come from "visibly" different cultures from "our" own (Bannerji 1987). The indigenous cultures of African immigrants are seen as inherently conservative and pathological, not oriented toward developing a high level of self-esteem, self-identity and, therefore, rendering them incapable of success in participating in Canadian social life (Agnew 1996).

Disadvantage experienced by Black migrant women may not merely be a question of racial discrimination in the job market, though there is indisputable evidence that it exists. Processes of economic restructuring must be taken into account. The overall effects of capital restructuring may have seriously affected these women, given their sectoral and subordinate position, through uneven economic growth, labour market segmentation and industrial relocation, which have detrimental consequences for all lower socio-economic groups in Canada.

Summary of Commonly Expressed Barriers and Challenges

Based on the survey of 100 women, the forty-two unemployed women identified the following problems as those constituting barriers to their access to gainful employment (see Table 2). Detailed analysis of each problem is not possible in the limited space of this chapter but will be incorporated into the discussion of the results.

- difficulty in gaining recognition for education already obtained in country of origin
- difficulty in gaining access to institutions of higher learning to upgrade their education
- lack of access to day care facilities that would enable them to engage in gainful employment
- accent and language seen by potential employers as problems
- lacking "Canadian experience" seen as a major setback to gainful employment
- perceived as overqualified for English as a Second Language classes
- personal circumstances, social pressure to stay at home, cultural barriers, the burden of double day and lack of support
- lack of support from employment agencies
- not knowing where to go, that is, a lack of knowledge of existing resources and inadequate knowledge of interview procedures
- ideological and stereotypical beliefs held by potential employers were acted out in interviews and resulted in poor performance of the women.

The survey also revealed that no mainstream agency was currently delivering effective employment services to ethno-cultural and racialized minorities which met the employment needs of African immigrant women. As alternatives, a few community-based ethno-cultural agencies have sprung up to fill the void. Ninety-eight percent of the respondents said that they did not find the mainstream agencies useful in finding jobs or in helping them prepare for job searches. The few African-focussed agencies which service this client group were found to be working under tremendous internal and external pressures that affected their ability to deliver services. The cultural diversity of African immigrants makes it difficult to design programs that meet their many and different needs.

Table 2: Identified Barriers to Gainful Employment (N=100)		
Identified Challenges	*Number of Respondents	Percent
Non-recognition of foreign qualifications	85	85
Lack of access to higher education	65	65
Lack of knowledge of English	25	25
Lack of access to childcare facilities	60	60
Having an "accent"	98	98
Family responsibility	70	70
Lacking "Canadian experience"	95	95
Personal circumstances	10	10
Cultural barriers, pressure to stay home	42	42
Lack of support from employment agencies	55	55
Lack of adequate information on how to find work	50	50
Limited knowledge of existing resources	40	40
Inadequate knowledge of interview process	50	50
Hostility from potential employers due to stereotyping	65	65
Religious reasons	16	16
Source: Field Survey 1994. *Note: Multiple categories indicated in subjects' responses.		

Existing resource allocation models are not effective in meeting the employment needs of the client group, especially in the area of childcare and the provision of community support. These trends are similar to those of previous studies' findings (see Boyd 1989) and are overwhelming for women who are overburdened with household chores, childcare and struggling with surviving in a new culture.

In ethnocultural organizations based on a monocultural model of delivery, it was also found that cultural, gender and racial barriers to service-delivery are not addressed. The services thus provided are based on the assumptions that—despite the obvious difference in cultural backgrounds and racial and gender identities of clients—all people share common needs and desires and, therefore, require similar modes of service and intervention.

Analysis and Discussion of Survey Findings

The questionnaire responses and interviews made it quite apparent that immigrant women confronted challenges/barriers to getting jobs for which they were qualified. These challenges/barriers were found to intertwine with institutional, systemic and socio-cultural discrimination. The findings of this study support those of previous studies which highlighted the "double-day" syndrome of paid and domestic labour (Armstrong and Armstrong 1990). The burden of the double day is intensified when the workplace becomes a place where immigrants experience segregation and isolation. Many of the women thus turn to their homes or ethnic communities for refuge from an alien environment. Many women were accustomed to participating in the paid labour force in their country of origin, and to the income, social support and independence which such participation represented. For these women who now find themselves either unemployed in Canada or hired domestic workers, the emotional effects of immigration are staggering. The situation these women face is worsened when they see their children and husbands being integrated into Canadian society because of their proficiency in the English language which they do not have. This exclusion from integration serves as a major source of alienation.

The work life of the African immigrant women in the sample changed after their arrival in Canada. Twenty percent of the respondents who reported housework as their sole occupation in their country of origin were employed in the paid labour force in Canada as janitors, nurse's aids, homemakers (cleaning the homes of middle-class white Canadian families or the elderly). This is consistent with Black women's historical work patterns in Canada. Sixty percent of immigrant women experienced a downward mobility trend in their occupational status when they entered the Canadian workforce. Twenty percent of the women continued working in similar occupations. Typical transitions reported were from nurse's aide to janitor, or from cleaner in hospital to cleaner in a hotel. Only five percent of the respondents reported upward mobility in the Canadian labour force. This included two women who worked as hair stylists in their country of origin and now owned their own beauty salons. Two other women reported owning their own restaurants after working as waitresses in their countries of origin. A former dress-maker in her country of origin now works as a social worker. Fifteen percent of the women reported that they could not find jobs even though they had an average education and had work experiences in their home countries. It was the lack of Canadian work experience that posed a barrier to employment. It is used as a yardstick by employers to measure immigrant women's suitability for the labour force. Although some women found employment despite lack of Canadian experience, mostly they were not employed in the areas in which they were trained or had experience. Additional studies examining African immigrant women's employment histories over time may provide insights into individual and group supports that facilitate entry into the labour market as well as eventual patterns of employment mobility for some.

The challenges confronted by African immigrant women in Canadian society are further compounded by the fragile positions of ethno-cultural agencies and community workers, who are supposed to play a pivotal role in providing services to racial and ethno-cultural communities but do not have formal degrees and certificates as social workers. A private member's bill that was proposed in the Ontario legislature to that effect would prohibit such workers without "credentials" from operating as certified social workers (Henry et al. 1995: 152). However, the bill was rejected because, according to Patricia O'Connor of Toronto George Brown College, the implication of the regulation limiting certification to university graduates was that funding agencies might be contingent on hiring only those with the right credentials (Webster 1992; Henry et al. 1995: 157).

There has been a continued push for increased professionalization and credentialization within the social service sector with resulting hierarchical work environments. Moreover, social workers and other human-service practitioners from diverse racial and cultural communities frequently experience major conflict between their cultural values and those of the dominant culture. This can seriously influence the practice and priorities of their organizations. They are frequently isolated and marginalized in mainstream agencies with the primary responsibility of serving clients who share the same racial or cultural background even if they have the required Canadian/provincial credentials. They tend to have limited power and status within larger mainstream organizations and in ethno-cultural organizations are confronted with limited sources of funding. Both of these limitations have resulted in typecasting of some ethno-cultural centres as places where all "problems with Blacks" are referred (Thomas 1987). As a result of these bottlenecks and stigmas, many clients under-utilize or terminate their involvement with some agencies, finding the manner of service delivery too institutionalized, fragmented and culturally insensitive (Agard 1987).

Interviews

In order to further validate this study's survey findings, summaries of the ten in-depth interviews of African immigrant women are described below. Four cases are described in detail because they are representative of immigrant and racialized women's experiences. The other six cases are paraphrased and described together. The cases capture the experiences, needs and concerns of women from Uganda, Ghana, Nigeria, Kenya, Sudan and South Africa and cover three regions of Africa—East, West and South. The four respondents whose interviews are individually presented below consist of two professionals and two non-professionals with a relatively good education.

Case I—A husband and wife, both medical doctors specializing in Gynecology and Obstetrics, moved from Ghana to Toronto as landed immigrants in 1989. They sat for the Canadian Evaluation and Qualifying Exams in 1990 and 1991 and passed, but could not attain opportunity for medical residency/training either in Toronto or in other provinces. They were told that if they could find a sponsor, for example, a pharmaceutical company to pay for their residency, then places might be made available. "The problem is money," they were told. They looked for research positions and could not find any. Neither could they find any opportunity to volunteer as research technicians to acquire some Canadian experience. "We were living like outcasts and were rejected everywhere we applied to," they said. "It was really a humiliating experience for us," said the wife. The couple was forced to live on social assistance for over three years and began exploring opportunities in the United States after passing the American qualifying exams.

A number of issues arise from this case: frustration, disappointment and emotional distress at both individual and family levels. The social and financial cost of wasted talent and the devaluation of the couple's knowledge because of their immigrant status is racist and problematic.

Case II—This case deals with another woman who was qualified as a veterinary trained at Makere University in Uganda. She described her experience here in Canada since her arrival five years ago as a "run around." Before emigrating to Canada for safety reasons, she had three years working experience and was familiar with the veterinary licensing process, including writing an exam. She tried gaining admission into an Ontario university to upgrade her skills and was invited for an interview but was unsuccessful in gaining admission. When she inquired about the reasons for her rejection, she was told that the competition was very stiff and that there were a limited number of spaces. She was advised to take three correspondence courses in order to improve her qualifications for admission the next year. The following year she again applied for admission. When she was not invited for an interview she inquired about the status of her application. This time she was told that the courses she had been advised to take were not needed for admission into the school. "They only served as a way of assessing your capacity to function at a certain educational level." Her admission was also turned down a third time. At the time of the study she was working with the Ontario humane society as a secretary and was still attempting to gain admission into a program for which she has qualifications from another country.

Case III—My third interview was with a woman from Nigeria who holds a degree in education. She came to Canada with her husband who is a graduate student. She is legally qualified to work in Canada, but all efforts to secure a job in her profession have been unsuccessful. In seeking accreditation for her degree from Nigeria she was told that it would not be recognized without make-up courses. "I was willing to take the make-up courses, but could not gain admission to any university because I was the spouse of a foreign student." In the past three years, she has worked as a home-care giver and at times has worked as a babysitter. While her husband is completing his studies, she is not even given the chance to upgrade her skills. "I feel very frustrated and have, at times, suffered from depression because of the loss of my privileged middle-class position in Nigeria and my lack of extended family support here, especially because I am a mother of two young children."

Case IV—The respondent in this case was a Black woman from South Africa who came to Canada as a refugee during the apartheid regime in South Africa. She completed high school education prior to coming to Canada but has had difficulty retrieving her original certificate from her country of origin. She has, therefore, not been able to further her education and has had to engage in menial jobs to survive. "I have had no luck finding a job in the formal labour force because of the stigma attached to my being a refugee who was forced to depend on social assistance. Every attempt I have made to improve my situation has not materialized," she said. "I am a single mother of three children who are now adolescents and who place high demands on my time. My children are all in high school and I have to make sure that their needs are met first before mine," she added. Although she is now a Canadian citizen, she had resigned herself to her low-income status. For low-income women in Canada, greater access to educational programs as an adult along with income and childcare supports might enable them to envision and plan for a different future. She was very glad to have been part of the focus group conducted as part of the research, and she was particularly happy that we were interested in her story. She has experienced a lot of discrimination and isolation since arriving to Canada, but has continued to make the best of her situation. Her children have successfully integrated into the Canadian social fabric and she was hoping that they would not have to experience what she went through both in her home country and in Canada.

Cases V–X—Three of these six women had backgrounds in elementary education, two with administrative skills and one with a background in health care. The three women (two Kenyans and one Sudanese) with degrees in education accompanied their husbands who were pursuing diploma programs. They were legally qualified to work in Canada, but all efforts to secure jobs in their fields of qualification were unsuccessful. They had sought accreditation for their foreign qualifications but were told that the degrees were not valid in Canada without make-up courses. They tried to find jobs as early childhood educators (ECE) but were turned down because they did not have ECE certificates. In the past three years, they had worked as occasional babysitters and as domestics. Ironically, there was a growing gap between their education and those of their husbands. They were concerned that this might create problems later in their marriages. Many women who have sacrificed their own careers to either support their husband's or accompany them have faced that reality down the line. Ways of addressing the situation of women who accompany their partners need to be examined from the early stages in which those plans are being made.

Two women, a Ghanaian and an Ethiopian, with backgrounds in administration said that their two-year effort to find employment yielded nothing, and one finally gave up trying and resigned herself to being a full-time housewife, while the other did typing work such as term papers, resume writing and theses for people from her home. Both respondents said that they occasionally volunteered their time at the African Research and Training Centre (Toronto) helping others to develop their resumes. They saw little hope for improving the opportunities for immigrant women to attain jobs for which they were qualified.

The woman from Eritrea with health care training did not succeed in having her qualifications recognized. She was not allowed to practice in her field except as a care-giver in a nursing home. She was particularly displeased by this because she was a nursing sister (a well-respected middle-class position) in her home country. She had worked for three years in the nursing home and was still not valued as a worker. She told of instances when she had been picked upon by her boss. On one occasion when she was ill and could not show up for work, she called her boss to inform him and rather than be sympathetic and understanding he threatened her with job loss if she did not report to work. As she was not in any position to lose her job, she went to work where she was so sick that the boss ended up sending her home. This woman felt trapped in her situation because her husband did not have a job. The thought of standing up for her rights was not a realistic option for her at that point. "I have to keep my job for now, until my husband finds a job so that we can continue to take care of our children. We do not want to depend on welfare as we were raised to earn our keep."

Analysis of In-Depth Interview Findings

In analyzing the findings of these ten highlighted in-depth interviews, it is obvious that racial and gender bias, stereotypic perceptions of immigrants, systemic discrimination and non-recognition of foreign qualifications all constitute barriers and are disadvantages to these racialized, migrant and ethnic African women. These disadvantages can be explained and linked to some of the following factors identified by Anthias and Yuval-Davis (1992):

1.   the women's position *as migrants* determines their legal, political and economic position differently from that of men, and points to their position in immigration and nationality laws
2.   the women's position *in racialized social relations,* and the specific forms which they take for men and women, and different ethnic groups points to racism and its effect
3.   the women's position *as women* and the sexism rampant in contemporary societies are overlaid by internal sexist relations and cultural practices of the groups. This ties in with patriarchal relations and sexist social policy and the different forms that they take
4.   the women's position *as members of particular classes* but who are ghettoized in particular areas of employment are overlaid by racist and sexist exclusion and discrimination. (p. 124)

It is, therefore, easy to conclude, from this study's findings, that the social construction of African immigrant women's race, the interaction of cultural norms, the experience of being transplanted into a new community, lack of perceived English language skills, pressures of raising a family, limited resources, lack of family connections and community support networks have exacerbated their marginalization from the labour force, limited their growth and development and, undoubtedly, have made their assimilation into the Canadian society difficult. The numerous unsuccessful attempts to enter their profession or trade has inevitable and deleterious effects on their self-esteem.

The study also reveals the degree to which African women's labour force participation conformed to the historical pattern for most immigrant women of colour. The pattern differed somewhat from that of white immigrant women when compared with other existing research findings. For example, Boyd (1984), in a study of the occupational attainment of foreign-born women in Canada, found that the situation was much better for those (Nordics) coming from Britain or Western Europe and with professional standing. They could more readily gain entry to well-paying white-collar jobs than those coming from Eastern or Southern Europe (Mediterraneans) or from Asia, Africa or the Caribbean (people of colour).[5] This differential occupational attainment can be mostly attributed to their race/ethnicity and class, and the ideological construct attached to them as already highlighted.

Cost-Effectiveness of Gatekeepers, Change Agencies and Social Networks

Three types of social agencies were found to be operating to address immigrant women's issues. I will refer to them as gatekeepers, change agencies and social networks. In attempts to assess the cost-effectiveness of these agencies in meeting the employment needs of immigrant women, gatekeepers (employment search and placement) and change agents (employment training) working with immigrants were interviewed and observed as they carried out their roles in three agencies. The gatekeepers were found to be mostly young, middle-class, Anglo-Saxon males who were either born in Canada or migrated with their parents to Canada at very early age. They were university educated and exercised a lot of control over the process of applying for jobs. Both the gatekeepers as well as change agents were similar in terms of race/ethnicity, class, language, gender, age and length of stay in Canada. On the other hand, most of the social workers were women who, although they were university educated, had limited clout. They were understaffed, quite frustrated and burnt out because of the heavy case loads they had to carry. Most of the immigrant women interviewed found the gatekeepers to be unfriendly and very paternalistic, while the social workers were not in a position to help them with their employment needs in a meaningful/practical way.

Mainstream agencies' effectiveness in meeting African women's employment needs when measured in terms of former clients' rate of participation in the labour force after various periods of time (up to ten years) was found to be inadequate and lacking. Of the 100 women surveyed, only fifteen found the agencies to be useful in meeting their employment needs. The resource allocation models used by the change agents to meet the employment needs of African women were found to be unstructured and developed on an ad hoc basis. They did not meet the employment needs of the women. They tended to focus on training in basic English as a second language. Although most of the African immigrant women already spoke and understood the English language, the "Canadian experience" which the women lacked was not provided by the agencies and their models for resource allocation.

As an alternative to existing agencies, the women formed social networks with an ethno-cultural base which they activated to get employment. These networks, although informal, were quite effective as some of the women were able to secure jobs as homemakers and childcare givers through information provided by their friends and network members. They were introduced and recommended to potential employers by members of these social networks who were doing similar work. These findings show that the need exists for social networks to be empowered through recognition and incorporation into a formalized system where they can collectively address some of the challenges that result in the marginalization of immigrant women in the labour force. These social networks, consisting mostly of ethnocultural groups where women have collective support and have a sense of belonging, could be funded by government to conduct research and develop policy statements that could be used in identifying and ameliorating systemic discriminatory practices against these women. Such an approach would help group members to develop a sense of belonging, usefulness and contribution to their newly adopted countries and integrate into a truly Canadian mosaic.

Conclusion and Strategies for Change

The findings of this research show that African immigrant women face problems similar to most immigrant women in Canadian society. However, these problems are compounded because of their social construction as immigrant women of colour. Discrimination, ghettoization in the paid labour force (that is, the restrictions that limit women to low-paying and low-status jobs), and the "double day" duty of both paid labour force activities and the domestic labour of caring for home and family are common experiences for women in Canada. In addition to the experiences faced by women (as a group) in Canada, immigrant women are required to adapt to the new society, to learn new language skills and to overcome the isolation and discrimination imposed by their new society. The dependence of immigrant women is dramatically perpetuated by their limited political clout and their isolation from the society at large. It is also important to note here the broader significance of networking in gaining employment. These women, as do many other groups, found employment primarily through informal networks. However, for those who are members of a group connected to well-paid professional and/or unionized jobs, the chances of accessing those jobs are higher than for persons from groups differentiated by gender, race, ethnicity and class. This, in part, explains the difficulty that well-educated immigrants and well-educated citizens of ethno/racial and lower-income backgrounds have in breaking barriers of access to higher-level paying jobs. While they may have the educational qualifications, they usually do not have the informal connections to those networks. Therefore, it is difficult for them to get a foot in the door. The situation of women from groups minoritized by race, ethnicity and class is compounded by the gender inequities that women's groups have continuously tried to have addressed (i.e., double work-day and the devaluing of women's reproductive work and the traditional caring professions).

If immigrant women of colour and African immigrant women, in particular, are to be adequately integrated into the Canadian mosaic, we must begin to construct community understandings that take positive social actions which celebrate, acknowledge and affirm difference and variety rather than denigrate them. Community-based approaches to ameliorating challenges confronted by immigrant women must include developing an understanding and appreciation of individuals and their different cultures and lifestyles. Such an approach must include viable avenues to formal recognition of immigrant women's foreign experience and qualifications, while providing a constructive path for design-ing community education and training programs. The establishment of broadly-based community coalitions would also be necessary to develop the strategies outlined here. The nature of this step is echoed by Bronfenbrenner (1979) who recommended partnering between organizations and agencies to build interconnectedness between various systems. Along the way, sensitivity in addressing issues of power and privilege, and a broadly-based system of collaboration that includes immigrants (both men and women) should be threads woven into the plan of action (DeBord and Thompson 1994).

It should be noted that in all of the preceding discussion regarding the analysis of the challenges confronted by African women, their stories of resist-ance and agency, may have been overshadowed and a picture of hopelessness may have been unintentionally painted. This is not, of course, the case. There is hope for the alleviation of the women's position because they are actively involved in ethno-cultural, racially specific and community-based agencies that are growing to fill the huge gap in service a delivery system created by the failure of mainstream institutions to serve the needs of a multiracial, multicultural and immigrant population. These agencies are, however, confronted by their isolation from the mainstream delivery system combined with a lack of support from government and other funding bodies for community-based agencies (Henry et al. 1995). Yet, they have undertaken the responsibility of providing more effective, responsive and equitable services to minority communities with little recognition and remuneration. It is within and through these very organizations that women of colour, including African immigrant women, must fight for their right to employment, access to training, housing and social services. These should be basic human rights in a country which they have come to regard as their home.

Notes

1. The terms "African immigrants" and Black immigrants are used interchangeably in this chapter to refer to immigrants of the same race with origins in Africa.
2. This study started out as part of a Social Sciences and Humanities Research Council of Canada–sponsored research co-investigated with Nakanyiki Musisi but subsequently ended up becoming a privately sponsored research by the author when the co-investigation terminated before the data was collected.
3. Mosaic is a metaphor to describe the ideal arrangement of various racial and ethnic groups in societies such as Canada. It is an image of disparate and distinct elements arranged into a patterned, cohesive whole.
4. Such work consists of cleaning white people's houses, bathrooms and hotel rooms; serving white people breakfast, lunch and dinner in private homes, in office cafeterias and hospitals; lifting, feeding, minding and washing white people's children and older white people; sweeping, boxing, scouring, washing and cooking (Brand 1987).
5. See also Tania Das Gupta (1994).

Chapter Six

Toward Anti-Racism in Social Work in the Canadian Context

Usha George

Recognizing the pervasiveness of racism and the importance of anti-racism in social work practice, this chapter attempts to provide a framework for anti-racist social work practice in Canada. I will begin with a brief overview of the literature on racism at different levels of intervention in social work practice. The second part of the chapter provides an analysis of the Canadian structural context in which social work is practised. The final section of the chapter outlines a framework for anti-racism in social work practice. The framework emphasizes multiple levels of analysis and engagement. At the individual level, this involves layers of understanding, which recognize the discourse of racism, the problem of intersecting oppressions, the historical experiences of different groups in Canadian society and the barriers they face, the role of the state in creating and sustaining oppressions, and the importance of active engagement towards the elimination of racism. At the organizational level, the framework emphasizes the importance of anti-racist organizational change. Anti-racist work at the structural level incorporates coalition building for collective action. The concluding section of the chapter reiterates the importance of white social workers and social workers of colour working together to bring about anti-racism change.

Racism and Social Work Practice

Race and ethnicity are important considerations in social work practice, however, social work has paid inadequate attention to them (Cooper 1973; Casas 1985; Proctor and Davis 1994; Sue, Arredono and McDavis 1992). Racism is inherent in social work practice (Dominelli 1988; Henry, Tator, Mattis and Rees 1995). In a content analysis of literature on social work practice with minorities, McMahon and Allen-Meares concluded that "most of the literature on social work practice with minorities is naive and superficial and fails to address their social context" (1992: 533). The colour-blind approach which prevailed until the late 1960s and the "blame-the-victim" approach which characterized much of the 1970s and part of 1980s (Cooper 1973; Proctor and Davis 1994) shared certain assumptions that racial/ethnic minorities were by nature pathological and, therefore, individual problems were the result of individual group characteristics. This approach encouraged racist practices and provided an excuse for counsellors not to challenge inequities within the system (Sue,

Arredono and McDavis 1992). Much of the research during this period focussed on race and ethnicity as client characteristics (Casas 1985; Ponterotto and Sabnani 1989). No attention was paid to variables such as counsellors' attitudes towards minority clients, the power differentials between counsellors and clients or the structural inequalities that limited minority access to services. Later models referred to in the literature as the culturally different model, the multicultural model or the culturally pluralistic or diverse model (Sue et al. 1992) pay attention to the culture, ethnicity and race of the clients, while ignoring the unequal power relations between the client and the social worker and the multiple oppressions that clients of colour experience in a stratified society (Dominelli 1988).

Racism is also rampant at the organizational/agency level. In a review of nearly 400 publications from Canada, the U.S., Britain and Australia, Reitz (1995) concluded that there is considerable evidence that immigrant groups do not use many important health and social services because of barriers related to language, cultural patterns of help-seeking, inadequate information about services, cultural insensitivity on the part of service providers and lack of service availability. In their study of Metropolitan Toronto, Doyle and Visano (1987) identified many barriers faced by racial and ethnic minorities in accessing health and social services. Racism in human services is manifested in "a lack of appropriate programs and services, ethnocentric values and counselling practices, a tendency to devalue the skills and credentials of minority practitioners, inadequate funding for ethno-racial community-based agencies, a lack of minority representation in social agencies, and monocultural or ad hoc multicultural models of service delivery" (Henry et al. 1995: 154). "Personal, institutional and systemic racism affect the kinds of service, training and employment opportunities available to members of racial minorities throughout the social and health-care system" (Tator 1996: 153).

At the organizational level, racism is manifested in the predominance of assimilationalist and multicultural models of organizations (Jackson and Holvino 1989; Henry et al. 1995; Tator 1996; Minors 1996). The assimilationist, or mono-cultural model, assumes that equality is achieved by treating everyone the same, that too much attention paid to differences will only perpetuate those differences, that the collective history of a group is irrelevant to work with clients from minority cultures, that workers are competent to deal with all issues, that racism is limited to a small number of people and that the values of the organization permeate every facet of the organization's functioning (Tator 1996: 155). The multicultural model leads to superficial changes in an organizations' functioning that do not alter their fundamental structure, functioning or culture. These organizations effect cosmetic changes to their operations, such as employing a small number of ethnic staff or translating some of their publications into languages other than English. The low-profile minority workers get very little support in their work and the needs and

perspectives of minorities get minimal attention. The culture of the organization is still mainstream and organizational inertia prevents real progress towards creating access and equity for ethno-racial minorities (Henry et al.
1995). "Social work exists in a racist society and, like other services that
target minority populations, social work is open to charges of racism"
(McMahon and Allen-Meares 1992: 533). Moreover, society undergoes changes
over time and so does the nature of racism created and perpetuated by the
dominant system.

The Structural Context of Racism in Social Work

"The world today is a racial battlefield" (Winant 1994: 267). True as it is, this
statement and others are being made at a time when the division of human
beings on the basis of racial characteristics is generally accepted as invalid as a
method of interpreting the complex nature of humankind. An examination of
the structural context of social work will further our understanding of the
persistence of racism in these times because "demographic shifts, political
realignments and economic pressures—both global and national—profoundly
affect the nature of racial identity" (Winant 1994: 286). Lee, McGrath, Moffatt
and George have identified "the critical trends facing geographic, functional
and identity-based communities in Canada" (1996: 223). Originally developed
to examine the context of community practice, their framework is broad enough
to provide an understanding of the context of social work practice. Four general
trends that impinge communities are the effects of globalization and technological development, ideological impositions upon the concept of community,
the devolution of social welfare responsibility to the local community, and the
growing diversity of communities (1996: 223–27). These trends do not operate
in isolation, they interact in complex ways on the lives of individuals and
groups. Brief explanations of these trends are given below.

Capitalism has become a global system as a result of the movement of
capital and people, enhanced by the development of information technologies.
These developments are often seen as historical imperatives and therefore they
escape close scrutiny of their impact on communities. However, they contribute
to the marginalization and disempowerment of a great number of people,
especially immigrants, refugees and poor people in Canada (1996).

The global era has also brought with it a new social contract, in which
rationality, technology and corporate power take precedence over community,
personal autonomy and humanity. Principles of mutual responsibility, equality
and empowerment acquire new meanings within a technological and individualistic paradigm (1996).

Massive changes have taken place in the area of social programs. Under
the pretext of deficit reduction, federal and provincial government support for
education, health and social programs is being slowly eroded. As a result, local
governments and local communities are asked to shoulder the responsibilities

of individual and community well-being. The concept of community capacity is promoted to evoke the nostalgic notions of caring neighbours, which masks the real intentions of the political masters (1996).

The demise of geopolitical colonialism, the development of a neocolonial political economic order, and the mass migration of people from former colonies to most Western societies have contributed to the growing diversity of hitherto homogeneous populations. Immigration trends in countries like Canada, Australia and the U.S.A. show an increase in people from non-European countries. Canada's population is becoming more and more diverse in terms of its ethnic composition (Statistics Canada 1996).

Much has been written on racism in Canadian society and how the policies and programs of the government have further marginalized poor people, immigrants and refugees. It is important to recognize the existence of racism in the contemporary Canadian context. For example: Martin Loney

> advances the unfashionable point that poverty and wealth, not race or gender, remain the key influences on life chances. The book details the millions of dollars of public money directed to groups like NAC and Alliance for Employment Equity to promote the fiction that, through race and gender, biology dictates destiny. (Loney 1997)

> The Ontario Coalition of Agencies Serving Immigrants states that community leaders feel that newspaper articles about immigrants, refugees and people of colour are neither fair nor balanced and that the effect of this imbalance on immigrant communities is substantial. (OCASI 1996).

> Although the proportion of visible minorities in the Canadian labour force rose from 5.9 percent in 1986 to 12 percent in 1996, their representation in the public service has increased from 2.7 percent in 1987 to only 4.1 percent in 1995. (Samuel 1997)

> A study which examined the impact of funding cuts on community services in Toronto observed: "the people who have lost the most in terms of access to services over the last two years of cuts have been immigrants and refugees." (Social Planning Council of Metropolitan Toronto and City of Toronto 1996: 46)

A number of steps by the current provincial government in Ontario including the cancellation of the Employment Equity Policy, the dismantling of the Anti-Racism Secretariat and cuts to many social programs that provided access and equity to minority populations have clearly indicated the lack of political will to address systemic discrimination in our society. Any systemic attempt to counter racism has been abandoned in favour of market-driven approaches. In keeping with the trend of the times, anti-racism as a system-wide strategy to bridge the power and opportunity gaps for minority populations has become decentralized. Racism is micro-managed and dealt with at the individual level even when it is reported.

A Framework for Anti-Racism in Social Work

Anti-racism is integral to the profession of social work. Social justice, the primary goal of social work, cannot be achieved in a racist society; it cannot be achieved through methods of practice that ignore the racialization and marginalization of vulnerable groups in society. Anti-racist social work theory, along with other critical social work theories, combines theory and practice to produce knowledge, interpret and change the world. It also argues for the unity of different levels of practice and policy work in social work (Banes 1998). "Thus, in a general sense, anti-racism refers to measures and mechanisms designed—by state institutions, organizations, groups and individuals—to counteract racism" (Henry et al. 1995: 39).

Although researchers and practitioners disagree over the best way to eliminate racism, they all recognize the importance of multiple levels of analysis and engagement. "I concur with those who have called recently for an explicit recognition of the multiple determination of racism, one that draws upon not only historical materialism but also psychoanalysis" (Miles 1994: 207). "Any strategy for effectively resisting racism, therefore, cannot be unitary—and probably not even unified" (Anthias and Yuval-Davis 1992: 157). According to Dominelli (1988), anti-racist social work focusses on transforming the unequal social relations between Black and white people into egalitarian ones; therefore, deconstructing racism requires changes at both systemic and individual levels. Recent attempts by Bishop (1994), Essed (1996) and Kivel (1996) have also emphasized the importance of multiple levels of anti-racism work.

The model proposed here has three components incorporating individual, organizational and structural levels: (1) anti-racism education and training for social workers, (2) anti-racism organizational change and (3) coalition building for collective action. These components should not be seen in isolation; their interactions are vital to an effective anti-racism strategy. Although a legal and policy framework is an important component of anti-racism work, it is not included in the model because the state is the final source of macro-policies. Social workers can influence the state mainly through collective action. In the following section, I will examine the three components of the proposed anti-racism framework in detail.

Anti-Racism Education and Training

At the individual level anti-racism requires that white social workers recognize their relative positions of power and privilege in a hierarchical social system that works in their favour. White social workers need to undergo anti-racism sensitivity training to enable them to unearth and discard avoidance strategies (Dominelli 1988). Social work education should provide the appropriate knowledge, values and skills to practice social work in an anti-racist way. The term "layers of understanding" denotes the convergence of knowledge, values and skills needed for ethnically sensitive social work practice (Devore and Schlesinger 1996). Cultural competence, that is, the ability to work effectively with individuals and groups belonging to different cultures (Green 1995; Lum 1986; Cross, Bazron, Dennis and Isaacs 1989), is also important in anti-racist social work. The layers of understanding which should form the basis of anti-racist social work education and training in the Canadian context are as follows.

Recognition of the Nature of Racism

This requires an understanding of the social construction of race and racism and the changing nature of racism. Although the notion of biological groupings of people on the basis of phenotypical characteristics is "no longer intellectually and politically viable as a public discourse" (Modood 1997: 154), new forms of racism have emerged. For example, in a climate of democratic racism policy or practice, initiatives to change oppressive conditions are undermined by the assumptions expressed in statements such as:

- "Racism doesn't exist in a democratic society."
- "Everyone experiences discrimination from time to time."
- "Racial conflicts occur because of diversity."
- "Minority groups refuse to adapt to Canadian society."
- "People of colour have cultural problems."
- "All we need is to treat everyone equally." (Henry et al. 1995: 308)

The discourse of cultural racism (Modood 1997) ascribes group differences to differences in culture. Under paternalistic and competitive racism (Essed 1996) the roles of dominated groups are defined by the dominant group's perception of the dominated groups.

Silva, after a thorough review of the existing views on racism (idealist, classical Marxist, neo-Marxist, institutional, internal colonialist and the racial formation perspective), advances a structural interpretation of racism that incorporates elements of the various theories. Silva defines racialized social systems as "societies that allocate differential economic, political, social and even psychological rewards to groups along racial lines; lines that are socially constructed." In a racist society, "a set of social relations and practices on racial distinctions develops at all societal levels." Races "historically are constituted according to a process of racialization" and opposition between racialized groups. This in turn gives rise to a racial ideology, which is not a superstructural phenomenon, but "the organizational map that guides the actions of racial actors in society." Racialized societies also produce racial contestation, which "reveals the different objective interests of the races in a racialized system" (Silva 1997: 10). This framework explains overt and covert racial behaviour as well as the changing nature of racism.

Changes are due to specific struggles at different levels among the races, resulting from differences in interests. Such changes may transform the nature of racialization and the global character of racial relations in the system (the racial structure). Therefore change is viewed as a normal component of the racialized structure (Silva 1997: 11). This perspective, however, does not answer the question: how do racialized systems come into existence? It has limited ability to explain the intersections of class and gender in racialized societies. The structural origins of racism demands a structural solution for its elimination and this has important implications for "curing" racism.

Understanding the overlapping relationships of race, ethnicity and culture and the interlocking oppressions of race, ethnicity, class, gender, sexual orientation, age, religion, language and other factors on the experiences of clients and the relationship between clients and social workers.

The overlapping definitions of race, ethnicity and culture complicate efforts to understand racism (Yinger 1994; Berry and Laponce 1994). "We are close to having come full circle. In the nineteenth century, race was used to mean culture as well as race. The twentieth century may well end with culture meaning race as well as culture" (Berry and Laponce 1994: 5). Although much work has been done in this area, theories about the complex relationships among race, class, gender and other forms of oppression are still inconclusive (Stasiulus 1990). For example, women of colour experience racism and sexism together. These oppressions interact and influence each other. "Multiple oppression is stressful and draining" (Gerrad 1991: 564). "Racisms cannot be understood without considering their interconnections with ethnicity, nationalism, class, gender and the state" (Anthias and Yuval-Davis 1992: viii).

The concept of integrative anti-racism represents recent attempts to capture the intricate relationship between race, class, gender and other sources of oppression (Dei 1995, 1996). Integrative anti-racism requires an understanding of the different yet intersecting forms of oppression based on race, gender, class, sexual orientation, religion, age, language or other factors, using race as the lens through which varied forms of oppression must be viewed (Dei 1995, 1996). Integrative anti-racism acknowledges the shifting and intersecting experiences caused by socially constructed race, gender and class categories and recognizes the saliency and visibility of certain forms of oppression. Integrative anti-racism draws on six interrelated issues:

1. understanding the process of articulation of social difference,
2. understanding the relevance of personal experience and knowledge,
3. understanding how differentials of power and privilege work in society,
4. understanding the saliency of race,
5. understanding the importance of global political economic issues, and
6. understanding how to engage in social transformation.

"When we also develop a consciousness about the numerous layers of oppressions that add up to subordinate the majority of people in society, we can better understand how these various oppressions also have a personal impact on our own lives" (Carniol 1991: 118).

Appreciating and understanding the historical experiences of different ethnic groups in Canada and the structural barriers they face in gaining access to services.
The history of Aboriginal peoples in Canada and the experiences of Black Canadians, Chinese–Canadians, Japanese–Canadians and South Asian–Canadians with respect to Canadian immigration policies reveal the extent of exploitation, domination and racism that has characterized the relationship between the dominant whites and others (Bolaria and Li 1988; Henry et al. 1995). Some of the theories that explain and predict the situation of ethnic groups in a post-industrial society are: assimilation, amalgamation, modified assimilation, modified pluralism, ethnic pluralism and ethnic conflict (Driedger 1996). The theory of pluralism and differential incorporation has been applied to the Canadian situation, in relation to Caribbean people in Toronto (Henry 1994). Henry argues that "societal racism," that is, the racism and discrimination in mainstream society, and its reluctance to respond to the needs of newcomers "create the marginal status for the Caribbean people and result in their differential incorporation into Canadian society" (Henry 1994: 16).

Acknowledging the role of the state in disempowering some population groups and understanding the impact of "neutral" policies on marginalized communities.
Recognizing the emerging heterogeneity of Canadian society, the government has a number of legislative measures to guarantee equal treatment of ethnic minorities in Canada. The Canadian Charter of Rights and Freedoms, the Canadian Policy on Multiculturalism, the Canadian Immigration Act, the Human Rights Code and federal Employment Equity legislation are examples of such attempts. It is important that social workers have a grasp of the strengths and weaknesses of these policies. Moreover, social workers should be equipped to examine the implications of new policies on minority populations. For

example, the proposed recommendations in the current legislative review of the Immigration Act have both economic and social implications for Canada's immigrants.

Working towards the elimination of all forms of oppression through reflective practice, critical thinking and collective action.
Social workers, due to their privileged positions, may not admit their own racism. This may happen through denial, omission, decontextualization, colour-blind approaches, dumping approaches, patronizing approaches and avoidance (Dominelli 1988). Anti-racism awareness training for social workers enables them to examine their individual attitudes and how they shape behaviour. It also helps social workers see the connection between individual and structural elements in racism, and how personal changes can contribute to structural changes through the design of policies and practices that are sensitive to the needs of non-dominant groups. Many of the models developed in cross-cultural training share three characteristics: a recognition of the role of one's own ethnic or cultural identity in determining one's world view, an emphasis on learning about other cultures, and the teaching of intervention and counselling skills for use with members of other ethnic groups (Corvin and Wiggins 1989). White social workers can become allies with marginalized people to break the cycle of oppression (Bishop 1994).

Feminist ideas have tremendous possibilities for combating racism. "The agreement to hear, see, and know about racism in ourselves is the core of making anti-racism a norm for ethical feminist therapy practice" (Brown 1995: 145). The three feminist principles: feminist consciousness and consciousness raising, the principle of integration and the idea that the personal is political are relevant to the development of an interactive perspective on ethnic minority issues (Gould 1987). Consciousness raising has two elements: it searches for dehumanizing social structures and it is oriented towards action to alter these social conditions (Mullaly 1993). The concept is very similar to the conscientization process by which individuals make the connections between the values, behaviours and attitudes they endorse and perpetuate and the social positions they occupy (Freire 1970). Conscientization enables social workers to understand their own privileges and this in turn helps them to change their attitudes and behaviours to treat others with openness and dignity (Dominelli 1988).

Anti-Racism Organizational Change
Social workers can encourage anti-racism organizational change by ending the conspiracy of silence about racism, by establishing equity in the workplace, by initiating discussions about the components of anti-racist social work and by establishing mechanisms to monitor the progress of anti-racism policies and programs within the agency (Dominelli 1988).

Anti-racism organizational change demands a holistic approach, commitment to the eradication of all forms of oppression and the elimination of racial disadvantage within the organization. It requires that social workers acknowledge that the perspectives of people of colour are relevant and real, and that people of colour should be included as full and equal participants in the organization. The organization must make fundamental changes to its policies and practices to be more inclusive. The "integrated multicultural/anti-racism model" of human service organizations gives high priority to the issues of minority access, participation and equity (Tator 1996).

James (1996) introduces an anti-racist model of service delivery which stands in sharp contrast to the multicultural model. The anti-racist model is characterized by the ongoing analysis of individual experiences in institutional contexts, challenges to existing power relations, the ongoing analysis of social systems in relation to its constituencies, the examination of the values of human service providers and institutions, and the provision of programs of employment equity and access for disadvantaged groups.

The models proposed by Dominelli (1998), Henry (1995), Tator (1996) and James (1996) incorporate both individual and organizational imperatives for change. Minors (1996) examines different models of change within organizations. The transition from "uni-versity" (discrimination) to "poly-versity" (anti-discrimination) represents anti-racism organizational change for the organization. In this process, the organization passes through six stages from an excluding organization, to a passive club, to token acceptance, to symbolic equity, to substantial equity, to an including organization. This is a linear model and actual organizational pathways may differ because of complex institutional patterns of behaviour.

Successful transition to anti-racism requires organizations to identify structures and behaviours that need to be changed, determine training and education needs, sanctions and supports, plan and implement necessary changes, and review, monitor and evaluate the changes (Thomas 1987, United Way 1991). At the organizational level there should be an anti-racism policy with goals, timetables and accountabilities that will promote access and equity for clients and for minority workers in service provision and the management of the organization.

Anti-Racism and Coalition Building

Social workers must help mobilize communities for action against discriminatory practices, policies and legislation. Social work tradition has always emphasized individual change along with social action, social change and community development (Elliott 1993).

Anti-racist social work recognizes the relationship between individual troubles and structural inequalities and works towards connecting the personal and the political. The community development continuum (Jackson, Mitchell and Wright 1989) takes into account the need for individuals to take charge of their lives. Jackson et al. (1989) suggest that this continuum consists of a number of stages: developmental casework, mutual support, issue identification and campaigns, participation in and control of services, and social movements. The goal of developmental casework is to create links between individual service users, so that they can mobilize for change for themselves and others. Developing mutual support involves strengthening families and establishing friendships and other networks. During the stage of issue identification, many "natural networks" come together to form coalitions interested in achieving change. The participation and control stage provide opportunities for people to become active in decision making to ensure that services are responsive to local needs. The final stage involves participation in social movements. At this point people become committed to ongoing change. This continuum does not describe an inevitably upward progression. Individuals can enter the continuum at any stage.

When social workers reject the strong push towards a conventional version of casework and act forcefully in favour of clients, they are at least temporarily able to interrupt the top-down flow of power and the associated social relations imposed by the welfare state. Granted such interruptions are by themselves insufficient to change the prevailing structures of society, they nevertheless constitute essential building blocks for basic change (Carniol 1991: 116). And unfortunately setbacks may occur.

Two important components of this model are empowerment and advocacy. According to Evans, the literature suggests three processes that facilitate empowerment (1992). These are skill building, the enhancement of feelings of efficacy and awareness of social realities which, taken together, are said to develop a sense of critical consciousness. Advocacy is an important element in anti-racist social work. "Advocacy involves acting as a broker among the community, institutions, and government—identifying unfair and unjust practices, advocating for new policies and programs, supporting external alliances or coalitions, working collaboratively with ethnospecific agencies, and lobbying for changes in education, policing, justice, and employment" (Tator 1996). The essence of anti-racism is to challenge the status quo through political activism. Therefore the anti-racist worker has to be a theorist and a practitioner at the same time (Dei 1996).

Conclusion

In concluding this chapter, I would like to draw attention to three important points. First, all social workers should be involved in anti-racism work. White social workers and social workers of colour should share the responsibility for bringing about change. Commenting on the complex relationship between race, ethnicity and nationalism, Rattansi (1992) points out "that racism and ethnocentrism are not necessarily confined to white groups" (p. 36). Varying levels of ethnocentrism, nationalism and even racism exist among people of colour, and social workers should be aware of the resulting ambivalence and contradictions. Secondly, the state has a major role to play in providing policy and fiscal supports to anti-racism efforts. The state has to create the required institutional framework to eliminate racism that affects the lives of people who are already vulnerable. Third, as discussed in the second part of this chapter, the context of social work practice is changing rapidly. Diminishing resources have prompted the development of short-term interventions and brief service models. In Ontario many programs and services specially designed for immigrant and refugee communities have been eliminated. In an environment of growing insecurity, anti-racism work should not be seen as a nonessential component of social work.

Chapter Seven

"Making" White Women through the Privatization of Education on Health and Well-Being in the Context of Psychotherapy

Kerstin Roger

This chapter explores how the practice of psychotherapy by white women in a large Canadian urban centre in the 1990s continues to structure hierarchical relations of race between women within the helping professions. The contemporary practice of psychotherapy will be shown to be a privatized and elite site, through which the social service professions have continued to provide Western white women with access to professional work that is based on an historically negotiated presence of the racial other. Not only are white women as psychotherapists seen to be elite helping professionals, assisting either other whites or a small group of people of colour, but they are also invested with kindness and innocence through this more elite helping work. This chapter highlights the hierarchies and contradictions that occur within such professionalized practices of helping. The broader implications of this essay will, I hope, lead to an understanding of how Western white women, who gained elite status through the professionalization of helping activities in the early twentieth century, as well as through gaining entry into the practice of psychotherapy through the emergence of a North American feminism in the mid-twentieth century, are reproducing historical relations of race, class and gender.

After describing the methodological foundations of this study, I will begin with an historical genealogy that makes clear how the creation of Canada as an imperial colony constructed the following hierarchies:

1. the health and helping professions in the early twentieth century,
2. how it constructed the white woman as a health expert, and
3. how the white woman and her particular professional use of empathy became a regulatory device for social relations of difference.

I will conclude by offering some suggestions for psychotherapy as a site for transformation within an anti-racist educational framework.

The Methodological Context of This Study

This research emerged as a study of race relations between women involved in the social services as helping professionals and their racially/ethnically constructed clients. What follows is a summary of this study's methodology. I had at my disposal a training centre where I had been trained as a psychotherapist and was now a resident/staff person. At this centre I could interview willing interns, ensuring a similar training model and theoretical modality. The majority of interns were white women who had all been previously involved in publicly-funded social service agencies prior to this training in a private setting. I discovered that none of the women of colour, a minority in this group, would be available to be interviewed. Since there were only a few men in training, I necessarily concentrated my focus on volunteer white women. I was intrigued that psychotherapy at this centre was primarily white and female. Exact figures on the race and gender distribution of resident/staff persons was not available. For me, practising in such a private sector setting made more visible and salient how, as privatized helping professionals, we were involved in educating others (new therapists and clients) about specific class norms, as well as Western values related to relationships, mental health and well-being.

I first selected ten women from this centre who would represent the broadest cross-section of ethnic, class and training backgrounds, as well as sexual orientations. Some of the psychotherapists I selected were currently in training, some had quit their training at some point after the interview and gone into private practice, and some had left the profession during the writing of this essay. Others had completed their training in the five years prior to the interview and were now in private practice. I proceeded with the interviews, reflecting with the women on their childhood experiences of race and difference, on why they decided to become trained as psychotherapists and on how they worked with their white and non-white clients.

Beginning the analysis of the first ten interviews, it became clear that these initial interviews would not be sufficient to support the text on empathy and whiteness that was emerging, and I included five further interviews to better describe the newer focus on empathy and how these psychotherapists were using empathy to help regulate social relations that constituted the race and gender of their practices. These final five interviews continued to develop themes which had emerged in the initial ten.

Finally, it became important to look at the history and evolution of the practices within psychotherapy which might have helped shape and facilitate how these fifteen white women came to access the profession of psychotherapy and how they depended on the racial "other" located both within and outside of psychotherapy in order to constitute their professional practices of helping. I began to refer to van Dijk (1993) for his discourse analysis on race, to Frankenberg (1993a) for her study on white women, to Burton (1994) for a European historical perspective on Christian white women as missionaries,

Stoler (1995) for how the bourgeois white woman as a social subject was shaped, and Valverde (1991) for a Canadian historical perspective. Fellows and Razack (1998) also presented methodological tools for looking at how race, class and gender interlock in order to shape social subjects.

Integrating this literature with what was emerging in the interviews suggested that the essential professional tools that were taught in psychotherapy functioned to shape these white women as innocent and kind, yet elite at the same time. The fact that we are educated and educate others on what it means to be "healthy" in the privatized setting of psychotherapy and the way in which health is performed by the health educator suggests that as psychotherapists we participate in constructing specific historical norms.

Why Study "Whiteness"?

The study of white subjects is a contradictory process. It is problematic because one reinscribes whiteness simply by describing it (Ellsworth 1997: 264). For example, the white researcher must almost exclusively refer to dominant discourses in writing about the white subject. She performs and regulates what it means to participate in a dominant group even while she is writing about it. This circular process denies that researchers of colour would interject a very different position on race and, therefore, break apart the practice of "how whites see whites." As Hurtado and Stewart suggest (1997), "people of colour are experts on whiteness, which we have learned whites most emphatically are not" (p. 308). In this way, whites researching whiteness can often reproduce a kind of individualistic and supposedly rational narrative, as if other narratives on whiteness neither matter nor exist. Chabram-Dernersesian (1997) suggests that "whiteness is [nor] should ever be a category of social analysis in the way that race, class and gender or other social categories are" (p. 111).

At the same time, failure to research whiteness (even by whites) threatens to entrench its invisible centrality, revealing practices within supposedly reified relations of race, class and gender so that those practices that maintain the invisibility of whiteness cannot be named or explored. As Roman (1997) states: "To get *off* white ... first requires that we get *on* it in critical and politically transformative ways" (p. 278). Omi and Winant (1993) suggest that such a critical and process-oriented analysis of race relies on political relationships, a global context and historical context in order to understand how race is performed as an ideology throughout all social practices.

The study of whiteness then possibly becomes a study, in part, of how "race" happens, how it is maintained and how different cultural and racial relations are shaped through various examples of social power situated through the previously invisible presence of whiteness. As Frankenberg (1993a) has stated, "naming 'whiteness' displaces it from the unmarked, unnamed status that is itself an effect of its dominance" (p. 6). In this chapter, the exploration of the practices of white women as privatized educators concerned with issues of health and well-being provides a means through which whiteness can be named in an attempt to continue the discussion of race, class and gender.

Historical Context of the White Woman as Health Professional

Through the context and practices of European imperialism, the British were involved in creating the nation Canada as a colony of Britain, and by the early to mid 1900s Canada had consolidated itself as a "white settler society" (Bakan and Stasiulus 1995: 97). In order to obtain the labour required to continue building this white settler society, British settlers encouraged immigration and developed Canadian citizenship and immigration procedures within a strongly racialized hierarchy (Calliste 1991: 153). These policies on immigrant selection were primary forces that shaped Canadian society's race, ethnic, gender and class relations (Ng 1991: 18). As Ng (1991) and Calliste (1991) argue, immigration policies were designed to support the building of a British colony and, therefore, subjugated those immigrants who were not seen to be British enough (both by placing them in lower-level paid work and by discriminating against all immigrants within social and public discourses). While ethnic and non-white immigrants were generally desirable for such work, these immigration policies gave preference to those who could assimilate more quickly, had an education and spoke English (Ng 1991: 18). The local "others," the Aboriginal population, had already become marginalized by state organization, and the desire for economic expansion demanded an increasing influx of external immigrant labour from outside of Canada (Valverde 1991: 15). This empowered the British Canadian community as governors of all other immigrant and Aboriginal people.

The British represented a community of Protestants who were mostly white and English-speaking, monogamous and heterosexual (at least publicly), middle-class and not first-generation British immigrants, who "[wanted] both immigrant and social deviants to embrace the culture and values of Anglo-Saxon, Protestant, middle-class urban Canadians" (Valverde 1991: 29). Protestants in particular were seen as moral guides and social helpers in fulfilling the duties that went along with the social reform movement (Valverde 1991: 16), thereby producing a privileged position for them even among other Christians.

The goal of the reform was, for its Christian Protestant members, to have an impact on all ethnic and non-white immigrants, as well as the working class, influencing views about how children should be raised in the home and school and defining attitudes for adults. For example, the moral value that emerged to "keep clean minds and bodies" for the sake of building Canada as a nation became incorporated within what Valverde describes as part of the social purity movement (Valverde 1991: 17). This goal of purity reproduced the values of the elite so that they might become the normative standards of sexuality, family life, and religious and work-related disciplines. This reflected imperial discourses that had already been shaping European culture (Burton 1994; Stoler 1995).

As the Christian church expanded its mission work to social sites, it hoped to infiltrate into society a renewed kind of mission that would continue the Christian reform project. These renewed reform projects included the designation of education or government-run agencies to reach out to the poor, the ethnic or racial "other" and the "sexually misaligned" (Newton 1992). As James (1996) documents, since these social projects were begun through the Christian mission, they were also bound in mandate and finances to the church, providing it with a continued ability to regulate their policies including the parameters in which they operated. This leadership heightened the church's continued ability to be involved in a reform that was social as well as religious and allowed the British Protestants to continue to participate in regulating the relations between themselves and those considered "other." For example, "government sanctioned social work programs ... depended on the funding of dominant organizations and not surprisingly reflected the social perspectives of middle- and upper-class Canadians" (Christensen 1996: 144).

As this social mission work came to be more organized and formalized, it was seen as work that required expertise, certain skills and training. This organization depended on a specific classification of social problems that removed the professionals from the larger problems of society and focussed their attention on the evident struggles of the individuals who were experiencing problems (Wharf 1990: 25). The public work of helping began to appear in the form of a new "science" where people's individual problems could be enumerated through a professionalized language of health and well-being. The activity of helping others was transformed into practices that included measurement, classification and organization on paper so that others could review, repeat and improve on these practices.

This environment shaped how the emerging health and helping professional could perform—a person could become a successful professional when they performed well as a non-judgmental and objective "scientist" promoting a better society through their practices of measurement and classification. The underpinning belief was that "the wealthier classes should be charitable to the 'deserving poor' [and could] enter into assessments of personal problems that have systemic roots" (Christensen 1996: 143). Christians and other whites who were already in a social position of privilege during this time could become such professionals and then transfer their knowledge about health management to other whites who wanted to become helping professionals. In a sense, they could teach and reproduce again and again the norms of Protestant membership and socially construct those "other" who did not belong.

Now, instead of providing others seen to be "less fortunate" with the enlightenment of Christianity, the professional nurse, social worker, shelter worker or teacher could improve upon their health, well-being and family relationships. Because access to this type of professional employment was restricted to people who were already in socially elite positions, assessment could then become a measurement of who most or least approximated these historical and social norms. This genealogy suggests how white women in Canada gained access to elite forms of professional practices such as health management, providing a means regulating of who was seen to be "healthy," knowledgeable and most representative of the "norm."

The process of professionalizing, helping and training white women as helping professionals marked their historical entry into an imperial system of education (Burton 1994). The historical white women who had been working in the community as social reformers could be trained to use these tools of classification and measurement that were shaping health professions as a science (Iacovetta and Valverde 1992). Their ability to use these scientific tools marked their success as professional helpers and solidified their economic place of privilege as health professionals. Through their ability to participate in writing down, classifying and signifying on paper how the racial "others" were different from them, they were seen to be working towards the hope of a "better society" (Iacovetta and Valverde 1992). This was a problematic and circular process, because while it gave the historical white women real privilege, it ensconced them within a system that was designed to pathologize all those, including themselves, who deviated from it.

The History That Shaped Feminist Psychotherapy

The North American feminist movement in the mid-twentieth century played an important role in disrupting some of the more traditional definitions and practices of this new health profession as a science. One of the most important influences of the North American feminist movement has been an exposé of a supposed universalized theory of development and a patriarchally based psychiatry and psychoanalytic theory. Several North American feminist theorists have suggested that behavior and personality were more closely linked to social contexts than to the traditional notion of biological drives (Belenky 1986; Jordan 1991; Miller 1976; Spelman, 1988). These feminists suggested that issues of development for women did not necessarily originate from penis envy, sexual drives or fantasies and fears about castration, as posited by earlier psychoanalytic processes, but that the issues of self and other for women were shaped through and within historical and social structures of power, as well as through world views based on the standpoint of women.

The idea that female experiences may be situated within non-male-based symbols fundamentally disrupted traditional theories of the development of the self and made more visible women's actual experiences (McClintock 1995). McClintock states, "the phobia of the 'nothing to be seen' of women is actually the male fear that we have different desires of our own" (1995: 191). Wright (1989) concurs with McClintock's critique that women have traditionally become the signifiers of men in symbolic and real ways. She suggests that "woman in patriarchy is condemned to occupy the place of signifier for the male other, who can give free reign to his fantasies and obsessions, and what is more, can implicate her in them" (Wright 1989: 142). Through a disruption of such traditional theories, North American feminists brought to light the need to theorize about the standpoint of women and their actual experiences within a patriarchally based world (see Chodorow 1989; Klein 1988). These critiques have included thinking which informed the anti-psychiatry movement and its pathologizing of women (see Miller 1976), theories of the body and body image as it pertained to women (see Bordo 1993; Brown and Jasper 1993) pronounced the significant presence of violence against women and the implications of this for working with adult survivors of incest and other violations (see Greenspan 1983; Jordan 1991; Miller 1976).

As North American feminists critiqued psychoanalysis on the basis of gender, they ultimately began to shape a new kind of helping profession that was similar to psychoanalysis yet resisted both its mandate and that of the developing "science" of the health professions. This new form of private feminist therapy "evolved from the feminist consciousness of those of us in the mental health field who found a discrepancy between our own experiences as women, and those described by the psychological theories we were required to learn and apply" (Laidlaw and Malmo 1990: 1).

During the early North American feminist movement, it was hoped that all women would come together in the context of this new therapy and break the silence about their experiences of discrimination, sexual harassment, rape or incest, and other forms of victimization. This new therapy was an acknowledgement that not all problems could be solved by political activism, but that the psychological dimension of women's experiences needed also to be addressed (Malmo 1985). For this reason, alternatives to the formalized mental health system were sought out in an attempt, through these combined conditions, to shape a private and individual place for all women to break their silence, begin to heal and continue with their activism (Chaplin 1988: 3). Laidlaw and Malmo (1990) specify three main components to this feminist therapy.

Firstly, they suggest that feminist psychotherapists recognize that anger is particularly difficult for women to express since they have been taught that anger is not valued. Secondly, they suggest that feminist psychotherapy attempts to teach women to nurture themselves, develop more friendships and continue talking about their relationship experiences in other contexts. Thirdly, feminist therapists hope to encourage their clients to continue to see that internal and external change is necessary so that the healthy client can continue being an activist outside the psychotherapy session (Laidlaw and Malmo 1990: 5).

These historical conditions marked the emergence of a North American white woman who was both resisting patriarchal practices, as well as becoming a privatized and privileged white educator on issues of health and well-being.

While she was hoping to disrupt all women's experience in patriarchy, by entering into a privatized professional space of self-reflection and education, she was entering into a more elevated and elite professional practice of helping others. This context provided North American white women with an opportunity "to test their independence from the constraints of patriarchal society" (Chauduri and Stroebel 1993: 9) while gaining status in a public realm and normalizing cultural standards of mental health and relationships.

The Discussion of the Interviews

This historical context frames how the fifteen contemporary white women in my interviews described their definitions of psychotherapy as a form of resistance to their own childhood experiences of patriarchy. Yet, marking the site of psychotherapy as primarily white, and of relative leisure (i.e., working-class women could not access it), self-reflection and private payment continues to shape these women as elite helpers and educators on health and well-being.

I reflect here on the women's stories about psychotherapy. These stories illustrate an awareness of resisting patriarchy by choosing to become psychotherapists. For example, Theresa suggests:

> I guess the way it started, I had seen my mother go through a lot, and my own ability to read people was pretty good, and so it became something I could put to use as a therapist. I felt that I could have an impact on other women who were also feeling the way I had, or had gone through what we had.

Many of the fifteen women described early childhood experiences related to gender as functional in their decision to become psychotherapists. Psychotherapy was imagined to be a professional site valued in its potential to transform some of these early "girl" experiences. As Goldhor-Lerner stated, "It is precisely the impact of patriarchy [that] is so profound and pervasive that it is not possible to fully comprehend how it shapes our theoretical assumptions and our practice of psychotherapy" (1988: xxi). Psychotherapy became a professional option for these women because it was imagined to provide a degree of solidarity among all women, initiate political action and increase a disruption of oppression.

The women in the interviews go on to describe how the possibility of becoming a psychotherapist marks their female experiences within patriarchy. Here, Serena defines her practice of psychotherapy:

> I guess it's looking at memories, memories of incest and things that have happened to people. Those are experiences you can't change and they do affect you in a social setting as well. I think therapy is about change and healing, and some kind of personal development.

As these women talk about their hope for and understanding of psychotherapy, it becomes easier to imagine it as a site of transformation and a disruption of social realities that refer to systems of patriarchy. This disruption caused by psychotherapy often occurs in the form of education, as Reta states:

> Therapy can be about education. Sometimes its about educating people that the system stinks. Sometimes its about their families. I feel deeply that therapy can be about mending some broken parts of ourselves that come out of an unhealthy society.

The prospect of educating themselves and other women about an "unhealthy society" emerges here. Nora calls herself a feminist in the interview and reflects on the possible transformative nature of psychotherapy:

> I do believe it is about deep change in terms of clarity and accepting people. It is not an overtly political front, but saying it's not political is very political. Educating people and empowering people, I think, goes hand in hand.

Nora is describing how psychotherapy can educate clients, empower women or transform society. She refers again to how these white women valued the possibilities that existed for them within the context of psychotherapy. Chaplin (1988: 6) describes this goal of psychotherapy when she suggests that:

> Feminist counselling rejects the prevailing hierarchical model of thinking, and recognizes the interconnection between different, even opposite, sides of life.... It is struggling towards greater justice and equality. It is about respecting and celebrating differences such as female/ male, Black/white.

Positioning psychotherapy in this way reflects these women's hope that they can participate in changing the realities of other women, but it does not always make clear that this hope for change through psychotherapy makes emancipation possible primarily for white middle-class women. Ophelia defines her approach to therapy:

> My history in a family with broken bodies and diseases, alcoholism and the negative affects of that, brought me to this profession, wanting something to be different, wanting something to be noticed. I feel that therapy has a large educational component to it and looking at social issues and how people hold onto stereotypes. It's not just about individual mental health but also about a community's sense of health.

Her hope for psychotherapy, as other women have mentioned, is based on the influences of feminism that suggest an empowerment for all women and oppressed people. Laidlaw and Malmo (1990: 3) support this view that psychotherapy is educational about a broader social change because

> as women began feeling safe in disclosing their pain to other women, they also looked for alternative therapeutic resources that would support their struggle to heal. As we, the therapists, listened to and worked with these women, the more we began to understand what they needed in order to become psychologically healthy and strong. As such, [feminist therapists] validate the clients' experiences, encourage them to fully examine their feelings, beliefs, intentions, and behaviour, and support their movement toward healthy growth and change.

While feminist psychotherapy initially included a re-visioning of oppression within society, and while this is reflected in the stories of the women above, it has in practice done little towards shaping a profession that is not exclusively white and North American based. As feminist psychotherapy has grown out of a resistance to patriarchy (and psychoanalysis) in the last thirty years, it has also become a helping profession for primarily white middle-class women. Psychotherapy, while it has value for the white women who can gain from it, does not address the disruption of race-based forms of oppression.

A Primarily White Clientele

As the fifteen women in the interviews now describe, their private practices have primarily white women as clients. Theresa suggests that:

> Most of my practice is white women ... interesting, I had always thought it was more diverse than that. I am not sure about therapy really, what its potential is or how it is limiting.

Erin states about psychotherapy:

> A place in me wants to be more radical, working more with the people [refugees] above. It strikes me that I didn't go into social work and why ... yet I seem more attracted to the one-on-one relationship.

While these women refer to the cost of psychotherapy as a barrier, this does not take into account barriers imposed by cultural differences and a history of racism. While cost remains an issue of access, barriers associated with psychotherapy being situated within Western and white methods and discourses, and that most of its practitioners are white, are not mentioned. Lize speaks clearly about access to psychotherapy when she says:

> It's not really accessible to anyone who doesn't speak English or doesn't come from that kind of framework. In a Canadian way, it's sort of white bread, middle-class, not immigrant. I think that's really important, the way that people get "othered" in therapy. Most women of colour that I know who are therapists are working in agencies. So that is very significant.

Lize's summary of the demographics of psychotherapy illustrates how it represents a singularly Western-based privileged population. Beth also suggests this, saying:

> Well, I think I do attract—although I am referred them [whites]—I think there is a process of attracting the kind of people you feel comfortable with and can work with. Somehow unconsciously that gets to be played out here. I love doing this work. I realize its not the majority, or the reality for most people. I guess I haven't realized how much I have been isolated and protected from the world.

Another therapist, Brandy, speaks eloquently in the interview about the possibilities for resistance that psychotherapy serves. However, while she has stated that she would quit if she "thought therapy was only white," she also refers primarily to white clients in her practice.

While these women are describing their hope for psychotherapy, their reflection on its primarily white practice identifies a history of psychotherapy as a more elite form of helping and health education. While they do refer to individual clients of colour throughout the interviews, these remain the exception to the rule. As the previous historical genealogy of the helping professions has already illustrated, the presence of the immigrant and racial other has shaped how the historical white woman in Canada first gained a public status as a social service worker. Through an existing affiliation to what had been considered normative, British and finally white, many white women gained access to these helping professions. As this study explains, this also provided them access to a more elite form of helping called psychotherapy.

According to Canadian employment trends of immigrants from non-Western countries in the early to mid 1900s, the racial other can also be seen as a professional helper (Calliste 1991). However, this is in the less elite work of the domestic or the nanny, work still primarily taken up by women. The entry of the racial other into this kind of helping marks a hierarchy within the health and helping professions that regulates the privilege of white women against the subordination of women of colour. This hierarchy is described by Bakan and Stasiulus, who remark that "parents who work evenings or on weekends ... have contributed towards a growing demand for full-time live-in caregivers ... [and] most such applicants for in-home caregiving positions are recruited from overseas" (Bakan and Stasiulus 1995: 308). Bakan and Stasiulus go on to state, "because of the poor working conditions associated with providing live-in care, few workers in advanced states seek this source of employment if any other labour is available" (Bakan and Stasiulus 1995: 308).

This statement highlights the less-elite working conditions of the person of colour as a domestic or nanny whose less-well-paid work makes the elevated work of other white women more possible. White women can gain access to the more elite helping professions based on a hierarchy between women in the helping professions. They have access to this form of helping work because of an imperial history that shapes white subjects as normative and the racial other as culturally and racially different from this norm. Psychotherapy becomes a site and practice that is defined by white women's resistance to patriarchy without necessarily acknowledging how this work and its professionals are shaped by a deeply regulated history of imperialism.

The Professional Tool: Empathy and the White Woman

While all fifteen women in these interviews began their helping careers in the public-sector helping services/professions—such as nursing, social work or Christian mission work—each of these white women eventually decided to become trained as a psychotherapist. Within this context, I now argue that the professional use of empathy as a technique continues to contribute towards their professional status and personal gain. Empathy becomes a professional tool that regulates and shapes their practices and their professional success with all white and non-white clients. As I will explain, this success depends not only on how they use empathy, but also because they have a mostly privileged white female clientele with whom empathy will be more successful when class and gender are also similar. In this way, empathy expressed by middle-class white women towards other white clients will be described as essential in regulating racial relations within psychotherapy and within a hierarchy of the helping professions.

Theorists of psychotherapy and psychoanalysis have described empathy, a concept much debated in the psychoanalytic field, in different ways. Moore and Fine define it as

> a special mode of perceiving the psychological state of experiences of another person. To empathize means to temporarily share, to experience the feelings of the other person. One partakes of the quality but not the quantity, the kind but not the degree of the feelings. (Berger 1987: 6)

Alternately, object relations theorists describe empathy as "an affective intuitive process involving a temporary breach of ego boundaries and regressive, symbiotic merger" (Jordan 1991: 27). Basch describes it as a combined collection of data including affect and formulating a structural understanding of the client's communications (Berger 1987: 37). Kohut (1995) speaks about empathy as vicarious introspection and as a type of observation. Feminist theorists such as Gilligan (1982), hooks (1988), Jordan (1991), Miller (1986) and others have also revised and significantly elucidated empathy. As Jordan (1991: 29) suggests, it

> always involves a surrender and cognitive structuring ... allowing perception of the other's affective cues, verbal and nonverbal ... thus producing a temporary identification with the other's emotional state. There is a momentary overlap of self and other representations and a resolution period in which one regains a sense of separate self that understands what has just happened.

In particular, as my description of feminist psychotherapy has illuminated, psychotherapy is a place in which the psychotherapist can offer her clients an awareness of a shared experience—for example, a shared experience of society. By acknowledging this shared experience, the psychotherapist can use empathy as a useful tool for both understanding the client and successfully educating her client on issues of identity, self-awareness and health, marking the professional success of the psychotherapist. Empathy becomes a successful educational tool for the client if the client feels heard, can accept the challenges presented by the psychotherapist and can go on to make healthy and strong decisions in her own personal and professional life. The success of the psychotherapist's use of empathy is measured by the client's subjective experience of well-being and actual ability to make good decisions and necessary changes in her life.

In this way, acts of empathy situate the psychotherapist within a personal/professional realm of emotive longings and cognitive organizations which are imprinted on her acts of empathy. The quality of the acts of empathy is situated within the fantasies and desires that the psychotherapist has for herself, for her social identity and for her professional relationships. This may include the desire of the psychotherapist to be seen as kind, highly empathic and understanding. Theresa suggests:

> Empathy is hard. It means that one has to be empathic about the feelings of the client towards oneself that may highlight things about oneself one doesn't want to see. If the client thinks I am being judgmental, and I don't want to acknowledge that, or don't want to see that, then how can I be empathic about the client's experience of me?

As Meyers (1994) has stated, empathy becomes something we learn from others who already practice it. This holds true between the white psychotherapist and her clients. As Nadia suggests about empathy, "it is getting as close as possible to their experience and staying there with them." Another psychotherapist, Zelda, states that empathy is

> feeling one's way into the experiences of another. How can I understand what this is for you? Saying to myself ... how can I apprehend the flavour of it?

Erin suggests:

> with my clients where I don't have common experiences, I have that experience through my background to find those places or to assume there are those places even if I don't recognize that.

It appears that the ongoing success of the work of these women as psychotherapists depends in part on the success of their use of empathy. As educators and professionals, these white woman continue to negotiate their use of empathy so that it can be more effective. Its successful use in psychotherapy becomes a path towards greater professionalism, greater fulfillment and thus also more referrals and clients. Continuing to have a primarily white practice, as most of these women do, can result in the direct success of their empathy. I am not suggesting that these women "seek" out primarily white clients, however, since psychotherapy is already constituted within a white and Western frame, its success (and its whiteness) is naturally regulated and reproduced simply through their (white) and successful use of empathy. Laura reflects on the therapist's needs to be empathic and giving:

> One can have selfish desires in being empathic, but that is not empathy at all. The exercise of being empathic brings us to our narcissistic vulnerabilities at times. It's more acute with someone who is radically different. We have our own needs in that openness and our desire for sameness. We have something invested in that sameness and it hurts when that is broken.

Pinderhughes (1989: 135) states that the critical concern in psychotherapy is that the process never be used to meet the needs of the clinicians to protect themselves or bolster their self-esteem, sense of competence, or power. However, being a successful white professional who uses empathy well is in direct conflict with this concern. It is through the successful application of her empathy that the white psychotherapist continues to enhance her professional status and it is the subjective experience of the client that marks the success of her empathy. In the case of these white psychotherapists, this reproduces a need for white clients and success in relation to them as well. Brandy suggests some of these contradictions when she states:

> There is a lot tied up with being a professional. There are layers and
> layers of meaning within that, what it means for us to be good
> therapists ... we want to be a safe, warm, nurturing container for the
> client.

Providing this "safe, warm, nurturing" experience is less possible when a
white psychotherapist engages with a client of colour who may be strongly
aware of her marginalization within a dominantly white culture. The fiction of
empathy as neutral or innocent for psychotherapy is belied by the fact that the
white professional's success will be undermined when she is faced with such
"different" cases that they appear to make empathy more difficult. The person
of colour becomes more marginalized within psychotherapy because of the
ways in which empathy depends on a large degree of similarity in order to be
successful. In this way, a majority of people of colour are regulated out of
psychotherapy by the very nature of empathy in the psychotherapeutic practice.
These are historical conditions that ultimately shape what the contemporary
white women have described above as an obvious whiteness in the context of
their psychotherapy practices.

This suggests that a small number of culturally and racially different
clients can elevate how the use of empathy by white women in this field is seen.
As I have discussed elsewhere (Roger 1998), psychotherapists can also gain
professional status by applying successful empathy with a small number of
"others." This continues to result in reproducing a middle-class culture of
whiteness as normative in the privatized context of psychotherapy. It continues
to regulate who appears to belong in this elite helping space and who does not.

Reta's hope to "understand the other" is situated in a practice that she says
is mostly white. She suggests here that "empathy is when you get as close as
you can to another person's experience, making the person see that you want to
understand them and that at least one person has heard them or really tried."
Race relations within the setting of psychotherapy are ultimately regulated by
the (white) demographic demands of successful empathy by white psychotherapists. This continues to signify psychotherapy as a profession that "fosters
essentialism ... so that women, and people of color, are implicitly viewed as
belonging to mutually exclusive categories, rendering women of color invisible" (Grillo 1991).

While psychotherapy originated out of "all" women having access to the
expression of "shared experiences" of patriarchy, these stories illustrate that
these fifteen women depend on their successful acts of empathy to mark their
professional success in a way that makes their reliance on a largely white
clientele invisible. As Lorde has stated, "as white women ignore their built-in
privilege of whiteness and define 'woman' in terms of their own experience
alone, then women of colour become 'other,' the outsider whose experience and
tradition is too alien to comprehend" (1980: 117). As with the category "woman,"

the white psychotherapist cannot ignore the built-in privilege that keeps a majority of white clients in the session and a majority of clients of colour out. It is through the use of empathy, which is more successful within a context of the higher level of shared experiences with white clients, that white psychotherapists can sustain their professional success and their elevated status as privatized health educators.

Shaping White Women as Kind Helpers

These professional practices and the dominant white clientele described by these psychotherapists help us to hypothesize what these fifteen white women might have invested in their professional acts of helping. This investment is not only professional but must be understood in terms of their core sense of self as helpers. As a number of women in the interviews have stated, they became professionals through skills they felt they had learned early in their families. They have also suggested that becoming a helping professional felt personally meaningful to them. As Serena stated, "I was going to be a loving, caring being who accepted everyone." This desire to become "helpful" and "kind" as female health professionals is based on a historical and personal process that shapes and requires these practices as a way of constituting a deeply invested sense of self as a kind and helpful person.

Historically, white women were already seen as powerful in their role as helpers despite not being seen as knowledgeable experts in other more "scientific" fields. As Stoler (1995: 135) states,

> Bourgeois women in colony and metropole were cast as the custodians of morality, of their vulnerable men, and of national character. Parenting, and specifically motherhood, was a class obligation and duty of empire.

The helping professions in Canada have also provided historical white women with the professional power and the personal satisfaction of becoming "the knowers" of the helping professions. Even the contemporary white women in these interviews chose helping professions because they felt as if they were responding to "a calling" that was "natural" and "right." This suggests an investment that white women have in these practices of helping. Walkerdine (1990) discusses the development of kindness in young girls in a school setting who see their female teachers as role models. However, Walkerdine does not discuss whether the young girls who are marked as racial minorities, or as different in other ways, have access to these same roles. Her study focuses on an implicit whiteness and does not name forms of marginalization, aside from gender, that might shape the relationship between the student and the teacher.

According to Walkerdine, the professional structure that shapes kindness for women is developed partly in the school classroom. She suggests that young girls watch the female teacher, one who observes and gently educates and learns about herself as gendered. The female teacher is a model for what can be described as female power through the activity of her pedagogic gentleness, which suggests that she is not "bad," "angry," "envious" or ragefully powerful. This prescribes for the young girl a schema of gendered qualities to which she either conforms or through which her difference is pathologized. Through this process of formal and unconscious education the relationship of teacher and girl student reinforce the concept of kindness as a naturally feminine attribute. The young girl discovers that the acts through which she can identify herself as powerful are paradoxically the same acts that are kind, helpful and somewhat passive (1990: 77). As Walkerdine states, "women can be educated enough to join the caring professions—to reproduce the knowers—yet not enough to know" (1990: 79).

Walkerdine talks about this process of regulating one thing while sublimating the rest as "splitting" (Walkerdine 1990: 47). She explores the process of this "splitting" in one of her own childhood fantasies where she imagines being a good and powerful little fairy. She talks about the desire to be fragile yet omnipotent, one of those "charming little fairies who have good and beautiful powers to transform" (Walkerdine 1990: 164). At the same time, Walkerdine recognizes that in growing up and out of this fantasy, the young girl as an adult must acknowledge what was sublimated within this imagined good fairy. Perhaps as these young white girls learn to have a sense of self, as they learn that being kind is being powerful in their families, they also begin splitting off other things that are not "fairy-like." These are not lessons of the "insane, but the basis of sanity" (Walkerdine 1990: 47). This "sanity" requires both a participation in acting like a "good fairy" and the suppression of all that does not appear to belong to the behaviour of a good fairy. As Serena mentions above, being loving and kind formed a core part of her sense of self, while she never acknowledged what it also suppressed.

This context of learning to become a female educator can be translated into the structure of the helping professions. Through the historical construction of the health and helping professions in Canada, shaping the white woman as a professional helper of others has been dependent on the presence of the racial other. It is through an ongoing hierarchy of race, class and gender shaped throughout Canadian history that white women have attained an elite and elevated status within the helping professions. It is through the ongoing economic subordination of the woman of colour as a less-elite helping professional that other white women have been able to become more elite and gain status within imperialism. The white woman who helps more vulnerable others in community settings, or who tends to her own mental health in the privatized setting of psychotherapy, or who depends on less privileged helping professionals to do other helping work (cleaning and housekeeping, for example) is deeply invested in these conditions in order to shape her social status, her privilege within a clean and privatized setting of health education and, in the case of the helping professions, her sense of herself as kind and helpful.

This represents what Walkerdine has described as a real split between being seen as powerful or being seen as kind. If one assumes that Walkerdine's thesis on the "good fairy" has shaped not only the young girl as an educator but also young girls' desire to become "helpers," then these same practices resemble what has historically defined an Eurocentric notion of middle-class femininity and how the white woman was supposed to act (Stoler 1995: 188). The white woman was seen to be a moral educator and a nurturer in a way that also defined her class status (Burton 1994). Through these activities it became possible to "[distinguish] oneself from that which was uncivilized, lower class and non-European" (Stoler 1995: 151).

The psychotherapist's profession in a privatized setting is constituted through historical definitions of a middle-class, white femininity that has demanded of white women not only a suppression of themselves in light of patriarchy, but also a suppression of their place of privilege in relation to the racial other. Psychotherapy appears to be a helpful and innocent profession, but it depends on particular historical and imperial conditions in order to spatially and economically mark it as an elite white space. This failure to acknowledge such hierarchies is reinforced through the successful use of empathy with a majority of white clients in the context of psychotherapy where "acts of resistance against patriarchy [are] often, simultaneously, acts of supporting imperialism" (Jeffrey 1997: 11).

While psychotherapy and the application of empathy appears to be an innocent, helpful activity which is potentially disruptive of privilege, it has the effect of marking "subordinate groups, and the unmarking of dominant groups leaves the actual processes of domination obscured, thus intact. Subordinated groups simply are the way they are; their condition is naturalized" (Fellows and Razack 1998: 341). Psychotherapy becomes a site that regulates who is seen to have privilege, who is invested in the higher forms of self-reflection and, finally, who is "invisible" within this privileged site.

White women's work as psychotherapists is not only about "helping" and "professionalism," it is also about marking a space that has historically been shaped as primarily middle-class and white. If this were to be disrupted, Walkerdine states, "new identifications are created, so too the potential for loss, annihilation and disavowal" (1990: 46).

If the kindness and elite professional work of these white women in the context of psychotherapy depends on their active and professional resistance to patriarchy, then what has been "split" from these professional spaces and activities must also be named. The power they gain through these apparent kind and innocent acts of helping mark their historical place within imperialism. Naming the professional helping work of the racial other in relation to this hierarchy also makes more visible the fragility that marks the imagined boundary and elite space of psychotherapy and how white women identify with this space. It highlights how their sense of power is gained by positioning themselves in a profession that borders between a white, male-based practice of psychoanalysis and other women, including women of colour, who occupy less-elite forms of helping professions.

Conclusion

In this chapter, I have discussed historical and social conflicts that have produced the labour of caring, and produced the white woman as a privatized psychotherapist and educator on issues of health. Through the historical and social conditions described, the contemporary white woman as a psychotherapist is shaped as a professional educator who continues to represent Western values related to emotions and relationships. Disrupting what the white feminist psychotherapist Brown (1994: 332) calls "the full weight of my privileged status" suggests that the conditions that shape such a psychotherapy (and that shape health education) must change.

First, the white woman as a psychotherapist can begin to acknowledge how deeply invested her sense of self as a good, kind helper is to her personal well-being and professional status. I have suggested that empathy is not seen to be aggressive within an imperial paradigm—it remains gendered as primarily female and gentle. Yet, empathy also provides one means through which white women as psychotherapists participate in constituting and regulating a myriad of powerful social relations. As I have described, their dependence on a majority of white clients within psychotherapeutic relationships circulates around the production of a successful empathy. Through its success they gain greater access and proximity to elite and professional forms of helping.

Second, the nature of education depends on shifts in social, institutional and pedagogical critiques through which whiteness and the racial other continue to be represented. The specific context of psychotherapy illustrates one educational setting through which white professionals are trained to re-constitute again and again their own normativity based on who is seen and not seen within these elite sites of helping. Psychotherapy depends on deeply ingrained imperial notions of such normativity in order for it to continue to exist. Acknowledging this reality will allow for new discussions and options for all the helping professions.

Third, psychotherapy (i.e., its professionals, its associations, its mandates) must visibly make cultural and racial others present as privileged health professionals who bring their own Western or non-Western methods of health care to elite forums of health education. While Roman (1997: 277) suggests that it is a "naive faith in native testimony" if whites assume that simply the presence of the racial other is a sufficient act of anti-racism, white psychotherapists must be accountable to the reality that they occupy a primarily white profession shaped by historically specific practices. Ensuring a disruption of what this history means is ongoing and complex in daily practice, yet it is also essential for our own growth, and awareness and depth of understanding about our participation in imperial histories.

This process frames what Freire (1970: 42) has determined is an essential project of educating not only the oppressed, but also the oppressor. White women as psychotherapists can be seen to occupy the contradictory position of being seen as more powerful as whites, yet within the broader context of psychotherapy as women, they are less powerful than men. As well, the categories of white, women and psychotherapist do not address other significant intersections related to sexual orientation and ability which also have implications in social relations of power.

Within a broader educational system, white educators must address how their acts of empathy can shape educational experiences in the classroom and how it might regulate normativity and imperially based gains. This essay attempts to point out that the white psychotherapist produces herself not only as a kind professional and an educator on health but that she also occupies a site of power and privilege in relation to her white clients and the less-visible racial other. She therefore has the option to participate in a form of education about emotional and mental health that can be seen as a site for transformation and change in relation to her white and non-white clients, and in relation to all helping professions.

Chapter Eight

Nurses and Porters
Racism, Sexism and Resistance
in Segmented Labour Markets
Agnes Calliste

Introduction

There are many similarities between African-Canadian women's resistance to professional exclusion and marginality in nursing from the 1970s to 1990s and sleeping car porters' anti-racist struggles against the submerged split labour market (Bonacich 1972) on Canadian railways in the 1950s and early 1960s (in which white men monopolized the higher-paid positions and "locked" Black men into the most menial, low-paying and low-status jobs). Like the porters, Black nurses tend to be streamed into the least skilled and least desirable areas (such as chronic care) irrespective of their qualifications and experience because of managements' perception that these women do not have the qualifications to work in other units (Calliste 1996b; Head 1986; OHRC 1992b). Moreover, the nurses' and porters' struggles for employment equity were carried on within their workplaces and unions, as well as within the political arena, since both groups of workers had to resist inequality practiced by their employers and unions. They also had to pressure the state to enforce fair employment practices and human rights legislation.

Despite the similarities in African-Canadian nurses' and porters' work experiences and anti-racist struggles, to date there is no comparative research on the two groups of Black workers. Recently, two African Canadian nurses were dismayed that I would even think of comparing professional nurses'[1] experiences and struggles with those of porters—as if I were declassing nurses. This view overlooks the evidence that although racism and gendered racism are historically specific (Essed 1991; Hall 1978), they have been embedded in labour markets and in other societal institutions, and they manifest themselves in different ways in different sites and contexts. Gendered racism refers to the racial oppression of racial/ethnic minority women and men as structured by historically situated racist perceptions of gender roles and behaviour (Essed 1991).

Blatant notions of racial inferiority such as that Blacks are inherently uncivilized and stupid are being replaced by a much more subtle ideology of cultural inferiority, which is articulated by the choice of carefully coded language—for example, portraying them as aggressive and loud (Gilroy 1987). However, the most persistent racist, sexist and classist stereotypes that have been used to justify the racial division of labour and the exploitation and de-valuation of Black workers', especially women's, labour are those that label Black workers as less intelligent, less competent, less skilled and less disciplined than white workers (Calliste 1996b; Essed 1991). For instance, although a porter in charge did the jobs of both a porter and a sleeping car conductor, in the 1950s and early 1960s Canadian railway companies and the Order of Railway Conductors (ORC), the Canadian Pacific Railway (CP) conductors' union, argued/implied that Black sleeping car porters were not suited for the position of sleeping car conductor (Blum 1958; Johnstone 1964; Smith 1964b). Similarly, in a human rights case in the early 1990s, management and some white staff members at the Dunfermline Hospital in Toronto tried to justify the dismissal or suspension of seven Black nurses on the grounds that they were either incompetent or unprofessional, thereby blaming the complainants for being the cause of their own misfortunes (Doris Marshall Institute and Arnold Minors & Associates 1994; OHRC 1992a; Ontario Ministry of Labour 1993a, 1993b; interviews, March 31, 1996). Scapegoating nurses and porters diverted attention from a critical analysis of the structures and practices of the workplace, which treated them inequitably and justified the status quo by blaming the victims.

This study focusses on African-Canadian women's resistance to professional marginality and exclusion in nursing and porters' resistance to the submerged split labour market on the railways from an eclectic theoretical perspective. The study draws on segmented and split labour market, social closure, anti-racism and feminist theoretical frameworks (Bonacich 1972, 1975, 1976; Brandt 1986; Calliste 1996b; Collins 1990; Dei 1996; Edwards 1979; King 1990; Parkin 1979). It examines the conditions under which these anti-racist struggles materialized, the constraints placed upon them and the effects of these struggles. Marginality is a process in which "a sense of otherness or peripherality is perpetuated and encouraged" (Brandt 1986: 104). Racial minorities are denied access to positions of power within institutions, and their experiences and perspectives are considered irrelevant. Although some Southern and Eastern Europeans were employed as porters in western Canada during and after World War II, before the war, "Blacks" and "sleeping car porters" were synonymous, and Blacks led the porters' anti-racist struggles in the 1940s to 1960s. Nurses of colour and a few whites have been involved in the nurses' struggle, but I have chosen to focus on the experiences of African-Canadians in Ontario and Quebec in the 1970s to 1990s. These provinces are chosen because there are large numbers of Black nurses there. For example, Reitz et al. (1981) found that Caribbean women[2] in Toronto's workforce were over-concentrated in nursing (except in supervisory positions), nurses' aide positions, orderly work and in other segregated occupations. The late 1970s demarcates the beginning of nurses' political organizing to combat increased racism during economic recession and cuts in health care budgets. The 1990s are characterized by nurses' and the African-Canadian community's intense anti-racism struggles.

Theoretical Framework

Racially segmented and split labour markets, racial and gender ideologies in segmented labour markets, gender ideology in family units and the capitalist structure in which Black men and women's specific race, gender and social class positions are embedded structure Black men's and Black women's work (Collins 1990: 46). Thus this study on nurses' and porters' resistance to racism and sexism in segmented labour markets draws on split and segmented labour market, social closure, anti-racism and feminist theoretical frameworks, while simultaneously according race, class and gender separate analytical statuses to develop a stronger explanatory model.

Split labour market theory was formulated by Edna Bonacich (1972, 1975, 1976) to explain economic sources of racial/ethnic conflict. She argues that a split labour market exists when the cost of labour differs substantially along racial lines for the same work, or would differ if they did the same work. In labour markets split along racial lines, conflict develops among employers desiring the cheapest possible labour, workers of the higher-paid, dominant racial group resist being undercut or displaced by cheaper labour from the racialized minority group, while the lower-paid racialized minority workers are struggling to find a niche in the economy. Such competition leads to four forms of racial conflict depending on the relative power of the three classes: (1) displacement, (2) exclusion of racialized minority workers, (3) a caste or submerged system which demarcates a colour line beyond which only white workers can advance and (4) radicalism in which the two labour groups form a coalition against employers. A racially split labour market results from the differential political and economic resources available to dearer or cheaper groups of workers in the struggle to improve wages and working conditions. However, split labour market theory overemphasizes the role of economics in the process and at best explains the results, not the origins, of white working-class privilege.

Segmented labour market theorists (Edwards 1979; Gordon, Edwards and Reich 1982; Piore 1971) adopt a more historical and structural account of the formation of labour markets segmented by race and gender. They argue that segmented labour markets emerged in the historical context of capitalist development with the formation of separate monopoly and competitive sectors, differential strategies of control in the workplace, changes in productive technology and the differential effects of working-class struggle across economic sectors. In segmented labour markets, jobs and industries are readily divided into a primary or core sector and a secondary or peripheral sector, and this division is reinforced by barriers that make it difficult for workers to move from one sector to another. In the primary sector, jobs are characterized by higher wages and fringe benefits, greater employment stability with possibilities of promotion, a higher degree of unionization, superior working conditions and due process in negotiating job rights. In contrast, the secondary sector includes work in marginal industries. These jobs are low-paying, often seasonal and sporadic, less likely to be unionized and offer little protection against the vagaries of either the individual employer or the ups and downs of the market-place. Allocations to these labour markets follow existing divisions of race and gender. The secondary sector uses the groups with little bargaining power such as racialized minorities and women who are pushed into particular race or sex-typed jobs to maximize profits, and partly because of systemic racism and patriarchy. Blacks are hired into the dirtiest, most physically demanding and lowest-skilled occupations, while women are pushed toward "helping" and nurturing occupations (Edwards 1979).

Segmented labour market theory helps to explain the segregation of women workers into female-typed jobs, and Blacks into race-typed jobs. However, it overlooks the relationship between social relations in production and race relations in unions, the connection between white labour's alliance with capital and labour's exclusion and marginality of Black and other racialized minority workers and women, and the role of radical labour leaders in promoting racial equality (Calliste 1996b; Glazer 1991; Hartmann 1976, 1981; Wilson 1996). Segmented labour market theory also overemphasizes the role of economics in the subordination of Black workers, and fails to entertain the possibility that racism and sexism are also ways in which "white workers (and men) have come to look at the world" (Roediger 1991: 10). Race and gender have always been crucial factors in the history of Canada's class formation (see Omi and Winant 1983; Roediger 1991).

The evidence suggests that racism, gendered racism and immigrant/migrant status interacted with class exploitation in the submerged split labour market on the railways, and in the informal segmented labour market in nursing, and that racism and sexism were not accidental to the process. For instance, the racially submerged split labour market practices on the railways developed initially from the employers' demand for cheap labour and systemic racism (Calliste 1987, 1995a; Foner 1981; Gould 1977; Marshall 1965). Racial and class divisions between Euro-Canadian and American railway workers and Black porters made for a fractured brotherhood. White railway unions helped to institutionalize and maintain a racial caste system in the industrial labour force by excluding Blacks as members, or by relegating them to auxiliary and segregated locals, and agreeing to segregated seniority systems which were written into collective agreements. The exclusion and marginalization of Black men by trade unions, especially industrial unions such as the Canadian Brotherhood of Railway Transport and General Workers (CBRT), cannot be explained simply in terms of economic self-interest. It also emerged out of the union's (white men's) quest for higher status and social privileges in the context of a highly stratified industry and a racist and sexist society (Marshall 1974; Roediger 1991; Wilson 1996). White railway workers wanted to maintain their social distance from Blacks; thus they emphasized the fraternal and social benefits of their organizations, and perceived racially mixed unions and integrated sleeping quarters to mean granting social equality to Blacks (Kamarowsky 1961; Marshall 1965; Northrup 1944).

Similarly, white health care administrators and nurses have historically marginalized/excluded racialized minority women to protect their jobs as well as to strive for an increase in the status of the profession. They rationalized the marginality/exclusion of the latter by using ideological constructions of racially specific femininity and sexuality, representing the opposite models of white, middle-class womanhood (Calliste 1993, 1996b, 2000; McPherson 1996). Social closure theory indicates that historical and contemporary patterns of exclusion involve not only discrimination or market mechanisms of job allocation but also privilege (Murphy 1988; Parkin 1979). Moreover, the theory postulates that the more desirable the job, the more likely subordinate groups (such as Black women) would be excluded, and the more a job is filled by Black women, the more it is devalued and deskilled by employers.

Anti-racism theory helps to explain the racialization of gender and class in nursing and on the railways as well as individual and collective resistance. Unlike segmented and split labour market theories that focus on class and treat racism as an epiphenomenon or manifestation of class, anti-racism theory centres racism while acknowledging its intersection with other forms of social oppression (Brandt 1986; Dei 1996). Anti-racism is a critical discourse of social oppressions (such as racism, sexism and classism) through the lens of race. It is also "an educational and political action-oriented strategy" for institutional systemic change to address racism and the interlocking systems of social oppression (Dei 1996: 25). The emphasis on racism is not intended to prioritize oppressions. Instead, the anti-racism discourse highlights that, though "race" is a "fundamental organizing principle of contemporary social life" (Winant 1994: 115) in racialized societies, the status quo continually denies there is racial discrimination in employment (for example, in hiring, promotion and work relations) and that the racial composition of jobs have an effect on how work is organized (that is, the labour process). However, the logic of capital is not "race" and "gender" blind. Access to work and justice are constrained by relations of oppression such as racism and gendered racism (Brandt 1986; Collins 1990; Essed 1991). Segmented labour theory and anti-racism can inform each other.

Some Black nurses acknowledge that they experience multiple oppressions in the workplace (Congress of Black Women of Canada [CBWC], Toronto Chapter 1991; Nurses, Woodlands Hospital 1992). For instance, in 1991, the Coalition in Support of Black Nurses stated: "Traditionally, Black women have been singled out to bear the brunt of economic hardships in our society, especially during recessionary periods" (CBWC 1991: 1). Similarly, porters argued that they were infantalized or treated like boys by railway management, white railway workers and unions and some passengers (Robinson 1941;

interviews, September 1, 1986). For example, porters recalled that some passengers called them "George" after George Pullman, the manufacturer and operator of railway sleeping cars, as if they were his boys or his property, which is similar to the practice of naming slaves after their masters, but also because adult Black males were considered as less than men (see Bederman 1995; Mergen 1974). Despite the interlocking systems of social oppression, Black nurses and porters emphasized racism because it was more visibly salient for them. Nursing, like portering, is a gendered occupation, and many of the oppressors of Black nurses are white female nurses who collaborate with management in harassing Black nurses (interviews, May 25, 1994, and September 8, 1996). Similarly, most of the oppressors of Black porters were white men (Calliste 1987, 1988, 1995a).

Anti-racism goes beyond acknowledging the material conditions that structure social inequalities to confront and question white power and privilege and its rationale for dominance (Dei 1996; Dyer 1997; Frankenberg 1993a; McIntosh 1990). Anti-racism questions the role that the state (including human rights commissions and labour arbitration systems) and societal institutions such as workplaces play in creating and maintaining inequalities. Anti-racism, like feminism (Armstrong and Armstrong 1990; Smith 1977), acknowledges that the state and societal institutions contain and manage the protests of oppressed groups (for example, by individualizing grievances), but they do not examine the underlying causes of discrimination or challenge systemic racism and patriarchy—especially racism—unless they are pressured into doing so (Bolaria and Li 1988; Calliste 1987, 1996b; Henry et al. 1995; Young 1992; Young and Liao 1992). Thus, the state's response to anti-racist, feminist and other minority struggles (whether it crushes, appeases or co-opts them) varies in accordance with the groups' economic, political and social power. Anti-racism theory questions the devaluation of knowledge, credentials and experience of subordinate groups (see Ontario, Ministry of Citizenship 1989a, 1989b), and the marginalization and silencing of certain voices in the workplace and in society. It recognizes the need to confront the challenge of social diversity and difference in Canadian society and the urgency for more inclusive and equitable workplaces and society (see Dei 1995).

The eclectic theoretical framework is relevant in explaining Black nurses' and porters' resistance to the interlocking systems of social oppression in the workplace. As mentioned previously, historically, Black nurses and porters in Canada (like their counterparts in the United States) have been simultaneously oppressed by racism, classism and sexism (see Barbee 1993; Calliste 1993, 1995a, 1996b; Head 1986; Hine 1989). The divisions between African-Canadian and Euro-Canadian women were most evident in the racist, sexist and classist images of Black women as "mammies," "Jezebels," and "matriarchs" (see Barbee 1993; Calliste 1991, 1993/94; Davis 1983; hooks 1981). These images, like the Black male images of "Sambo," "Buck" and "Rastus," emphasized physical attributes over social (Fox-Genovese 1988). Sambo captured the image of the stereotypical childlike and subservient male slave or servant—the antithesis of white male honour, masculinity and intelligence (Bederman 1995; Fox-Genovese 1988). Similarly, the "mammy" image of the faithful and obedient domestic servant was created to justify the economic exploitation of female house slaves. These racially specific notions of femininity and masculinity played an important role in justifying the restriction of Black women and men to menial and backbreaking jobs, such as domestic work, chronic care nursing and portering, as well as conditioning managerial strategies of control, and they represented the "normative yardstick used to evaluate" Black women and men (Collins 1990: 71). Porters recalled that some passengers called them "Sam" (Sambo)[3] and "Rastus" (interviews, September 1, 1986, and May 1, 1987; see Beckford 1990; Williams 1978; Williamson 1986). Racism, sexism and classism continue to permeate workplace culture which stereotypes Black nurses as childlike, lazy, aggressive, emotional, uncommunicative and trouble-making (Calliste 2000; CBWC 1995; Doris Marshall Institute and Arnold Minors & Associates 1994; OHRC 1992a; interviews, May 25–27 and July 3, 1996). This image of the Black nurse is the antithesis of the Florence Nightingale image of the soft-spoken, compassionate, nurturing, rational and professional nurse (Ehrenreich and English 1973). An African-Canadian nurse also notes that "the Black nurse is still treated as the servant girl in the kitchen" (interview, July 1, 1994). Thus, the Black woman nurse becomes an "undesirable" entity in this context. Black nurses and nursing assistants have helped to maintain a segmented nursing labour force that was initially based on class (see Doyal et al. 1981; Gamarnikow 1978).

Although segmentation usually refers to distinctions between occupations, it includes differentiation within an occupation between professional and non-professional strata, for example, between registered nurses (RNs), graduate nurses and registered practical nurses (RPNs). Black nurses in Canada, like their counterparts in Britain, South Africa and the United States, are concentrated at the lower levels of the nursing hierarchy as staff nurses and RPNs—a reflection of persistent inequalities in nursing and in the wider society (Calliste 1996b; Doyal et al. 1981; Glazer 1991; Head 1986; Marks 1994).

In addition to this formal segmentation to protect the class-based and racial/ethnic privileges of some nurses, there are informal ways of segmenting RNs to protect the racial privileges of white RNs. The Dunfermline Hospital in Toronto serves as an illustration of the racially segmented nursing labour force. In 1992 its management was predominantly white, while 56 percent of its nursing staff were people of colour with 30 percent being Black (Das Gupta 1993: 39; OHRC 1992a: 3). Most of the Black nurses were working in the chronic and acute care units and they were the least represented in high-technology and high-status specialty units (where there are greater opportunities for further training and the nurses are encouraged to take courses) (Caissey

1994; Head 1986; OHRC 1992a; ONA 1996). For instance, 41 percent of the nurses in the chronic and acute care units were Black compared to 15 percent white and 44 percent other nurses of colour (such as Canadians of Chinese and Filipino descent). Conversely, only 13 percent of the nurses in the intensive care unit were Black, compared to 55 percent white and 32 percent other nurses of colour (OHRC 1992a: 9).

The state helped to create and maintain segmented labour markets and the subordination of Black nurses and porters through differential immigration policies. As I have argued elsewhere (Calliste 1993, 1993/94, forthcoming), before 1962 the process of immigration control of Black people entering Canada and the manner in which they were incorporated into the labour market—as free immigrant labour with citizenship rights, or unfree migrant labour—were structured by a dialectic of economic, political and ideological relations (the demand of employers for cheap labour and the state's desire to exclude Blacks as permanent settlers). Perceiving Black women and men as inferior, undesirable and likely to create permanent economic, social and race relations problems, immigration officials sought to avoid this difficulty by restricting entry to those whose services were in urgent demand, and only when sources of white labour were unavailable. In the 1950s and early 1960s, a small number of Caribbean nurses were allowed into Canada under differential immigration policy, which stipulated that one of the conditions for admitting them into the country was that the hospital administration which offered them employment had to be "aware of their racial origin" (Acting Chief, Admissions 1956). Moreover, in order for Black nurses to enter Canada as permanent immigrants, they were required to have nursing qualifications that exceeded those of white nurses. Among Black nurses, only those who were eligible for registration with the provincial Registered Nurses Association (RNA) were admitted as landed immigrants. Others were allowed to enter as migrant workers. This differential immigration policy helped to reinforce Black nurses' subordination within a gendered and racially segmented nursing labour force (Calliste 1993).

Similarly, the Canadian state helped the Canadian Pacific Railway (CP) to create and maintain a double split labour market between African-Canadian and imported African-American labour on the one hand, and between Black and white Canadian labour on the other, by allowing the company to import African American porters, particularly from the southern states, both as seasonal workers and also as regular workers on six-month contracts which could be renewed. In 1949, approximately 50 percent of the CP's 600–700 porters were American born. Many of these migrant porters had been with the CP for several years (Calliste 1987: 6, 10). Migrant status hindered solidarity among some Black nurses and porters, given they had no political and citizenship rights, and made them extremely vulnerable to an employer's exploitation (Burawoy 1976; Calliste 1987, 1993; Miles 1982).

The Canadian government played a more direct role in creating and maintaining the submerged split labour market on the CN since it was a crown corporation. Thus in the CN porters' anti-racist struggle, they were pitted against the state, the very institution which was responsible for enforcing the Canada Fair Employment Practices (FEP) Act.

Research Methods

My discussion of porters is based upon data drawn from extensive archival research in Canada and the United States, review of literature, oral history interviews of one hundred porters and former porters, and to some extent, porters' families and union leaders conducted mainly in Winnipeg in 1982–83 and in Truro, Halifax, Montreal, Toronto and Vancouver in 1986–89. The sample was drawn through snowball sampling, referrals and from the seniority lists of porters.

My discussion of nurses is based upon data drawn from forty semi-structured interviews conducted in Toronto and Montreal, mainly in 1994–97. The sample consists of thirty registered nurses, three officers from nurses' unions and seven members of community organizations which assisted Black nurses in their anti-racism struggles. The sample was drawn through snowball sampling and referrals, as well as from the membership list of two nurses' organizations. I was also a participant observer at three conferences in Toronto centred on anti-racism and/or integration and advancement of Black nurses in health care. I wrote one of the conference reports (Calliste 1995c). The primary data on nurses were supplemented with analysis of records of the OHRC, the Quebec Human Rights Commission (QHRC), labour arbitration cases and community organizations and other secondary sources. The secondary data also served as checks for possible biases in the primary data. In order to maintain confidentiality, I use fictitious names to identify nurses and health care institutions except those who are already named in secondary sources.

Racism on Canadian Railways

Black sleeping car porters had become a fairly entrenched Canadian tradition after the 1880s. Except for the Grand Trunk Railway (GTR) which employed Black male cooks and waiters in its dining cars, the Canadian railway companies followed the southern American practice of hiring Black men almost exclusively as porters until the amalgamation of the porters' and dining car locals of the CBRT in 1964.

The Canadian railway companies employed Blacks as porters because they were cheaper than white workers for comparable work. Moreover, the assumed social distance that existed between whites and Blacks meant that the presence of Black male porters on sleeping cars was considered as part of the furniture and did not serve as a complicating factor in the intimacies which travel by sleeping cars necessitated. Thus, Black men were de-sexed as porters because of the social distance. The railway companies also knew that Blacks were traditionally assigned physically demanding and service roles, and that it was a sign of status among whites to be waited on by them (Anderson 1986; Brazeal 1946; Harris 1977). Portering was a male form of domestic work which reinforced social relationships of white superiority that had been established by slavery. Each Canadian Pacific Railway (CP) porter had to sign a contract acknowledging that the company had the right to dispense with his service at any time without being required to give any reason for doing so (*The Labour Gazette* 1920: 241). The company claimed that this clause was necessary because sleeping car porters' work was of a domestic nature and involved close personal relations between the porters and sleeping car travellers. Dining car employees were not required to sign such a contract. It was the porter's job to give total personalized human service to the passengers, including even the shining of their shoes. In order to guarantee the porter's efficiency and to maximize profits, the railway companies took care that the porter's welfare should be inextricably tied up with the type of service he gave passengers. The porter was paid a low monthly wage and had to depend upon passengers to augment his income through tips. For example, CP porters' monthly salaries in 1920 ranged from $75 to a maximum of $85 after three years (*The Labour Gazette* 1920). Out of his meagre salary, a CP porter had to buy his meals, uniform, a shoe-shine kit and even the polish for the passengers' shoes. Porters in charge performed the duties of both the porter and the conductor (except the porter was usually in charge of one or two cars) but received substantially less pay than conductors. For example, in 1951 a CN conductor's monthly salary during his first year of service was $268 compared to a porter in charge who made $213, and a porter made $188 (CBRT and CN 1951: 37–38). Thus Black porters experienced interlocking systems of social oppression: racism, sexism, class exploitation and, in some cases, super-exploitation based also on their migrant status.

The process of forming a racially submerged split labour market on Canadian railways began in the 1880s and continued in the 1920s when the CN reclassified work categories in order to limit Blacks, except for those already otherwise employed, to being porters only. In 1926 when the CN took over the GTR, it began replacing Black waiters in the dining car service of former GTR cars with white help. Consequently, an arbitration board heard a complaint made by the Black employees that their displacement was contrary to agreement, a violation of status and of seniority rights, which they argued could be attributed to racism. A compromise arrangement was agreed to, allowing the displaced Black waiters to take employment as porters with full seniority. The Black cooks were gradually eliminated through attrition (*The Labour Gazette* 1927; McGuire 1942).

The racially segregated job classification and seniority system in the sleeping and dining car department of the CN were institutionalized in 1927

when the company and the CBRT agreed to a group classification system for
seniority purposes (CBRT and CN 1927). Group 1 was for dining car employees
and sleeping car conductors. Group 2 was set up exclusively for porters. These
groups coincided with the CBRT's segregated dining car and porters' locals. The
collective agreement between the CN and the CBRT stated that seniority and
promotion of employees would be confined to the groups in which they were
hired. The selection of supervisors, such as platform and road inspectors, took
place within Group 1. A strictly logical occupational line of promotion for
porters, particularly porters in charge, would include the position of sleeping
car conductor since porters in charge performed the duties of conductors.
However, some whites with far less railway experience and far less education
than some Blacks were promoted as inspectors and sleeping car conductors
(Grayson 1953; Tobin 1959). Porters often had to assist inexperienced sleeping
car conductors.

White dining car employees collaborated with the CN to exclude Blacks
from higher-paying and higher-status jobs because of economic reasons and,
partly because of institutional, systemic and everyday racism. The central white
labour force wanted to insulate itself from the peripheral Black labour force,
especially during the post–World War I contraction in the railway industry. In
addition, whites were probably unwilling to do such undesirable jobs as portering,
which included distasteful tasks (such as cleaning spittoons). The CBRT's
exclusion and marginalization of porters also illustrate systemic racism in
unions. The CBRT (formerly the Canadian Brotherhood of Railway Employees)
formed in 1908 to represent non-operating railway employees on the Intercolonial
Railway, restricted membership to whites only (Arab 1978; Greening 1961;
Robinson 1945). In 1917, porters on the Canadian Northern Railway (which
became part of the CN) organized an Order of Sleeping Car Porters (OSCP) and
applied for membership in the CBRT (Robinson 1941). A.R. Mosher, CBRT's
president, informed Winnipeg's John Robinson, OSCP's president, of the membership restriction and suggested that the OSCP accept as its name the Canadian
Brotherhood of Coloured Railway Employees (Robinson 1945). However,
under pressure from the OSCP, in January 1919 the CBRT decided to give the
OSCP auxiliary status. In September of that same year, the exclusionary clause
was removed and the OSCP was given segregated status within the brotherhood.
The segregated porters' and dining car locals were used as the basis for the
segregated seniority system.

The CP refrained from using Black dining car employees until World War I,
when the company imported African-American men during the busy periods in
1916 and 1917. In May 1918 some African-American men were imported as
migrant workers to displace white dining car employees in the Western Division, who had joined the CBRT. The dismissed men demanded an investigation
under the Industrial Disputes Investigation Act, claiming that they were dismissed because of union activity and they resented being replaced by American

Black men. As one of the dismissed men told the conciliation board, "they didn't like being replaced by 'black labour' as Canadians and 'as white men'" (*The Labour Gazette* 1918: 603). Racism and sexism were also evident in the CP's testimony. The company argued that it was implementing a 1918 policy decision to introduce Black dining car employees because it had difficulty obtaining white male employees during the war. The company stated that it had given serious consideration to hiring white women, but it could not provide proper sleeping quarters. Thus the only alternative was "to engage coloured men who seem more adaptable to that service" (*The Labour Gazette* 1918: 602). Management seemed to have determined the suitable characteristics for the job on the bases of race, gender and class. Although the company could not produce any evidence of the 1918 policy decision, the case was dismissed. The Black dining car employees were laid off after the war and the CP resumed its tradition of hiring whites (Greaves 1930: 55).

Porters' Struggle Against the Racially Segmented Labour Market

The CN porters began the struggle against the submerged split labour market in 1942, but it only became a legitimate discrimination grievance after the enactment of the Canada Fair Employment Act (FEP) in 1953 when they intensified their pressure for promotion. The FEP Act, which prohibited discrimination in employment by employers, unions and employment agencies on the basis of race, national origin, colour and religion, had several weaknesses. For instance, it focussed on intentional and individual cases of alleged discrimination. Thus the law was ineffective in dealing with systemic discrimination because it was difficult to prove intent to discriminate (Vizkelety 1987). Moreover, as the United States Supreme Court (*Griggs* v. *Duke Power Co.*, cited in *Albermarle Paper Co.*, v. *Moody* 1975) and the Fifth Circuit (*Oatis* v. *Crown Zellerback* 1968) argued, racial discrimination in employment is by definition class discrimination because it is the result of institutional systemic discrimination (i.e., the adverse effects of employment policy and practices rather than motivations for the act) (see Keene 1992). The 1927 collective agreement between the CN and the CBRT discriminated against porters as a group; thus CN porters successfully took class action to effectuate change.

The CN porters' struggle for promotion was difficult and drawn out. From 1955 to 1963, the Winnipeg Local 130, chaired by Lee Williams, and with the support of the other porters' locals, lodged repeated protests of the discriminatory clause in the collective agreement—which barred porters from being promoted to sleeping car conductor's positions—to the CBRT, the CN, the Canadian Labour Congress (CLC) and the federal government. Porters also wanted the right to promotion to non-unionized positions such as inspectors (CBRT 1955; Local 130 1959; Williams 1957b, 1958). Both the company and the CBRT denied discrimination. The CN management tried to avoid negative publicity by suggesting that the union should initiate any request for change in the collective agreement. Meanwhile, management employed counter resistance strategies, such as trying to flood the sleeping car conductors' seniority list with dining car employees and to bar porters from promotion (Williams 1957c). Many porters confirm that the ringleaders, particularly Williams, were targeted. In Williams' words:

> It wasn't easy. It was a lot of pressure.... You know that you are in danger.... There were investigators following me on every trip and they were trailing me every trip just trying to fire me; anything that they could use to fire me. (Interview, June 14, 1982)

In the 1950s, the CBRT attempted to solve the discrimination charge problem through amalgamation of Groups 1 and 2 without eliminating classification seniority. Both groups voted against amalgamation. Indeed, Group 2 was interested in amalgamation only if full seniority rights were granted, in which case they could displace junior sleeping car conductors (Bailey 1963). As Williams (1961) acknowledged, promotion with seniority rights would not eliminate systemic inequalities against porters. It would be an attempt to rectify the situation without further inflicting unfairness and inequality on them. Group 1 was opposed to amalgamation because of racism and the greater seniority held by Group 2. Passenger service was declining and they feared they might be the first dropped in the elimination of runs (Blum 1961; CBRT 1955).

The FEP officers seemed to have administered the act half-heartedly. The Minister of Labour, for example, did not acknowledge that segregated seniority groupings were a violation of the act or that rights could not be bargained away. He claimed that the issue of promotional rights had to be settled "within the family" of the CBRT (Starr 1958a). It did not pacify the porters who felt unfairly treated as "only distant cousins" by the CBRT (Williams 1958), and humiliated by the CN, a crown corporation (Williams 1957a, 1957b).

In 1961, the porters launched a massive national media campaign against the discrimination practiced by the CBRT and the CN ("Porters would Like Probe" 1961; Werier 1961). This prompted the National Committee on Human Rights of the CLC to conduct an inquiry. The committee found discrimination but blamed the railway for its discriminatory employment policy (Blum 1961). Williams labelled the CLC report as "a whitewash to suit the trade union hierarchy" (*Winnipeg Free Press,* September 1961). The porters contended that fault lay with the union contract. It is difficult to accept the committee's argument that the national officers of the CBRT did not discriminate against Blacks, given their segregated locals and seniority groupings, as well as a history of inadequate representation of porters (Robinson 1941; Swift 1945). The committee's recommendation that Groups 1 and 2 be amalgamated was rejected by both groups. The Winnipeg porters threatened to take legal action against both the company and the union ("CN Porters to Battle" 1962; "Porters to take union" 1962).

In July 1963, Winnipeg Local 130 laid an official discrimination complaint under the FEP Act (Williams et al. 1963). After investigation, it was finally decided that amalgamation of the two groups and a combining of seniority lists was the only fair solution to the charges of discrimination. However, Group 1 demanded another referendum on the question (Smith 1963a, 1963b). The result of the referendum was an approval of the merger ("Merger of seniority groups" 1964). Group 1 locals unsuccessfully sought an injunction to block the amalgamation on the grounds that the referendum was misleading and, consequently, the amalgamation and subsequent loss of positional rights were forced on them by the union (Wright 1964). Their petitions and attempts to win the support of passengers against porters trying "to take away the white man's jobs" also failed.

The post-amalgamation period led to the ascendancy of Blacks as many porters displaced sleeping car conductors and dining car employees (Matthews 1965; McAllister 1965; Smelter 1964; Smith 1964b; interviews, August 26–27, 1986). However, Blacks' ascendancy was short-lived partly because of technological changes and economic recession, which had a greater effect on Black railway workers than on whites. Many were elderly employees nearing retirement age who were likely to be replaced by non-Blacks. With job integration and wage equalization, the railways no longer had a vested interest in employing them, especially since improved working conditions had made portering attractive to whites.

Unlike CN porters, who took class action, CP porters used test cases to pressure the CP management to promote Black porters to sleeping car conductors' positions. After the enactment of the Canada FEP Act, several porters in Toronto filed official discrimination complaints against the company after they were denied promotion (Ontario Labour Committee for Human Rights [OLC] 1956; Petgrave 1956; interviews, June 15–16, 1987). Management continued to use evasive techniques such as "doubling out"[4] rather than fill vacant sleeping car conductors' positions, and introduced an irrelevant "aptitude test" to avoid promoting the porters while simultaneously avoiding more FEP complaints. It took almost two years of conciliation and persuasion before George Garraway, a mulatto, was promoted to the position of junior conductor without seniority rights in 1955. Following continued pressure from the federal Department of Labour and labour organizations (such as the Toronto Labour Committee for Human Rights), five porters were promoted on a "trial basis" (Blum 1956; "CPR to hire" 1955; OLC 1956).

The Black conductors also had to file FEP complaints against the Toronto Division of the Order of Railway Conductors (ORC), a craft organization, which refused to accept them as members even though union dues were automatically checked off from their wages. The ORC then solicited the membership of

Garraway, who was speedily inducted into the division. The officers of the division felt that by giving Garraway a membership they could successfully reject all other Black conductors. The Minister of Labour argued that he could not force the ORC Brotherhood to accept the Black conductors as members given that there was no proof of intent to discriminate. However, after a period of negotiations, the union accepted the Black conductors as members (Blum 1956b, 1958; Petgrave 1956).

The loss of seniority rights effectively discouraged some porters from becoming conductors, particularly since some conductors had to revert to junior porters' positions, either because they could not get sufficient work on the spare board to support their families or they were demoted. Some conductors also sought employment outside of the railways, for example, at the Post Office (interviews, June 9 and 12, 1987). In 1964, Arthur Blanchette, the Brotherhood of Sleeping Car Porters' (BSCP) Field Organizer in Canada, successfully negotiated with the CP for the promotion of a few porters in Montreal and Toronto to junior conductor while retaining their seniority as porters. Approximately three Blacks on the CP were also promoted to office positions (BSCP 1964; interviews, August 25–September 2, 1986, June 8–15 and 22, 1987).

Although there were no major changes for most Black employees on the CP, the BSCP played a leading role in the anti-racism movement in the 1940s to 1960s (*The Black Worker* 1952; BSCP 1956; Calliste 1995b). For instance, in 1944–1945, the BSCP Divisions in Canada with the assistance of their international president, A. Phillip Randolph, organized a multiracial organization, the Canadian League for the Advancement of Coloured People (CLACP), "to fight for a civil rights bill, and provincial and federal Fair Employment Practices laws" ("Canadian Blacks Fight" 1945; Coward 1944). The CLACP succeeded in helping a few African-Canadians to find employment in commerce and sales, jobs which were formerly closed to Blacks (Calliste 1995b). Moreover, in the 1950s to early 1960s, the BSCP Divisions in Toronto and Montreal collaborated with other organizations (such as the Negro Citizenship Association) in pressuring the Canadian government to change its discriminatory immigration policy and facilitated the immigration of a small number of Caribbean Blacks, including nurses, to Canada (Calliste 1993; *The Black Worker* 1952). The formation of VIA Rail Canada to assume responsibility for passenger service marked the demise of the BSCP in Canada.

The CN porters were more successful than the CP porters in their struggle for promotion because they were strongly organized. It took sustained class action from 1955 to 1964 to eliminate the racially segregated job classification and seniority system. Although the CP porters' method of using test cases provided some redress for the aggrieved individuals, the CP maintained its segregated job classification and seniority system until it got out of passenger service in 1978. In addition to CN porters being better organized, as members of the CBRT, they were able to exert group pressure on the Brotherhood. CP porters and conductors were organized by two different unions, the BSCP and the ORC, respectively. This complicated the problem of promoting porters with full seniority rights. The junior conductors who were allowed to retain their seniority as porters had to be members of both unions. The CN porters had another advantage. The CN management was more susceptible to public pressure than the CP, given that the former was a crown corporation. Given the ineffectiveness of the FEP laws, a member of Parliament argued that the most the federal government could do to eliminate CP porters' grievances against lack of promotion was "to use moral persuasion" (Alexander 1972). Both the CN and CP porters' victory effected a significant reduction of outrageous discrimination in Canada. This section examined porters' resistance to the submerged split labour market on Canadian railways. The following section discusses the professional exclusion and marginality of African-Canadian women in nursing.

Marginality and Exclusion in Nursing

Black women were allowed into nursing as a floating reserve army of labour during the postwar expansion of industrial capitalism and severe nursing shortages. However, they were then and are today marginalized and treated as the "Other." For instance, even at the present time they are concentrated at the bottom of the gendered and racially segmented nursing labour force as staff nurses; they are also more likely than their white counterparts to be employed through the nursing registry, and to be employed part-time and as casuals. Thus, they are less likely to be entitled to fringe benefits. Moreover, Black nurses who work full-time are more likely than their white counterparts to be underemployed, to be denied access to promotions and to be assigned the least desirable shifts and duties involving mostly menial work (Caissey 1994; CBWC 1995; Das Gupta 1996; Head 1986; OHRC 1992a; interviews, September 1, 1996).

During economic crises Black nurses are the first to be suspended, demoted and summarily dismissed, often for alleged incompetence or for not following standard nursing procedures, or for "unacceptable behaviours," especially if they resist racism. In the 1990s, it seemed as if they were being further marginalized and excluded as economic restructuring and rapid downsizing of the health care system had been combined with new (and very old) forms of racism and racialization that had a disproportionate impact on Black health care workers, particularly those who worked in chronic care units and those who were assertive (Calliste 1993 and 1996b; Franklin 1995; Hardill 1993). Black nurses who work in chronic care units are more vulnerable and powerless, given "peripheral" workers are the first to be laid off or displaced by cheaper labour. ONA notes:

> More so than on other units, chronic [care] unit nurses are being
> replaced by [low-skilled unregulated assistive personnel or] generic

workers, while at the same time these same nurses are told they lack the skills to bump into other areas of the hospital, even if they have the seniority to do so. (1996: 5)

Overt racism, sexism and other forms of social oppression in nursing, as in other areas of employment, increased during the economic recession and cutbacks in health care budgets in the late 1970s to early 1980s, and intensified during the 1990s fiscal crisis (Bolaria and Li 1988; Hardill 1993; Henry and Ginzberg 1985). As I have discussed elsewhere (Calliste 1996b, 2000), harassment of racialized minority nurses by hospital management takes several forms, including targeting them for discriminatory treatment, and differential documentation and discipline for minor or non-existent problems for which white nurses are not disciplined. For instance, at a meeting of le Ralliement des Infirmiieres Haitiennes de Montreal (RIIAH) in October 1997, after some Haitian nurses reported on alleged racial discrimination and harassment at their workplaces, forty-two Haitian nurses decided to form a crisis committee to prepare a petition to send to their employers denouncing the numerous allegations of harassment against Black nurses and demanding a work environment free of harassment (Dominique 1997: 6).

Health care institutions reinforce the marginality of Black nurses by denying their experiences of racism. Instead they focus on interpersonal dynamics such as "communication skills" and "personality problems," and blame Black nurses for "their problems" rather than investigate the issue of racism (Doris Marshall Institution and Arnold Minors & Associates 1994; interviews, March 30, June 24 and July 3, 1996). Donna Jones' case serves as an illustration. In 1992, Donna, a public health nurse in Toronto, received her first unsatisfactory performance appraisal in fifteen years of employment at the Belair Health Unit, partly because of a "negative perception of her personality." However, she was not given a satisfactory explanation for the performance appraisal. She notes: "When I inquired as to why I was not told about the negative perception of my personality and my work prior to this date, I was told that I would have reacted negatively.... Most of the comments lack concrete data" (Jones 1993: 1). Donna argues that she began experiencing racial harassment when she began to be more assertive and to resist (gendered) racism and ageism in the workplace, such as infantalization by her peers and directors (interview, June 24, 1996). Donna filed several grievances and a human rights complaint of racial discrimination against her employer. However, she resigned in 1994, citing continuing discrimination. She felt that the stressful work environment was impacting upon her health (Ontario Ministry of Labour 1996; Jones 1994; interview, June 24, 1996). This also indicates some of the hidden injuries of racism and sexism as well as the emotional and psychological costs of resistance.

Black women's assertiveness and resistance to the multiple oppressions they experience are perceived as threatening to white patriarchal definitions of femininity. Donna was also harassed to control her assertive behaviour, to discourage solidarity among nurses and to undermine her ability to influence others. Management's divisive strategy also served as a form of containment; at the same time it was a factor in producing a "poisoned" work environment. Hospitals' denial of racism is also reflected in their lack of support for Black nurses who are subjected to racism, sexism or physical assault by patient's families. Management tends to deal with such incidents as crisis management issues, rather than dealing with the issue of racism (OHRC 1992b). Hospital managers who acknowledge racism tend to attribute it to individual biases or misconduct rather than understanding it as systemic (see Young 1992). For instance, in 1990, a public relations director at the Paradise Hospital in Montreal said that she had "never heard of a problem [of racism at the hospital].... I'm sure that it occurs. We have approximately 2500 employees. I'm just going on the assumption that someone will step out of line" (Brown 1990). Given management's denial of racism, it is not surprising that, in 1990, hospitals in Montreal and Ontario did not have racial harassment policies.

Black nurses' everyday experiences of racism reflect systemic racism in the workplace (for example, subjective recruitment, evaluation and promotion processes, as well as differential work assignments). Management practices and employment systems in these hospitals adversely affect Black nurses. The recruitment and promotion processes are often subjective and arbitrary and lead to discriminatory treatment of applicants. For example, some hospitals recruit through employee referrals or word-of-mouth methods that tend to reproduce the status quo. Pre-screening of applications, checking of references, interviewing and internal transfers are often left to one person, a white manager. Moreover, there are no standard questions that are consistently asked when interviewing for nursing staff. This could result in culturally laden questions being asked as well as arbitrary, biased and subjective decisions being made (Henry and Ginzberg 1985; OHRC 1992b). In sum, systemic and everyday racism produce and reproduce each other. The following section discusses Black nurses' resistance to the interlocking systems of social oppression in the health care system.

Resistance in Nursing

Black nurses in Quebec and Health care workers of colour in Ontario began organizing themselves and making formal as well as informal complaints of racial discrimination and harassment in the late 1970s and the early 1980s, as racism and sexism increased with the downturn in the economy and cuts in health care budgets (Calliste 1996b, 2000; Head 1986; interviews, July 5, 1994, June 20, 1998, and June 19, 1999). For instance, in the 1980s, the Black Nurses Association of Quebec (BNAQ) initiated a series of investigations into long-standing cases of racial discrimination against its members at a Montreal hospital and made representations on their behalf before the QHRC (Robertson 1985a, 1985b; Sam 1986; interviews, November 17, 1997). In Ontario, Eva filed a human rights complaint against a university hospital in 1980, alleging racial harassment and wrongful dismissal. Several organizations (such as the local chapter of the International Committee Against Racism and the Afro-Caribbean Students Association) demanded that the university and the hospital "end racist practices in employment and education, rescind the dismissal" of Eva and "drop all charges before the College of Nurses" (Hathiramani 1980; Quigley 1980; "Racism at McMaster" 1980: 1; interview, July 5, 1994).

Although a few Black nurses won individual cases in the 1980s (Ontario Ministry of Labour 1983; Calliste 1996b), neither their organizations nor their communities had the power to pressure local governments and health care facilities for institutional and systemic changes. The status quo (sometimes including the nurses' unions) was able to block resistance because economic and political power resources are unequally distributed. For instance in 1982–90 in Montreal, there were sixteen human rights complaints of racial discrimination and harassment in the health care sector. All were dismissed (Brown 1990).

In the 1990s, some Ontario hospitals' use of blatant classist and gendered racism against a number of nurses of colour galvanized some nurses, particularly African-Canadians and their advocates. They realized that they needed a multilayered or multidirectional agenda to achieve institutional and systemic changes. As I discussed elsewhere (Calliste 1996b), in 1994–1995 the CBWC, with the support of several organizations, was instrumental in pressuring the OHRC to investigate claims of systemic racism and discrimination against two Toronto hospitals—the Dunfermline Hospital and the Birchgrove Hospital. In addition to the nurses obtaining human rights settlements, the hospitals also agreed to adopt and implement policies and practices that would hopefully transform them into institutions free of racism. These piecemeal reforms were also intended to placate the nurses and the community who were demanding a public inquiry into systemic racism and other forms of discrimination in the health care system (Calliste 2000; CBWC 1996: 1–2; NAFAD 1996; ONA 1996; interviews, May 25, 1994, and September 1, 1996). As a result, nurses of colour continued to file grievances and individual human rights complaints in a more regressive economic, political and social climate that militates against anti-racist and feminist politics. Fighting for human rights, however, is moving more and more to legal challenges in the court system given that the OHRC has refused to deal with the complaints of unionized workers to reduce its caseload (ONA 1997; Ontario Court of Justice 1998: 2) and arbitration boards rarely deal with complaints of racial discrimination and harassment.

In Quebec, despite many informal complaints of racial harassment in some Montreal hospitals in the 1990s, there have been relatively few official complaints. The low reporting of racial harassment has been attributed to nurses' fear of reprisals from employers and other employees, problems of documentation, as well as lack of confidence in arbitration tribunals at the QHRC (Brown

1990; Dominique 1997; interviews, June 19, 1999). There is some evidence to support nurses' apprehension. The QHRC files indicate that racial discrimination complaints are more often dismissed or tended to be resolved in a more ad hoc fashion than those based on age, gender and disability (QHRC 1997a: see Frideres and Reeves 1989; Young 1992). Out of fourteen racial discrimination and harassment complaints of health care workers of colour in 1990 to June 1998, only one was successful.

In May 1997, Janet was awarded $40,000 (including $30,000 for loss of salary during her demotion in 1994–96 and $10,000 for moral damages). She filed her complaint against the Paradise Hospital after she was forced to resign from her position as Head Nurse of the Hospital's neonatal unit. The defendant also had to submit to the QHRC a letter of apology to the complainant for wrongful demotion (QHRC 1997b: 1–2). Janet's effective resistance strategy included obeying the hospital's orders while she quietly documented the incidents of discrimination and harassment.

There are some similarities between the nurses' and the porters' resistance to social oppression in their workplaces. Nurses and porters had to pressure their employers and unions as well as the state to investigate and settle their complaints. For instance, in the Dunfermline Hospital's case in Toronto, neither the OHRC nor the ONA wanted to investigate the nurses' complaints. The ONA advised the nurses to go to the Commission because the union did not deal with human rights complaints. The Commission, however, characterized their complaints as a labour relations problem that should be dealt with through the ONA (CBWC 1995; interview, May 25, 1994). As a result, the CBWC Toronto Chapter organized the Coalition for Black Nurses to pressure the OHRC to investigate the nurses' complaints as a systemic complaint. The Coalition also lobbied the ONA to support the complainants through the OHRC process and to raise the problem of racism at their arbitration hearings before the Labour Board. As June Veecock of the Ontario Federation of Labour, also a CBWC member and one of the nurses' strongest advocates, explains:

> We advised the nurses to file individual complaints and we also asked the Human Rights Commission to bring a Commission-initiated complaint. Well, all hell broke loose. The Commission's systemic unit was not so inclined. So, that too became a struggle. So, we were fighting the hospital.... We were ... trying to gain support from the ONA; and we were challenging the systemic unit of the Commission. (CBWC 1995)

Another similarity between the nurses' and porters' resistance strategies were the effective media campaigns to gain public support and to exert pressure on their employers and unions, as well as the state. The media's support coupled with the nurses' and porters' and their allies' effective use of networks of contact, including political connections and coalitions, contributed to the movements' success (interviews, June 1982 and May 1994). Veecock emphasizes the importance of the media in the Dunfermline Hospital's case: "I was ... playing the media and trying to keep it [the case] alive because I knew if we lost the media's interest we would lose the case" (interview, May 25, 1994). Similarly, Lee Williams argues that the massive media campaign was a crucial factor in the success of the CN porters' struggle for promotion (interview, September 1983).

Conclusion

This study centred on nurses' and porters' resistance to racism and sexism in segmented labour markets supports an eclectic theoretical perspective: anti-racism, feminism, split and segmented labour markets and social closure by illustrating the relational aspects of social difference. The study also reveals some of the emotional, psychological and social costs of resistance. The settlements of some nurses' and porters' complaints indicate symbolic redress. Black railway workers were not fully compensated for the losses incurred as a result of discrimination (such as years worked with lower salaries and the cyclical effect of discrimination in housing and their children's education). Similarly, the OHRC and the QHRC's maximum compensation ($10,000) for mental anguish is grossly inadequate given some nurses are suffering from severe emotional, physical and psychological effects from their experience with racism, sexism and, in some cases, ageism and ableism (CBWC 1995; interviews, May 25–26, 1994, and July 6, 1994). In order to minimize reprisals for resisting and to achieve institutional and systemic change, while at the same time addressing the politics of everyday racism and sexism, racialized minority nurses must take political action. They must unite and organize a strong association as well as actively participate and get elected to the executive of their unions, professional associations (Registered Nurses Association) and their licensing bodies (the College of Nurses of Ontario and the Order of Nurses of Quebec) where they could influence policy. Moreover, nurses must form meaningful coalitions and networks at the local, national and international levels with other anti-oppression movements in nursing as well as in other institutions (such as universities and colleges) and workplaces. We cannot eliminate racism, sexism and other interlocking systems of social oppressions in the health care system without simultaneously combatting them in education and transforming the social and economic institutions of capitalist society.

Notes

1.   Although Black nurses perceive themselves as educated professional women, white women define the boundaries of professionalism, delineating separate standards for white and Black women, ensuring that the latter are assigned the lowest jobs in nursing, thus maintaining a racially stratified workforce (Calliste 1993,

1996b; Flynn 1998).
2. Although not all Caribbeans are Black, a large proportion are.
3. Some researchers (Beckford 1990; Williams 1978; Williamson 1986) argue that Black slaves never accepted the world view of the white capitalist class—they used the Sambo personality as a guerrilla strategy or role-playing technique to deceive and pacify whites—and that the latter needed the Sambo to feed their egos and mask their terror of slave revolts. Thus the Sambo image functioned to reinforce whites' view of themselves as Christian and civilized and their perspective of the slave as happy and childlike. It is plausible that in the pre–World War II period, some porters "samfied," a behaviour that was encouraged by the tipping system and the absence of due process (for example, a complaint from a passenger could result in demerit marks and even dismissal).
4. To double out meant that when an employee returned from a trip—which may have lasted for as long as a week—he could be ordered out on the very next train, without a rest period.

Special Note:
    I would like to thank the nurses, porters and their families, community nurses' organizations, union officers and others who shared information with me. I would also like to thank Debbie Murphy at the Department of Sociology and Anthropology at St. Francis Xavier University.

Chapter Nine

Anti-Racist Feminism
A Conclusion to a Beginning
Agnes Calliste and George J. Sefa Dei

It is always significant to work with the "philosophy of hope," even in circumstances when challenges appear so enormous and the pace of change is too slow. Hopefully, this book will help contribute to a theorization of insurgent responses to racialized and gendered discourses of "nation" and "democratic citizenship." The essays have to varying degrees articulated how women of colour negotiate their multiple identities and pursue politics across several political, historical and social domains. This collection, in asking critical questions of national identity and citizenship from the perspective of gender and race, opens the social reality of nation and citizen past and present in a manner that ruptures myths. Knowing as we do the history and status of women and racial minorities within the formation of nation-states makes this location one of the best suited from which to ask certain key questions. For example, at whose expense have nations been built? What have been (and continue to be) the conditions of entry for some groups and the condition of groups indigenous to the conquered lands? In whose interests have our institutions and social policies been structured? Whose interests have these institutions served?

Some of these questions have been historically examined in Enakshi Dua's piece on immigration policies towards South Asian–Canadian women as portrayed in the British Columbia press in historical and contemporary times. A more contemporary media analysis was taken up in Helle-Mai Lenk's piece on a more contemporary/modern debate on national identity. The question of Quebec and those identified as "Others," in this case the wearing of Islamic headscarf (*hijab*) in high school, is seen as a reason for excluding a female student from a public high school.

Throughout the collection, overt denial of entry into the nation and into societal institutions, including covert denial through obstacles to jobs and employment, unions and social services are a recurring theme. So is the historical and present reality that those who were/are denied equal entry or access were/are welcomed through different points of entry. For example, their "cheap labour" has been/is required for building the nation, its institutions and the economy. Agnes Calliste and Patience Elabor-Idemudia examined some of these questions, more specifically, the relationship between employment and immigration policies. In Calliste's article, the relationship between employment and labour that historically marginalized and excluded Black porters and currently still marginalizes women of colour in the health care system was examined. Social services, psychotherapy and the academy were also explored from the intersecting perspective of race and gender in the chapters of Sherene Razack, Kerstin Roger and Usha George. Exclusion, marginalization and the naming as "Other" of women of colour is much of what emerges from the historical and present examination of these sites. In the early periods of nation-building, women and all persons from racialized and minoritized groups were denied full status and participation. They were denied the right to name themselves and their reality and this denial has continued through to our present social institutions in a myriad of ways that deny equitable access and outcomes.

Reflecting on these histories and contemporary practices should lead us not to forget. It should also break the *desire* to forget and not name what does not fit the myths that are constantly perpetuated about so-called "immigrants." It should sound a loud and cautionary note as national governments and institutions are being restructured to adapt to a new macro-structure that seeks to exclude and find sources of cheap labour for the new global economy. In reading these studies on past and present practices, we cannot help but reflect that it is those services carried out primarily by women—services in health care, social services and the public funding of education, both schools and universities—which have received the brunt of cost cutting by this global restructuring. From which groups, communities and countries does this global economy seek cheap labour? Not only do these articles ask questions about past and present "nation-making," but they also add to a counter dialogue that sounds cautionary notes about the direction that some with power want to take the nation. Seeking to arrest equity and access gains that have been made is not supported by the authors of this collection. But this direction is becoming even more problematic when "community" or "nation" is being restructured in such a way that it regresses to the detriment of women, particularly poor women and women from racially different backgrounds and their families.

But there is hope that sound anti-racist feminist politics may be able to offer. There can be no academic closure to either the discourse or practice of anti-racist feminisms. Anti-racist feminist discourse and practice is addressing fundamental issues as we enter the new millennium. The discourse is acknowledging the power of subjectivity, subjective knowing and political agency. So we would close (but not end) the discussion by briefly exploring some of the alternative racist feminist strategies for change that this collection of essays bring forth. There is the question of how to conceptualize the politics of anti-racist feminisms broadly in way that recognizes the intellectual agencies of different subjects as they resist their marginality in society. The processes of racialized, gendered classifications continue to have profound implications for human relations and conflict. The contextual specificities of raced and gendered subjectivity means that individuals and groups negotiate their entry into society at different levels. The process of entry ensures that groups and individuals are differentially positioned in their access to the material goods and services of society. While, for some, race and gender become sites of punishments and oppression, for many others these identities continue to be sites of rewards and privilege. Even today, the practice of encoding bodies with racist and sexist meanings prevails. The Victorian discursive practice of using Black women's bodies as markers of abnormality and deviancy and a reference point in discussion regarding sexual deviance among white women still persists in contemporary society. The perception of the Black female as a sexualized deviant and abnormal female, a source of corruption and disease, while not without opposition and counter-voices, is rife. This is one area where anti-racist feminism has become a challenging discourse. A new approach to anti-racist feminist politics begins by asking, what is the discursive site through which raced and gendered knowledge is produced, organized and regulated? Beyond the visibility of skin colour, marginalized communities are continually silenced and rendered invisible. To resist this "unhealthy knowledge," anti-racist feminist politics is challenging colonial and imperial practices. Through the production of counter-hegemonic narratives, racially minoritized women and peoples of colour are resisting dominant perceptions by producing their own discourses about themselves. For example, it is no longer acceptable to attribute social issues in Black communities to a lack of strong patriarchal figures. Critical anti-racist feminist practice also challenges the staticism and permanence of racial and gender boundaries. Marginalized subjects are not bringing static and restrictive definitions to their identities. Thus the accentuation of a "Black woman identity" implies fluidity and dynamism. It also signals a gesturing to the powerful symbolic and material consequences that cut across ethnic, gender, religious lines/differences. There are multiple and contesting meanings of identity claimed as an entry point to the pursuance of anti-racist feminist politics. The dominative perceptions that encode "Blackness" with criminality, violence, dysfunctional family life, compulsive heterosexuality, maleness, chaos, fear, low academic achievement, a sense of nihilism or hopelessness and detachment is being seriously challenged (see also John 1999).

There is also great resistance to anti-racist feminist change because the dominant groups want to maintain their power and privileges. Thus, it is necessary that those who engage in anti-racist feminist praxis form meaningful coalitions, networks and alliances with other groups/organizations (i.e., gay, lesbian, bisexual, anti-poverty, fair trade (not free trade), human rights and environmental groups, etc.) that are also committed to eliminating oppression at the local, national and international levels. This is because solidarity is powerful. And it is even more crucial in this era of globalization, characterized by a neo-liberal/neo-conservative regressive climate which militates against institutional and systemic anti-racist feminist change. There are, depending on whether the goals are long-term or short-term, various ways of working together. For instance, in choosing to form an alliance, a network or a coalition, it is important to consider that a network is a more permanent and ongoing relationship than an alliance or coalition. As anti-racist feminists we need to be flexible, critical and explicit about our goals and our conceptual meanings of community. We cannot assume that an ethno-racial community such as a Black community is less heterogenous than cross-racial/ethnic communities. For instance, should membership in a Black academic association be based on African ancestry or on one's politics of race, class, gender and sexuality as well as political commitment to anti-oppression in education and in academe? As we enter the new millennium we hope that the colour and gender problems of the one we exited will not be continued as the legacies of the twenty-first century (DuBois 1903; Franklin 1993).

References

Abella, I. and H. Troper. 1991. *None Is Too Many: Canada and the Jews of Europe 1933–1948*. Toronto: Lester Publishing.

Acting Chief, Admissions. 1956. Letter to the Acting Director, Immigration, May 9. Public Archives of Canada (PAC), Immigration Branch Records, RG 76, Vol. 847, File 553-110.

Adebayo, A.G. 1996. Personal communication, September 15.

Agard, R. 1987. "Access to the Social Assistance Delivery System by Various Ethnocultural Groups." *Social Assistance Review Committee Report* Ontario Ministry of Community and Social Services.

Agnew, V. 1996. *Resisting Discrimination: Women from Asia, Africa, and the Caribbean and the Women's Movement in Canada*. Toronto: University of Toronto Press.

Ahmad, A. 1994. *In Theory*. London: Verso.

Ahmed, L. 1992. *Women and Gender in Islam*. New Haven/London: Yale University Press.

Albermarle Paper Co. v. *Moody*. 1975. 422 U.S. 405: 16, 417–18.

Alexander, L. 1972. Letter to J. Ewing, August 22.

Allola, M. 1986. *The Colonial Harem*. Minneapolis: University of Minnesota Press.

Alonso, A. 1994. "The Politics of Space, Time and Substance: State Formation, Nationalism, and Ethnicity." *Annual Review of Anthropology* 23:379–405.

Anderson, B. 1983. *Imagined Communities: Reflections on the Origin and Spread of Nationalism*. London/New York: Verso.

Anderson, J. 1986. *A. Phillip Randolph*. Berkeley: University of California Press.

Anthias, F. 1992. "Connecting 'Race' and Ethnic Phenomena." *Sociology* 26: 421–38.

Anthias, F. and N. Yuval-Davis. 1992. *Racialized Boundaries: Race, Nation, Gender, Colour and Class and the Anti-Racist Struggle*. New York and London: Routledge.

Arab, J. 1978. "The Struggle for Equality Rights for Porters and Questions Regarding Canadian Racism." Mimeo.

Armstrong, P. and H. Armstrong. 1990. *Theorizing Women's Work*. Toronto: Garamond.

_____. 1994. *The Double Ghetto: Canadian Women and Their Segregated Work*. Toronto: McClelland and Stewart.

Avery, D. 1995. *Reluctant Host: Canada's Response to Immigrant Workers, 1896–1994*. Toronto: McClelland and Stewart.

Bailey, J. 1963. December 2. Letter to D. Secord. PAC, MG 28, I215, Vol. 5,

Baines, C. 1988. *Women's Reform Organizations in Canada, 1870–1930: Historical Perspective*. Thesis: University of Toronto.

Bakan, A. and D. Stasiulus. 1995. "Making the Match: Domestic Placement Agencies and the Racialization of Women's Household Work." *Signs: Journal of Women and Culture in Society* 20(2): 303–35.

Balibar, É. 1991a. "Racism and Nationalism." In Étienne Balibar and Immanuel Wallerstein (eds.), *Race, Nation, Class: Ambiguous Identities*. London/New York: Verso.

_____. 1991b. "The Nation Form: History and Ideology." In Etienne Balibar and Immanuel Wallerstein (eds.), *Race, Nation, Class: Ambiguous Identities*. London/New York: Verso.

Banes, D. 1998. *Everyday Practice of Race, Class and Gender.* Unpublished Ph.D. dissertation. Faculty of Social Work: University of Toronto.

Banks, J. 1994. "The Historical Reconstruction of Knowledge About Race: The Implication for Transformative Teaching." Paper read at the Annual Meeting of the American Educational Research Association, New Orleans, La. April 4–9.

Bannerji, Himani. 1987. "Introducing Racism: Notes Towards an Anti-racist Feminism." *Resource for Feminist Research* 16(1): 10–12.

Banton, M. 1977. *The Idea of Race.* London: Tavistock.

Barbee, E. 1993. "Racism in U.S. Nursing." *Medical Anthropology Quarterly* 7(4): 346–62.

Beckford, G. 1990. "Plantation Capitalism and Black Dispossession." In A.W. Bonnett and G.L. Watson (eds.), *Emerging Perspectives on the Black Diaspora.* Lanham, Maryland: University Press of America.

Bederman, G. 1995. *Manliness and Civilization: A Cultural History of Gender and Race in the United States, 1880–1917.* Chicago: University of Chicago Press.

Bélanger, C.A. and A. Émond. 1996. *Au Nom d'Allah.* Montréal: Radio-Canada. Video. 17:00.

Belenky, M.F. 1986. *Women's Ways of Knowing: The Development of Self, Voice and Mind.* New York: Basic Books.

Berger, D. 1987. *Clinical Empathy.* London: Jason Aronson.

Berger, F. 1994. "Les Québécois: la nouvelle minorité visible." *La Presse*, 21 novembre: A4.

_____. 1995. "La défense des droits individuels est-elle menacée?" *La Presse,* 25 mars: A4.

Berry, J.W. and J.A. Laponce. 1994. *Ethnicity and Culture in Canada: The Research Landscape.* Toronto: University of Toronto Press.

Bertley, L. 1985. "Discrimination against Black nurses?" *Afro-Can* 5(2): February:1, 5.

Bhabha, H. 1994. *The Location of Culture.* London/New York: Routledge.

Biddiss, M. 1979. "Towards a History of European Racism." *Ethnic and Racial Studies* 2(4): 508–13.

Billig, Micheal. 1987. *Arguing and Thinking: A Rhetorical Approach to Social Psychology.* Cambridge: Cambridge University Press.

Bishop, A. 1994. *Becoming an Ally: Breaking the Cycle of Oppression.* Halifax: Fernwood Publishing.

Bissonnette, L. 1994. "Le choix du *Devoir.* Le Parti québécois, avec nonobstant." *Le Devoir,* 7 sept: A6.

Black Worker, The. 1945. "Canadian Blacks Fight for Civil Rights." September.

_____. 1952. "Immigration by Discrimination." March: 1.

Blum, S. 1956a. Letter to K. Kaplansky, May 25. PAC, MG 28, I173, Vol. 7, File Correspondence. Jewish Labour Committee of Canada.

_____. 1956b. Letter to M. Swerdlow, December 8. PAC, MG 28, V75, Vol. 14, File 14-13.

_____. 1958. "Report of the National Committee on Human Rights." January 5, PAC, MG 28, V75, Vol. 14, File 14-13.

_____. 1961. "Inquiry into Charges of Racial Discrimination against the CBRT by Mr. Lee Williams, Chairman, Local 130, CBRT." PAC, MG 28, V75, Vol. 34.

Bolaria, S. and P. Li. 1988. *Racial Oppression in Canada.* 2nd edition. Toronto: Garamond Press.

Bonacich, E. 1972. "A Theory of Ethnic Antagonism: The Split Labour Market." *American Sociological Review* 37: 547–59.

_____. 1975. "Abolition, the Extension of Slavery, and the Position of Free Blacks: A Study of Split Labour Markets in the United States, 1830–1863." *American Journal of Sociology* 81(3): 601–28.

_____. 1976. "Advanced Capitalism and Black/White Relations in the United States: A Split Labour Market Interpretation." *American Sociological Review* 41: 34–51.

Bordo, S. 1993. *Unbearable Weight: Feminism, Western Culture and the Body.* Berkeley: University of California Press.

Bourgeault, Ron. 1988. "Race and Class Under Mercantilism: Indigenous People In Nineteenth-Century Canada." In Singh Bolaria and Peter Li (eds.), *Racial Oppression in Canada.* Toronto: Garamond Press.

Boyd, Monica. 1984. "At a Disadvantage: The Occupational Attainment of Foreign-born Women in Canada." *International Migration Review* 18 (Winter).

_____. 1986. "Immigrant Women in Canada." In R.J. Simon and C. Brettell (eds.), *International Migration: The Female Experience.* New Jersey: Rowman and Allanheld Publishers.

_____. 1987. *Migrant Women in Canada: Profiles and Policies.* Employment and Immigration Canada and The Status of Women, Canada.

_____. 1989. "Immigration and Income Security Policies in Canada: Implications for Elderly Immigrant Women." *Population and Policy Review* (8) 5–24.

Boyzon-Fradet, D. and S. Boulot. 1991. "Le système scolaire français: aide ou obstacle à l'intégration?" In Pierre-André Taguieff (ed.), *Face au racisme. Tome 2.* Paris: La Découverte.

Brah, A. 1994. "'Race' and 'Culture' in the Gendering of Labour Markets: South Asian Young Muslim Women and the Labour Market." In Haleh Afshar and Mary Maynard (eds.), *The Dynamics of 'Race' and Gender: Some Feminist Interventions.* London: Taylor and Francis.

Brand, D. 1984. "Black Women in Toronto: Gender Race and Class." *Fireweed* Summer/Fall: 26–43.

_____. 1985. "Black Women in Toronto: Gender, Race and Class." *Fireweed* 19: 26–43.

_____. 1986. *The Realization of Anti-Racist Teaching.* London: Falmer.

_____. 1987. "Black Women and Work: The Impact of Racially Constructed Gender Roles on the Sexual Division of Labor." *Fireweed* (25): 35.

_____ 1991. *No Burden to Carry: Narratives of Black Working Women in Ontario, 1920s to 1950s.* Toronto: Women's Press.

_____. 1993. "A Working Paper on Black Women in Toronto: Gender Race and Class." In Himani Bannerji (ed.), *Returning the Gaze: Essays on Racism, Feminism and Politics.* Toronto: Sister Vision Press.

Brantlinger, P. 1985. "Victorians and Africans: The Genealogy of the Myth of the Dark Continent." In Henry Louis Gates, Jr. (ed.), *"Race," Writing, and Difference.* Chicago/London: University of Chicago Press.

Brazeal, B. 1946. *The Brotherhood of Sleeping Car Porters.* New York: Harper and Brothers.

Brewer, R.M. 1993. "Theorizing, Race, Class and Gender: The New Scholarship of Black Feminist Intellectuals and Black Women's Labour." In Stanlie James and Abena Busia (eds.), *Theorizing Black Feminisms.* New York: Routledge.

Bristow, P., D. Brand, L. Carty, A. Cooper, S. Hamilton and A. Shadd. 1994. *"We're*

Rooted Here and They Can't Pull Us Up": Essays in African Canadian Women's History. Toronto: University of Toronto Press.

Bronfenbrenner, U. 1979. *The Ecology of Human Development: Experiments by Nature and Design.* Cambridge, MA: Harvard University Press.

Brown, C. and K. Jasper (eds.). 1993. *Consuming Passions: Feminist Approaches to Weight Preoccupation and Eating Disorders.* Toronto: Second Story Press.

Brown, E. 1990. "Hospital Colours: Nurses of Racial Minorities Suffer Harassment in Silence." *Montreal Mirror,* October 18–25.

Brown, L. 1994. *Subversive Dialogues: Theory in Feminist Therapy.* New York: Basic Books.

_____. 1995. "Anti-Racism as an Ethical Norm in Feminist Therapy Practice." In J. Adelman and G. Enguidanos (eds.), *Racism in the Lives of Women: Testimony, Theory, and Guides to Antiracist Practice.* New York: Haworth Press.

Brown, L. and M. Root (eds.). 1990. *Diversities and Complexities in Feminist Therapy.* New York: Haworth Press.

BSCP. 1956. Resolutions submitted by the Toronto CP Division, BSCP, to the First Constitutional Convention of the Canadian Labour Congress, Toronto, April 23.

_____. 1964. "Minutes of the meeting of the International Executive Board." January 7-9. Chicago Historical Society, BSCP Papers, Box 19.

Burawoy, M. 1976. "The Functions and the Reproduction of Migrant Labour." *American Journal of Sociology* 81(5): 1050–87.

Burton, A.M. 1992. "The White Woman's Burden." In Nupur Chaudhuri and Margaret Stroebel (eds.), *Western Women and Imperialism: Complicity and Resistance.* Bloomington: Indiana University Press.

_____. 1994. *Burdens of History: British Feminists, Indian Women, and Imperial Culture, 1865–1915.* Chapel Hill: University of North Carolina Press.

Butler J. and J. Scott (eds.). 1992. *Feminists Theorize the Political.* London: Routledge.

Caissey, I. 1994. "Presentation to the City of North York's Community, Race and Ethnic Relations Committee." Toronto, October 13.

Calliste, A. 1987. "Sleeping Car Porters in Canada: An Ethnically Submerged Split Labour Market." *Canadian Ethnic Studies* 19(1): 1–20.

_____. 1988. "Blacks on Canadian Railways." *Canadian Ethnic Studies* 20(2): 37–52.

_____. 1991. "Canadian Immigration Policy and Domestics from the Caribbean: The Second Domestic Scheme." In Jesse Vorst et al. (eds.), *Race, Class, Gender: Bonds and Barriers.* Toronto: Garamond.

_____. 1993. "Women of Exceptional Merit: Immigration of Caribbean Nurses to Canada." *Canadian Journal of Women and the Law* 6(1): 85–102.

_____. 1993/94. "Race, Gender and Canadian Immigration Policy: Blacks from the Caribbean, 1900-1932." *Journal of Canadian Studies* 28(4): 131–48.

_____. 1995a. "The Struggle for Employment Equity by Blacks on American and Canadian Railroads." *Journal of Black Studies* 25(3): 297–317.

_____. 1995b. "The Influence of the Civil Rights and Black Power Movement in Canada." *Race, Gender and Class* 2(3): 123–40.

_____. 1995c. *End the Silence on Racism in Health Care. Conference Report.* Written for the CBWC, Toronto Chapter. Toronto: CBWC.

_____. 1996a. "Anti-Racism Organizing and Resistance: Blacks in Urban Canada, 1940s–1970s." In J. Caulfield and L. Peake (eds.), *City Lives and City Forms.* Toronto: University of Toronto Press.

_____. 1996b. "Antiracism Organizing and Resistance in Nursing: African Canadian Women." *Canadian Review of Sociology and Anthropology* 33(3): 361–90.

_____. 2000. "Resisting Exclusion and Marginality in Nursing: Women of Colour in Ontario." In M. Kalbach and W. Kalbach (eds.), *Race and Ethnicity in Canada.* Toronto: Harcourt Brace.

_____. Forthcoming. "Immigration of Caribbean Nurses and Domestic Workers to Canada, 1955–1967."

Canada FEP Act, S.C. 1952–1953, Chap. 19.

Canada, Secretary of State. 1988. Programme for the Promotion of Immigrant Women. *The Canadian Observer.* September 18, 25, and December 11, 1915.

Canady, H.G. 1936. "The Effect of 'Rapport' on the I.Q.: A New Approach to the Problem of Racial Psychology." *The Journal of Negro Education* (April) 5(2): 209–19.

Carby, H. 1990. "The Politics of Difference." *Ms.* (September/October): 85.

_____. 1986. "White Woman Listen! Black Feminism and the Boundaries of Sister-hood." In *The Empire Strikes Back: Race and Racism in 70s Britain.* London: Centre for Contemporary Cultural Studies.

Carniol, Ben. 1991. *Case Critical: Challenging Social Work in Canada.* 2nd edition. Toronto: Between The Lines.

Carter, R. 1991. "The Relationship Between Racism and Racial Identity Among White Americans: An Exploratory Investigation." *Journal of Counselling and Development* 69: 46–50.

Casas, J. Manuel. 1985. "A Reflection on the Status of Racial Ethnic Minority Re-search." *The Counselling Psychologist* 13: 4581–98.

CBRT. 1955. Minutes of the Joint Protective Board, September 24-26. PAC, MG 28, I215, Vol. 6.

_____, Local 130. 1959. "Petition to CNR & CBRT." September 18. PAC, MG 28, I215, Vol. 14.

CBRT and CN. 1927. "Collective Agreement Between the CN and the CBRT for Employees in Sleeping, Dining and Parlour Car Service." June 1: 37–38.

_____. 1951. "Collective Agreement Between the CN and the CBRT for Employees in Sleeping, Dining and Parlour Car Service."

CBWC (Congress of Black Women). 1991. Toronto Chapter. Press Conference, 27 March.

_____. 1995. "End the Silence on Racism in Health Care: Build a Movement Against Racism, Discrimination and Reprisals." Conference. Toronto, May 25–26.

_____. 1996. "Presentation to the Metropolitan Toronto Anti-Racism, Access and Equity Committee." October 16.

CEIC (Canadian Employment and Immigration Center). 1994. Immigration Act and Regulations. Ottawa: Minister of Supply and Services.

Chabram-Dernersesian, A. 1997. "Whiteness in Chicana/o Discourses." In R. Frankenberg (ed.), *Displacing Whiteness: Essays in Social and Cultural Criticism.* London: Duke University Press.

Chan, A. 1983. *Gold Mountain.* Vancouver: New Star Books.

Chaplin, J. 1998. *Feminist Counselling in Action.* London: Sage Publications.

Chauduri, N. and M. Stroebel. 1993. *Western Women and Imperialism.* Bloomington: Indiana University Press.

Chodorow, N. 1989. *Feminism and Psychoanalytic Theory.* New Haven: Yale University Press.

Chow, R. 1993. *Writing Diaspora. Tactics of Intervention in Contemporary Cultural Studies.* Bloomington: Indiana University Press.

Christensen, C.P. 1996. "The Impact of Racism on the Education of Social Service Workers." In C. James (ed.), *Perspectives on Racism and the Human Services Sector: A Case for Change.* Toronto: University of Toronto Press.

"CNR Porters to Battle Discrimination." 1962. *Winnipeg Tribune,* January 4.

Colen, S. 1995. "Like a Mother to Them: Stratified Reproduction and West Indian Childcare Workers and Employers in New York." In Faye D. Ginsburg and Rayna Rapp (eds.), *Conceiving the New World Order: The Global Politics of Reproduction.* Berkeley: University of California Press.

Collins, P. 1990. *Black Feminist Thought. Knowledge Consciousness and the Politics of Empowerment.* New York: Routledge.

_____. 1993. "Toward a New Vision; Race, Class and Gender as categories of Analysis and Connection." *Race, Sex and Class* 1(1): 25–45.

Commission des droits de la personne du Québec. 1995. *Religious Pluralism in Québec: A Social and Ethical Challenge.*

Cooper, Shirley. 1973. "A Look at the Effects of Racism on Clinical Work." *Social Casework,* February.

Corvin, Sue Ann and Fred Wiggins. 1989. "An Anti-Racism Training Model for White Professionals." *Journal of Multicultural Counselling and Development* 17: 105–14.

COSTI. 1991. *Report on Immigrant Women: Education, Training and Employment.* Toronto: COSTI.

Coward, V. 1944. Letter to A.P. Randolph. Library of Congress, BSCP Papers, Box 73, September 27.

Cox, O. 1976. *Race Relations: Elements and Social Dynamics.* Wayne State University Press.

"CPR to Hire First Negro Conductor." 1955. *Canadian Labour Reports,* March 10: 2.

Crosby, M. 1991. "Construction of the Imaginary Indian." In Stan Douglas (ed.), *Vancouver Anthology: The Institutional Politics of Art.* Vancouver: Between the Lines.

Cross, Terry L., Barbara J. Bazron, Karl W. Dennis and Mareasa Isaacs. 1989. *Towards a Culturally Competent System of Care: A Monograph on Effective Services for Minority Children Who are Severely Emotionally Disturbed.* Washington, D.C.: Georgetown University Child Development Center.

Das Gupta, T. 1993. *Analytical Report on the Human Rights Case involving Northwestern General Hospital.* Toronto, September.

_____. 1994. "Political Economy of Gender, Race and Class: Looking at South Asian Immigrant Women in Canada." *Canadian Ethnic Studies* 26(1): 59–73.

_____. 1996. *Racism and Paid Work.* Toronto: Garamond Press.

Davis, A. 1983. *Women, Race and Class.* New York: Vintage Books.

DeBord, K. and A. Thompson. 1994. *Community Diversity Issues: Strategies for a Comprehensive Multicultural Framework.* Unpublished manuscript.

Dei, George J. Sefa. 1995a. "Integrative Anti-Racism: Intersections of Race, Class and Gender." *Race, Gender and Class: Special Edition* 2(3): 11–30.

_____. 1995b. "Examining the Case for African-centred Schools." *McGill Journal of Education* 30(2): 179–98.

_____. 1996. *Anti-Racism Education: Theory and Practice*. Halifax: Fernwood Publishing.

_____. 1997. "Race and the Production of Identity in the Schooling Experiences of African Canadian Youth." *Discourse* 18(2): 241–57.

_____. 1999. "The Denial of Difference: Reframing Anti-Racist Praxis." *Race, Ethnicity and Education* 2(1): 17–38

Dei, George J. Sefa and c. connelly. 1999. "Review Essay" In M. Bloch, J. Beoku-Betts and R. Tabachnick (eds.), *Women and Education in Sub-Saharan Africa: Power, Opportunities and Constraints*. London: Boulder [forthcoming].

Dei, George J. Sefa and I.M. James. 1998. "'Becoming Black': African-Canadian Youth and the Politics of Negotiating Racial and Racialised Identities." *Race, Ethnicity and Education* 1(1): 91–108.

Delgado, R. and J. Stefancic. 1997. *Critical White Studies: Looking Behind the Mirror.* Philadelphia: Temple University Press.

Devore, Wynetta and Elfriede G. Schlesinger. 1996. *Ethnic-Sensitive Social Work Practice*. 4th edition. Boston: Allyn and Bacon.

Dhaliwal, Amarpal K. 1994. "Reading Diaspora: Self-Representational Practices and the Politics of Reception." *Socialist Review* 24(4): 13–44.

Dickenson, H. and T. Wotherspoon. 1992. "From Assimilation to Self-Government: Towards a Political Economy of Canada's Aboriginal Policies." In Vic Satzewich (ed.), *Deconstructing A Nation: Immigration, Multiculturalism and Racism in '90s Canada*. Halifax, Nova Scotia: Fernwood Publishing.

Dominelli, Lena. 1988. *Anti-racist Social Work*. London: Macmillan.

Dominique, M. 1997. "Racial Harassment in the Workplace and Building a Solidarity to Change the Situation." Address delivered to Professional Training in Health Relations, Program to Help Employers. November. Montreal.

Doris Marshall Institute and Arnold Minors & Associates. 1994. *Ethno-Racial Equality: A Distant Goal? An Interim Report to Northwestern General Hospital*. Toronto: authors.

Doyal, L., G. Hunt and J. Mellor. 1981. "Your Life in Their Hands." *Critical Social Policy* 1(2): 54–71.

Doyle, Robert and Levy Visano. 1987. *Access to Health and Social Services for Members of Diverse Cultural and Racial Groups, Reports 1 and 2*. Toronto: Social Planning Council of Metropolitan Toronto.

Driedger, Leo. 1996. *Multi-ethnic Canada: Identities and Inequalities*. Toronto: Oxford University Press

Dua, E. and A. Robertson. 1999. *Scratching the Surface: Canadian Anti-Racist Feminist Thought*. Toronto: Women's Press.

Dubinsky, K. 1992. "'Maidenly Girls' or 'Designing Women?' The Crime of Seduction in Turn of the Century Ontario." In F. Iacovetta and M. Valverde (eds.), *Gender Conflicts: New Essays in Women's History*. Toronto: University of Toronto Press.

Du Bois, W.E.B. 1903. *The Souls of Black Folks*. New York: Penguin Books.

DuCille, A. 1994. "The Occult of True Black Womanhood: Critical Demeanor and Black Feminist Studies." *Signs: Journal of Women in Culture and Society* 19(3): 591–628.

Duclos, N. 1992. "Disappearing Women: Racial Minority Women in Human Rights Cases." Paper presented at the Seminar on Racial, Ethnic and Cultural Equity, Saskatchewan.

Dyer, R. 1997. *White*. London: Routledge.

Edwards, R. 1979. *Contested Terrain*. New York: Basic Books.

Ehrenreich, B. and D. English. 1973. *Witches, Midwives, and Nurses: A History of Women Healers*. Old Westbury, New York: Feminist Press.

Eke, C. (ed.). 1997. *Race and the Enlightenment: A Reader*. London: Blackwell Publishers.

Elliott, D. 1993. "Social Work and Social Development Towards an Integrative Model for Social Work Practice." *International Social Work* 36(1): 21–37.

Ellsworth, E. 1997. "Double Binds of Whiteness." In M. Fine, L. Weiss, L. Powell and L.M. Wong (eds.), *Off White: Readings on Race, Power, and Society*. New York: Routledge.

Enloe, C. 1989. *Bananas, Beaches and Bases: Making Feminist Sense of International Politics*. London: Pandora Press.

_____. 1993. *The Morning After: Sexual Politics at the End of the Cold War*. Berkeley: University of California Press.

Espinet, R. 1989. "The Invisible Woman in Caribbean Fiction." *World Literature Written in English (WLWE)*, Summer.

_____. 1992. "Representation and the Indo-Caribbean Woman in Trinidad and Tobago." In Frank Birbalsingh (ed.), *Indo Caribbean Resistance*. Toronto: TSAR Publications.

_____. 1994. "A Sense of Constant Dialogue—Writing, Woman and Indo-Caribbean Culture (A Dialogue with Elaine Savory)." In Makeda Silvera (ed.), *The Other Woman: Women of Colour in Contemporary Canadian Literature*. Toronto: Sister Vision Press.

Essed, Philomena. 1991. *Understanding Everyday Racism*. Newbury Park, California: Sage Publications.

_____. 1996. *DiVeRSiTY: Gender, Colour and Culture*. Amherst: University of Massachusetts Press.

Estable, A. and M. Meyer. 1986. *Women Immigrant in Canada: Current Issues*. Ottawa: Canadian Advisory Council on the Status of Women.

_____. 1989. A Discussion Paper on *Settlement Needs of Immigrant Women in Ontario*. Canada: Immigrant Settlement and Adaptation Program. March.

Evans, E.N. 1992. "Liberation Theology, Empowerment Theory and Social Work Practice with the Oppressed." *International Social Work* 35: 135–47.

Fanon, F. 1963. *The Wretched of the Earth*. [Constance Farrington, trans. from French]. New York: Grove Press.

_____. 1967. *Towards the African Revolution*. New York: Monthly Review.

Fellows, M. and S. Razack. 1994. "Seeking Relations: Law and Feminism Roundtables." *Signs. Journal of Women in Culture and Society* 19(4): 1048–83.

_____. 1998. "The Race to Innocence: Confronting Hierarchical Relations Among Women." *Iowa Journal of Gender, Race and Justice* 1(2): 335–52.

Ferber, A.L. 1995. "'Shame of White Men': Interracial Sexuality and the Construction of White Masculinity in Contemporary White Supremacist Discourse." *Masculinities* 3(2): 1–24.

FIIQ and Royal Victoria Hospital. 1993. Quebec Arbitration, Grievance 90/296-211054 16.

Fischer, W. 1996. "Deconstructing Whiteness in a Canadian University Year Abroad Program." Unpublished paper, Graduate Department of Education, University of

Toronto.

Fleras, A. and J.L. Elliot. 1996. *Unequal Relations: An Introduction to Race, Ethnic and Aboriginal Dynamics in Canada*. Scarborough: Prentice Hall.

Flynn, K. 1998 "Proletarianization, Professionalization, and Caribbean Immigrant Nurses." *Canadian Woman Studies* 18(1): 57–60.

Foner, P. 1981. *History of the Labour Movement in the United States. Vol. III: The Politics and Practices of the American Federation of Labour, 1900–1909*. New York: International Publishers.

Fordham, S. 1988. "Racelessness as a Factor in Black Students' School Success: Pragmatic Strategy or Pyrrhic Victory?" *Harvard Educational Review* 58(1): 54–84.

Foucault, M. 1980. *Power/Knowledge: Selected Interviews, 1972–77*. (C. Gordon, ed.). Brighton: Harvester Press.

Fox-Genovese, E. 1988. *Within the Plantation Household: Black and White Women of the Old South*. Chapel Hill: University of North Carolina Press.

Francis, D. 1993. *The Imaginary Indian: The Image of the Indian in Canadian Culture*. Vancouver: Arsenal Pulp Press.

Frankenberg, R. 1993a. *White Women, Race Matters: The Social Construction of Whiteness*. Minneapolis: University of Minnesota Press.

_____. 1993b. "Growing Up White: Feminism, Racism and the Social Geography of Childhood." *Feminist Review* (Autumn) 45: 51–84.

Franklin, C. 1995. "Presentation at OHA Conference on Anti-Racism." Toronto, May 29.

Freeman, F. 1934. "The Interpretation of Test Results with Especial Reference to Race Comparisons." *Journal of Negro Education* (July) 3(3): 519–22.

Freire, Paulo. 1970. *The Pedagogy of the Oppressed*. Hammondsworth: Penguin.

Frideres, J. and W. Reeves. 1989. "The Ability to Implement Human Rights Legislation in Canada." *Canadian Review of Sociology and Anthropology* 26(2): 311–32.

Gamarnikow, E. 1978. "Sexual Division of Labour." In A. Kuhn and A. Wolpe (eds.), *Feminism and Materialism*. London: Routledge.

Gangulee, N. 1947. *Indians in the Empire Overseas*. London: The New India Publishing House.

Geadah, Y. 1996. *Femmes voilées, intégrismes démasqués*. Montréal: VLB.

Gerrad, N. 1991. Racism and Sexism, Together, in Counselling: Three Women of Colour Tell Their Stories. *Canadian Journal of Counselling* 25(4): 555–66.

Gilligan, C. 1982. *In a Different Voice*. Cambridge: Harvard University Press.

Gilroy, P. 1987. *There Ain't no Black in the Union Jack*. London: Hutchison.

Ginsburg, F.D. and R. Rapp (eds.). 1995. *Conceiving the New World Order*.

Giroux, H. 1994. "White Utopias and Nightmare Realities: Film and the New Cultural Racism." In *Disturbing Pleasures: Learning Popular Culture*. New York: Routledge.

_____. 1997. *Channel Surfing: Race Talk and the Destruction of Today's Youth*. Toronto: Canadian Scholar's Press.

Glazer, N. 1991. "'Between a Rock and a Hard Place': Women's Professional Organizations in Nursing and Class, Racial, and Ethnic Inequalities." *Gender & Society* 5(3): 351–72.

Goldberg, D. (ed.). 1990. *Anatomy of Racism*. Minneapolis: University of Minnesota.

_____. 1993. *Racist Culture*. Oxford: Blackwell.

Goldhor-Lerner, H. 1988 *Women in Therapy*. New York: Harper and Row.

Gordon, D., R. Edwards and M. Reich. 1982. *Segmented Work, Divided Workers*.

London: Cambridge University Press.

Gould, K. 1987. "Feminist Principles and Minority Concerns: Contributions, Problems and Solutions." *Affilia*, Fall: 6–19.

Gould, S.J. 1981. *The Mismeasure of Man*. New York: W.W. Norton and Company.

_____. 1994. "Curveball." *The New Yorker,* November 28: 139–49.

Gould, W. 1977. *Black Workers in White Unions*. Ithaca: Cornell University Press.

Gouvernement du Québec. 1977. *Charte de la langue française*. Québec: Éditeur officiel.

Grayson, M. 1953. Letter to H. Parr, September 15. PAC, MG 28, I 173, Vol. 34.

Greaves, I. 1930. *National Problems of Canada: The Negro in Canada*. Montreal: McGill University Economic Studies, No. 16, p. 55.

Green, J.W. 1995. *Cultural Awareness in the Humans Services*. Boston: Allyn & Bacon.

Greening, W. 1961. *It Was Never Easy, 1908–1958: A History of the Canadian Brotherhood of Railway, Transport and General Workers*. Ottawa.

Greenspan, M. 1983. *A New Approach to Women and Therapy*. New York: McGraw Hill.

Grewal, I and C. Kaplan. 1996. *Home and Harem: Nation, Gender, Empire, and the Cultures of Travel*. Durham: Duke University Press.

_____. 1994. *Scattered Hegemonies: Postmodernity and Transnational Feminist Practices*. London and Minneapolis: University of Minnesota Press.

Grillo, T. and S. Wildman. 1991. "Obscuring the Importance of Race: The Implication of Making Comparisons between Racism and Sexism." *Duke Law Journal* 397.

Hall, S. 1978. *Policing the Crisis*. London: Macmillan.

_____. 1991. "Old and New Identities: Old and New Ethnicities." In A. King (ed.), *Culture, Globalization and the World System.* New York: State University Press.

Hardill, K. 1993 "Discovering Fire where the Smoke Is: Racism in the Health Care System." *Towards Justice in Health* 2(1): 17–21.

Harris, W. 1977. *Keeping the Faith*. Urbana: University of Illinois Press.

Hartmann, H. 1976. "Capitalism, Patriarchy, and Job Segregation by Sex." *Signs* 2: 137–69.

_____. 1981. "The Family as the Locus of Gender, Class, and Political Struggle: The Example of Housework." *Signs* 6(3): 366–94.

Hathiramani, H. 1980. "Tribunals Study Nurse Dismissal at Mac-Chedoke." *Silhouette,* September 18.

Head, W. 1986. *An Exploratory Study of Attitudes and Perceptions of Minority and Majority Group Health Care Workers*. Toronto: OHRC.

Henry, F., et. al. 1985. *Who Gets the Work?: A Test of Racial Discrimination in Employment*. Toronto: Urban Alliance on Race Relations.

_____. 1994. *The Caribbean Diaspora in Toronto: Learning to Live with Racism.* Toronto: University of Toronto Press.

Henry, F., C. Tator, W. Mattis and T. Rees. 1995. *The Colour of Democracy: Racism in Canadian Society*. Toronto: Harcourt Brace.

Henry, K. 1981. *Black Politics in Toronto since World War I*. Toronto: Multicultural History Society of Ontario.

Hill, D.G. 1981. *The Freedom Seekers: Blacks in Early Canada*. Agincourt, Ontario: Book Society of Canada.

Hine, D. 1989. *Black Women in White*. Bloomington: Indiana University Press.

Hobsbawm, E. 1990. *Nations and Nationalism Since 1780*. Cambridge: Cambridge University Press.

Hoodfar H. 1993. "The Veil in Their Minds and On Our Heads: The Persistence of Colonial Images of Muslim Women." *Resources for Feminist Research/Documentation sur la recherche feministe* 22(3/4): 5–18.

hooks, b. 1981. *Ain't I a Woman: Black Women and Feminism.* Boston: South End Press.

_____. 1984. *From Margin to Centre.* Boston: South End Press.

_____. 1988. *Talking Back.* Toronto: Between the Lines Press.

_____. 1992. "Representing Whiteness in the Black Imagination." In L. Grossberg et. al. (eds.), *Cultural Studies.* New York: Routledge.

Horna, Jarmila. 1990. "Acculturation, Dual Cultural Identity or Somewhere Between: A Sociological Summary. "Paper presented at the 42nd Congress of Czechoslovak Association of Canada, Edmonton, Alberta. May.

Houda-Pepin, F. 1993. "Les Musulmans font face à de nombreux préjugés." *La Presse,* 15 jan.: B3.

Hurtado, A. and A. Stewart. 1997. "Through the Looking Glass: Implications of Studying Whiteness for Feminist Methods." In M. Fine, L. Weiss, L. Powell, L.M. Wong (eds.), *Off White: Readings on Race, Power, and Society.* New York: Routledge.

Huttenback, R. 1976. *Racism and Empire.* Ithaca: Cornell University Press.

Iacovetta, Frances. 1986. "From Contadina to Workers: Southern Italian Immigrants Working in Toronto, 1947–1962." In Burnet (ed.), *Industry, Science and Technology in Canada.* Ottawa: Ministry of Industry, Science and Technology.

_____. 1998. "Making New Canadians: Social Workers, Women, and the Reshaping of Immigrant Families." In Franca Iacovetta, Paula Draper and Robert Ventresca (eds.), *A Nation of Immigrant Women, Workers, and Communities in Canadian History, 1840s–1960s.* Toronto: University of Toronto Press.

Iacovetta, Frances and M. Valverde (eds.). 1992. *Gender Conflicts.* Toronto: University of Toronto Press.

Ibrahim, A. 1996. "Race, Language and the Politics of Identity: A Black Franco-Ontarian Case Study." Ph.D research proposal, Department of Education, OISE/ University of Toronto.

Immigrant Women of Saskatchewan. 1985. *Doubly Disadvantaged: The Women Who Immigrate to Canada.* Saskatoon: Immigrant Women of Saskatchewan (Monograph).

Jackson, B.W. and E. Holvino. 1989. "Working with Multicultural Organizations: Matching Theory to Practice." *Proceedings of a Workshop on Diversity: Implications for Education and Training,* 109–21.

Jackson, T., S. Mitchell and Maria Wright. 1989. "The Community Development Continuum." *Community Health Studies* XIII(1): 66–73.

James, C.E. 1995. "Multicultural and Anti-Racism Education in Canada." *Race, Gender and Class,* Spring 2(3): 31–48.

_____, (ed.). 1996. *Perspectives on Racism and the Human Services Sector: A Case for Change.* Toronto: University of Toronto Press.

Jeffery, D. 1997a. "Feminist Social Workers: Reconciling Theory with Practice." Master's Thesis, University of Toronto, Ontario Institute for Studies in Education (OISE), Department of Adult Education.

_____. 1997b. "Helping as an Imperial Discourse: Social Work in Canadian History." Unpublished paper.

Jenkins, M. 1936. "A Socio-Psychological Study of Negro Children of Superior Intelligence." *The Journal of Negro Education,* April 5(2): 175–90.

John, M. 1989. "Postcolonial Feminists in the Western Intellectual Field: Anthropologists and Native Informants." *Inscriptions* 5: 49–73.

_____. 1999. Racialized Bodies: The Social Construction of Black Identities in Popular Cinema. Unpublished MA Thesis. Toronto: Department of Sociology and Equity Studies, OISE/University of Toronto.

Johnston, H. 1989. *The Voyage of the Komagat Maru: The Sikh Challenge to Canada's Colour Bar.* Vancouver: University of British Columbia Press.

Johnstone, T. 1964. Letter to B. Wilson, January 3. PAC, MG 28, I215, Vol. 14.

Jones, D. 1993. Letter to F. White, January 25.

_____. 1994. Letter to F. Gallant, September 23.

Jordan, J. 1991. *Women's Growth in Connection.* New York: Guilford Press.

Kamarowsky, A. 1961. Letter to S. Blum, May 25. PAC, MG 28, V75, Vol. 15, File 8.

Kazosi, A.B. 1988. "The Integration of Black African Immigrants to Canadian Society: A Case Study of Toronto." *CMA,* 1986. Toronto: CANACT.

_____. 1992. "Adjustment of Black African Immigrants to Canadian Society, 1980–1982" (mimeo).

Keene, J. 1992. *Human Rights in Ontario.* 2nd edition. Toronto: Carswell.

Khan, S. 1993. "Canadian Muslim Women and Shari'a Law: A Feminist Response to 'Oh! Canada!'" *Canadian Journal of Women and the Law* 6(1): 52–65.

Khouri, N. 1992. "Des classifications labiles: ordres politiques et métissages." In Nadia Khouri (ed.), *Discours et mythes de l'ethnicité.* Montréal: Acfas.

King, D. 1990. "Multiple Jeopardy, Multiple Consciousness: The Context of Black Feminist Ideology. In M. Malson, E. Mudimbe-Boyi, J. O'Barr and M. Wyer (eds.), *Black Women in America.* Chicago: University of Chicago Press.

_____. 1994. "Perceiving Reality in a New Way: Rethinking the Black/White Duality of Our Time." Paper presented at the Annual Meeting of the American Educational Research Association: New Orleans, La.: April: 4–9.

Kivel, P. 1996. *Uprooting Racism: How White People Can Work for Racial Justice.* Gabriola Island, B.C.: New Society Publishers.

Klein, M. 1988. *Envy and Gratitude.* London: Virago.

Kohut, H. 1995. *The Analysis of the Self: A Systematic Approach to the Psychoanalytic Treatment of Narcissistic Disorders.* Connecticut: International Universities Press Inc.

Kondapi, C. 1951. *Indians Overseas, 1838–1949.* London: Oxford University Press.

La Violette, F. 1973. *The Struggle for Survival: Indian Cultures and the Protestant Ethic in British Columbia.* Toronto: University of Toronto Press.

Labour Gazette, The. 1918. August (18): 597–604.

_____. 1920. March (20): 241.

_____. 1927. January (27): 17–18.

_____. 1964. "Merger of Seniority Groups." April (64): 262.

Laïdaoui, H. 1994. "La question ethnique. Autochtones et immigrants se perçoivent-ils des citoyens à part entière?" *Le Devoir,* 16 oct.: E6.

Laidlaw, T.A. and C. Malmo. 1990. *Healing Voices: Feminist Approaches to Therapy with Women.* San Francisco: Jossey-Bass Publishers.

Law Union of Ontario. 1981. *The Immigrant's Handbook.* Montreal: Black Rose.

Laxer, G. 1989. *Open for Business: The Routes of Foreign Ownership in Canada.* Don Mills, ON: Oxford University Press.

Laxer, R. 1973. *(Canada) Limited: The Political Economy of Dependency.* Toronto:

McClelland and Stewart.

Lazreg, M. 1988. "Feminism and Difference: The Perils of Writing as a Woman on Women in Algeria." *Feminist Studies* 14(1): 81–107.

_____. 1994. *The Eloquence of Silence: Algerian Women in Question.* London/New York: Routledge.

Leah, Ronnie. 1991. "Linking the Struggles: Racism, Sexism and the Union Movement." In Vorst et al. (ed.), *Race, Class, Gender: Bonds and Barriers.* Toronto: Between the Lines.

_____. 1993. "Black Women Speak Out: Racism and Unions. In Linda Briskin and Patricia McDermott (eds.), *Women Challenging Unions: Feminism, Democracy, and Militancy.* Toronto: University of Toronto Press.

Lee, B., S. McGrath, K. Moffatt and U. George. 1996. "Community Practice Education in Canadian Schools of Social Work. *Canadian Review of Social Work* 13(2): 221–36

Lee, I. 1990."Multiculturalism: The Dilemmas of Implementation." In C. Hedrick and R. Holton (ed.), *Cross-Cultural Communication and Professional Education.* Adelaide: Centre for Multicultural Studies, Flindas University.

Legault, J. 1994. "New Film on October Crisis Brings Back Memories." *The Gazette,* Sept 30: B3.

Li, P. 1988. *The Chinese in Canada.* Don Mills, Ontario: Oxford University Press.

Li, P. and S. Bolaria (eds.). 1983. *Racial Minorities in Multicultural Canada.* Toronto: Garamond Press.

Loney, M. 1997. Letter to the Editor. *Toronto Star,* Nov. 1.

Lopez, L.J. 1995. "The Social Construction of Race." In R. Delgado (ed.), *Critical Race Theory: The Cutting Edge.* Philadelphia: Temple University Press.

Lorde, A. 1980. *Age, Race, Class and Sex: Women Redefining Difference.* Copeland Colloquium. Amherst College, Amherst, MA.

Lui, M. 1996. "Mixed race People, Racism and Challenging Boundaries." Unpublished paper, Graduate Department of Education, University of Toronto.

Lum, D. 1986. *Social Work Practice and People of Colour: A Process-stage Approach.* Monterey, CA: Brooks/Cole.

Macchiusi, J. 1992/93. "The Origins of Racism and the Rise of Biological Determinism." *Paradox of Racism, Prize Winning Essays* 6: 53–63. Toronto: York University.

Malarek, Victor. 1987. *Haven's Gate: Canada's Immigration Fiasco.* Toronto: Macmillan.

Malmo, C. 1985. *Issues and Strategies in Counselling Girls and Women.* Athabasca: University of Athabasca Press

Manpower and Immigration. 1974. *The Immigration Program.* Ottawa: Information Canada.

Marks, S. 1994. *Divided Sisterhood: Race, Class and Gender in the South African Nursing Profession.* New York: St. Martin's Press.

Marshall, R. 1965. *The Negro and Organized Labour.* New York: John Wiley & Sons.

_____. 1974. "The Economics of Racial Discrimination: A Survey." *Journal of Economic Literature* 12: 849–71.

Martin, D.C. 1995. "The Choices of Identity." *Social Identities* 1(1): 5–20.

Martineau, R. 1995. "Leçons d'Alger." *Voir* 25–31 (mars): 5.

Matthews, W. 1965. Letter to W. Smith, January. 4. PAC, MG 28, I215, Vol. 15.

McAllister, J. 1965. Memo to file, March 1. PAC, MG 28, I215, Vol. 15.

McAlpin, A.S. 1932. "Changes in the Intelligence Quotients of Negro Children." *The Journal of Negro Education* (April) 1(1): 44–48.

McCarthy and Warren Crichlow (eds.). *Race, Identity, and Representation in Education*. New York: Routledge.

McClintock, A. 1995. *Imperial Leather: Race, Gender, and Sexuality in the Colonial Conquest*. London: Routledge.

McGuire, J. 1942. Letter to A. Mosher, November 6. PAC, MG 28, I 215, Vol. 81, File— the Race Issue.

McIntosh, P. 1990. "White Privilege: Unpacking the Invisible Knapsack." *Independent School* 49 (2): 31–36.

McLaren, A. 1990. *Our Own Master Race: Eugenics in Canada, 1885–1945*. Toronto: McClelland & Stewart.

McMahon, A. and P. Allen-Meares. 1992. "Is Social Work Racist? A Content Analysis of Recent Literature." *Social Work* 37(6): 533–39.

McPherson, K. 1996. *Bedside Matters*. Toronto: Oxford University Press.

Meijer, M. 1993. "Countering Textual Violence. On the Critique of Representation and the Importance of Teaching Its Methods." *Women's Studies International Forum* 16(4): 367–78.

Mergen, B. 1974. "The Pullman Porter: From 'George' to Brotherhood." *South Atlantic Quarterly* 73(Spring): 224–35.

Meyers, D.T. 1994. *Subjection and Subjectivity: Psychoanalytic Feminism and Moral Philosophy*. New York: Routledge.

Mies, M. 1986. *Patriarchy and Accumulation on a World Scale*. London: Zed Books.

Miles, R. 1982. *Racism and Migrant Labour*. London: Routledge & Kegan Paul.

_____. 1989. *Racism*. London: Tavistock.

_____. 1994. "Explaining Racism in Contemporary Europe." In A. Rattansi and S. Westwood (eds.), *Racism, Modernity and Identity*. London: Polity Press.

Miles, R. and R. Torres. 1996. "Does Race Matter? Transatlantic Perspectives on Racism after Race Relations." In. V. Amit-Talai and C. Knowles (eds.), *Re-Situating Identities: The Politics of Race, Ethnicity and Culture*. Peterborough, ON: Broadview Press.

Miller, J.B. 1976. *Toward a New Psychology of Women*. Boston: Beacon Press.

Minors, A. 1996."From Uni-versity to Poly-versity: Organizations in Transition to Anti-Racism." In C.A. James (ed.), *Perspectives on Racism and the Human Services Sector: A Case for Change*. Toronto: University of Toronto Press.

Mirza, Heidi Safia. 1997. *Black British Feminism*. London and New York: Routledge.

Modood, T. 1997. "'Difference,' cultural racism and anti-racism." In P. Werbner and T. Modood (eds.), *Debating Cultural Hybridity: Multi-cultural Identities and the Politics of Anti-Racism*. London: Zed Books.

Moghissi, H. 1994. Personal (class) communication. October 20.

Mohanty, C. 1991. "Under Western Eyes." In Chandra Talpade Mohanty and Lourdes Torres (eds.), *Third World Women and the Politics of Feminism*. Bloomington: Indiana University Press.

Moodley, Kogila. 1983. Canadian Multiculturalism as Ideology. *Ethnic and Racial Studies* 6(3): 320–21.

Mootoo, S. 1993. *Out on Main Street*. Vancouver: Press Gang.

Morrison, T. 1992. *Playing in the Dark: Whiteness and the Literary Imagination*. New York: Vantage Books.

Morton, P. 1991. *Disfigured Images*. New York: Greenwood Press.

Moussa, Helene. 1993. *Storm and Sanctuary: The Journey of Ethiopian and Women Refugee*. Dundas, ON: Artemis Publishers.

Mullaly, R. 1993. *Structural Social Work, Ideology, Theory and Practice*. Toronto: McClelland and Stewart.

Murphy, R. 1988. *Social Closure: The Theory of Monopolization and Exclusion*. New York: Oxford University Press.

Musisi, Nakanyiki. 1994. "Meeting the Employment Needs of African Immigrant and Refugee Women in Toronto" (Working Paper).

NAFAD. 1996. "Presentation to the Anti-Racism and Equity Committee, Metro Council." October 16.

Nasrulla, A. 1994. "Educators outside Quebec mystified by *hijab* ban." *The Globe and Mail*, Dec. 13: A1.

Naylor, T. 1975. *The History of Canadian Business, 1867–1914*. 2nd edition. Toronto: McClelland and Stewart.

Nestel, S. 1995. "Other Mothers: Race and Representation in Natural Childbirth Discourse." *Resources for Feminist Research* 23(4), Winter: 5–19.

_____. 1996. "Immigration, Proletarianization and Racialization: Constructing the Nursing Labor Force in Ontario." Unpublished paper, Department of Adult Education, OISE/ University of Toronto.

Neuwirth, Gertrude. 1989. *The Settlement of Ethiopian Refugees in Toronto: An Exploratory Study*. Ottawa: CEIC (November).

Newsinger, J. 1986. "Lord Greystoke and Darkest Africa: The Politics of the Tarzan Stories." *Race and Class* 28(2): 59–71.

Newton, J. 1992. "The Alchemy of Politicization: Socialist Women and the Early Canadian Left." In F. Iacovetta and M. Valverde (eds.), *Gender Conflicts*. Toronto: University of Toronto Press.

Ng, R. 1988. *Politics of Community Services: Immigrant Women, Class and the State*. Toronto: Garamond Press.

_____. 1991. "Sexism, Racism and Canadian Nationalism." In J. Vorst (ed.), *Race, Class and Gender: Bonds and Barriers*. Toronto: Garamond Press.

_____. 1993. "Racism, Sexism and Nation-Building In Canada." In Cameron McCarthy and W. Crichlow (eds.), *Race, Identity and Representation in Education*. New York: Routledge.

Ng, R. and A. Estable. 1987. "Immigrant Women in the Labour Force: An Overview of Present Knowledge and Research Gap." *Resource for Feminist Research* 16(1): 29–33.

Ng, R., P. Staton and J. Scane (eds.). 1995. *Anti-Racism, Feminism and Critical Approaches to Education*. Toronto: OISE Press.

Northrup, H. 1944. *Organized Labour and the Negro*. New York: Harper and Brothers.

Northrup, H., H. Risher Jr., R. Leone and P. Jeffrerss. 1971. *Negro Employment in Land and Air Transport*. Pennsylvania: Wharton School of Finance and Commerce.

Nurses, Woodlands Hospital. 1992. Letter to the OHRC, 5 Dec.

Oatis v. *Crown Zellerback Corp.* 1968. 5th Circuit. 398 F.2d 496.

OCASI (Ontario Council of Agencies Serving Immigrants). 1996. "Community agency survey." *A Nation of Immigrants*. Toronto: OCASI.

OCL (Ontario Labour Committee for Human Rights). 1956. "FEP Complaints, CPR." PAC, MG 28, I173, Vol. 34.

OHRC (Ontario Human Rights Commission). 1992a. "Case Report." Toronto.
_____. 1992b. "Dunfermline Hospital: Systemic Analysis." Toronto.
Omi, M. and H. Winant. 1983. "By the Rivers of Babylon. Part One." *Socialist Review* 13(5): 31–65.
_____. 1993. "On the Theoretical Status of the Concept of Race." In McCarthy and W. Crichlow (eds.), *Race, Identity, and Representation in Education.* New York: Routledge.
_____. 1994. *Racial Formation in the United States.* New York: Routledge.
ONA. 1996. "Presentation to the Metro Anti-Racism, Access and Equity Committee." October 16.
_____. 1997. "Judicial Reviews filed for Human Rights Commission's Refusal to Investigate Unionized Workers' Complaints." *The ONA News,* June–July: 26.
_____. 1998. "Ontario Human Rights Commission takes up the Fight for Grad Nurses." *The ONA News,* January–February 25(1): 24–25.
Ontario Court of Justice. 1998. *Three Nurses and the OHRC and Toronto Hospital* file 342/96. Toronto. February 5.
Ontario Hospitals' Anti-Racism Task Force. 1996. *Ontario Hospitals Anti-Racism Project Report.* Toronto, Feb.
Ontario Ministry of Citizenship. 1989a. "Nursing: Background Study Prepared by the TFAPTO." Toronto.
_____. 1989b. *Access! Task Force on Access to Professions and Trades in Ontario.* Toronto: Queen's Printer for Ontario.
Ontario Ministry of Culture and Recreation. 1979. *Ontario Ethnocultural Profits.* Toronto: Ministry of Culture and Recreation.
Ontario Ministry of Labour. 1983. *Sudbury and District Health Unit and ONA.* Toronto.
_____. 1993a. *ONA and Dunfermline Hospital.* File 910215, October 13: 199.
_____. 1993b. *ONA and Dunfermline Hospital.* File 900727, November 29.
_____. 1996. *Belair Health Unit and ONA.* File 940354, July.
Palmer, D. 1997. *Canadians' Attitude toward Immigration: November and December 1996, and February 1997 surveys.* Report Prepared for Program Support, Strategic Policy, Planning and Research Branch, Citizenship and Immigration, Canada.
Parkin, F. 1979. *Marxism and Class Theory: A Bourgeois Critique.* New York: Columbia University Press.
Paur, J. 1994. "Writing My Way 'Home': Travelling South Asian Bodies and Diasporic Journeys." *Socialist Review* 24(4): 75–108.
Peterson, J. 1934. "Basic Considerations of Methodology in Race Testing." *The Journal of Negro Education* (July) 3(3): 403–10.
Petgrave, V. 1956. Letter to Maclean, November 19. PAC, MG 28, V75, Vol. 14, File 14-13.
Petrowski, N. 1995a. "Derrière le hijab: La femme asexuée." *La Presse,* 25 mars: A1.
_____. 1995b. "Derrière le hijab: Ce que nous sommes bons." *La Presse,* 26 mars: A1.
_____. 1995c. "Derrière le hijab: Le hijab qui excite." *La Presse,* 27 mars: A1.
Phillips, C. 1995. "Feminisms, Post-modern Theory and Trouble-Making: Social Work (Education) by Another Name." Master's thesis, University of Toronto, OISE, Department of Sociology.
Pinderhughes, E. 1989. *Understanding Race, Ethnicity, and Power.* New York: Macmillan.
Piore, M. 1971. *The Dual Labor Market.* Lexington, MA: D.C. Heath.
Ponterotto, J. and Haresh B. Sabnani. 1989. "'Classics' in Multicultural Counselling: A

Systematic Five Year Content Analysis." *Journal of Multicultural Counselling and Development* 17: 23–37.

"Porter would Like Probe." 1961. *Winnipeg Free Press*, May 11.

"Porters to Take Union to Court." 1962. *Winnipeg Free Press*. January 3.

Proctor, E.K. and L.E. Davis. 1994. "The Challenge of Racial Difference: Skills for Clinical Practice." *Social Work* 39(3): 314–23.

QHRC (Quebec Human Rights Commission). 1997a. *Maggie* v. *QHRC*. File 500-53-000008-936. Montréal, February 21.

_____. 1997b. *Janet* v. *Paradise Hospital*. File 7947. Montréal, May 23.

Quigley, M. 1980. "Racism: A Growing Problem at McMaster." *Silhoutte,* September 18.

"Racism at McMaster." 1980. August 11 (statement).

Raj, S. 1980. "Some Aspects of East Indian Struggle in Canada, 1905–1947." In K.V. Ujimoto and G. Hirbayashi (eds.), *Visible Minorities and Multiculturalism: Asians in Canada*. Toronto: Butterworths.

Ramcharan, S. 1982. *Racism: Nonwhites in Canada*. Toronto: Butterworths.

Rattansi, A. 1992. "Changing the subject? Racism, culture and education." In J. Donald and A. Rattansi (eds.), *Race, Culture and Difference*. London: Sage Publications with The Open University.

Rattansi, A. and S. Westwood (eds.). 1994. *Racism, Modernity, and Identity*. London: Polity Press.

Razack, S. 1994. "What Is the Cost of Looking White People in the Eye?" *Signs: A Journal of Women in Culture and Society* 19(4): 894–923.

_____. 1995. "Policing the Borders of Gender, Race and Nation: Domestic Violence and Gender Persecution." *Canadian Journal of Women and the Law* 8(1): 891–922.

_____. 1998. *Looking White People in the Eye: Gender, Race and Culture in Courtrooms and Classrooms*. Toronto: University of Toronto Press.

Recourt, V. and M. Alcindor. 1990. "Notes pour Disparaître." *La Parole Métèque* 15: 32.

Reitz, J. 1995. *A Review of the Literature on Aspects of Ethno-racial Access, Utilization and Delivery of Social Services*. Report prepared for The Multicultural Coalition for Access to Family Services and Ontario Ministry of Community and Social Services.

Reitz, J., L. Calzavara and D. Dasko. 1981. *Ethnic Inequality and Segregation in Jobs*. Research paper, No. 3. Toronto: Centre for Urban and Community Studies, University of Toronto

Report of the Special Committee on Visible Minorities in Canada. 1984.

Reynolds, L.T. and L. Lieberman. 1993. "The Rise and Fall of 'Race'." *Race, Sex and Class* 1(1): 109–28.

Rezai-Rashti, G. 1995. "Multicultural Education, Anti-Racist Education, and Critical Pedagogy: Reflections on Everyday Practice." In R. Ng, P. Staton and J. Scane (eds.), *Anti-Racism, Feminism, and Critical Approaches to Education*. Toronto: OISE Press.

Richmond, A.H. 1994. *Global Apartheid: Refugees, Racism, and the New World Order*. Toronto: Oxford University Press.

Rioux, M. 1978. *Quebec in Question*. Toronto: James Lorimer.

Roberts, B. 1979. "'A Work of Empire': Canadian Reformers and British Female Immigration." In L. Kealey (ed.), *A Not Unreasonable Claim: Women and Reform in Canada, 1880–1920*. Toronto: Women's Press.

Robertson, Judith. 1994. "Cinema and the Politics of Desire in Teacher Education."
    Ph.D. Thesis. Toronto: Department of Education, University of Toronto (OISE).
Robertson, M. 1985a. "A Victory for Black Nurses." *Afro-Can* 5(5), May: 1, 11.
_____. 1985b. "Black Nurse Loses Petition." *Afro-Can* 5(10): 1
Robinson, J. 1941. Letter to J. McGuire, March 27. PAC, MG 28, I 215, Vol. 81, File—
    The Race Issue.
_____. 1945. Letter to A. Mosher, August 1. PAC, MG 28, I 215, Vol. 81, File—The
    Race Issue.
Roediger, D. 1991. *The Wages of Whiteness*. London: Verso.
_____. 1994. *Towards the Abolition of Whiteness*. London/New York: Verso.
Roger, K. 1998. "'Fairy Fictions': White Women as Helping Professionals." Thesis:
    University of Toronto.
Roman, L. 1993. "White is Colour! White Defensiveness, Postmodernism and Anti-
    racist Pedagogy." In Cameron McCarthy and Warren Crichlow (eds.), *Race, Iden-
    tity and Representation in Education*. New York: Routledge.
_____. 1997. "Denying (White) Racial Privilege: Redemption Discourses and the Uses
    of Fantasy." In M. Fine, L. Weiss, L. Powell, L.M. Wong (eds.), *Off White:
    Readings on Race, Power, and Society*. New York: Routledge.
Roy, P. 1989. *White Canada Forever*. Vancouver: University of British Columbia Press.
Ruedy, J. 1992. *Modern Algeria: The Origins and Development of a Nation*. Bloomington:
    Indiana University Press.
Said, E.W. 1979a. *Orientalism*. New York: Vintage Books.
_____. 1979b. *Culture and Imperialism*. New York: Vintage Books.
_____. 1993. *Culture and Imperialism*. New York: Alfred A. Knopf.
Sam, Y. 1986. "Black Nurses' Association Still Fighting against Discrimination." *Afro-
    Can* 6(9), September.
Samuel, J. and Associates Inc. 1997. *Visible Minorities and the Public Service of
    Canada*. Report submitted to the Canadian Human Rights Commission. Ottawa: J.
    Samuel and Associates Inc.
Satzewich, V. 1989. "Racisms: The Reaction to Chinese Immigrants in Canada at the
    Turn of the Twentieth Century." *International Sociology* (September) 4(3): 311–27.
_____. 1998. "Race, Racism and Racialization: Contested Concepts." In V. Satzewich
    (ed.), *Racism and Social Inequality: Concepts, Controversies and Strategies of
    Resistance*. Toronto: Thompson Educational Publishing.
Scott, J. 1992. "Experience." In Judith Butler and Joan Scott (eds.), *Feminists Theorise
    the Political*. New York: Routledge.
Sharma, S. 1976. "East Indians and the Canadian Ethnic Mosaic: An Overview." *South
    Asian Bulletin* 3: 53–69.
Sharpe, J. 1994. *Allegories of Empire*. Minn.: University of Minnesota Press.
Shiose, Y. and L. Fontaine. 1995. "La construction des figures de l'<<autre>>: les
    communautés culturelles au Québec." *Canadian Review of Sociology and Anthro-
    pology/Revue canadienne de sociologie et d'anthropologie* 32(1): 91–110.
Silva, E. 1997. "Rethinking Racism: Toward a Structural Interpretation." *American
    Sociological Review* 62(3): 465–86.
Silvera, M. 1989. *Silenced*. Toronto: Sister Vision Press.
Simmons, A. 1998. "Racism and Immigration Policy." In. V. Satzewich (ed.), *Racism
    and Social Inequality: Concepts, Controversies and Strategies of Resistance*. To-
    ronto: Thompson Educational Publishing.

Sleeter, C. 1994 April. "Multicultural Education, Social Positionality and Whiteness." Paper presented at the Annual Meeting of the American Educational Research Association, New Orleans, La.:12-18.

Smelter, L. 1964. Letter to W. Smith, November 14. PAC, MG 28, I 215, Vol. 15.

Smith, D. 1977. *Feminism and Marxism*. Vancouver: New Star Books.

_____. 1987. *The Everyday World as Problematic: A Feminist Sociology*. Toronto: University of Toronto Press.

_____. 1999. *Writing the Social: Critique, Theory and Investigations*. Toronto: University of Toronto Press.

Smith, W. 1963a. Letter to M. Wright, October 17. PAC, MG 28, I 215, Vol. 14.

_____. 1963b. Letter to D. Fenton, December 5. PAC, MG 28, I 215, Vol. 14.

_____. 1964a. Letter to M. Wright, January 21. PAC, MG 28, I 215, Vol. 14.

_____. 1964b. Letter to L. Smelter, November 26. PAC, MG 28, I 215, Vol. 15.

Smith-Rosenberg, C. and C. Rosenberg. 1972. "The Female Animal: Medical and Biological Views of Woman and Her Role in Nineteenth-Century America." *Journal of American History* 60: 332–56.

Social Planning Council of Metropolitan Toronto and City of Toronto. 1996. *Profile of a Changing World*:

Solomos, J. and L. Back. 1995. "Marxism, Racism and Ethnicity." *American Behavioural Scientist* 38(3): 407–20.

Spelman, Elizabeth. 1988. *Inessential Woman: Problems of Exclusion in Feminist Thought*. Boston: Beacon Press.

Spivak, G. 1992. "Acting Bits/Identity Talk." *Cultural Inquiry* 18(Summer): 770–803.

_____. 1993. *Outside in the Teaching Machine*. New York: Routledge.

_____. 1996a. "Diasporas Old and New: Women in the Transnational World." *Textual Practice* 10(2): 245–69.

_____. 1996b. "Commentary. 'Woman' as Theatre." *Radical Philosophy* 75(Jan/Feb): 2–4.

St. Clair Price, J. 1934. "Negro-White Differences in General Intelligence." *The Journal of Negro Education,* July 3(3): 424–52.

Starr, M. 1958a. Letter to L. Williams, March 15. PAC, MG 28, I 215, Vol. 14.

_____. 1958b. Letter to L. Williams, April 24. PAC, MG 28, I 215, Vol. 14.

Stasiulis, D. 1990. "Theorizing Connections: Gender, Race, Ethnicity and Class." In P. Li (ed.), *Race and Ethnic Relations in Canada*.

Stasiulis, Daiva and Radha Happan. 1995. "The Fractitious Politics of a Settler Society: Canada." In Daiva Stasiulis and Nira Yuval-Davis (eds.), *Unsettling Settler Societies*. London: Sage.

Statistics Canada. 1991. Census of Canada.

_____. 1996. *Canada's Changing Immigrant Population*. Catalogue 96-311E.

Stevens, J. 1981–90. "Feminist Fictions: A Critique of the Category 'Non-Western Woman' in Feminist Writings on India." In Ranajit Guha (ed.), *Subaltern Studies, I-VI*. Delhi: Oxford University Press.

Stoler, A.L. 1995. *Race and the Education of Desire: Foucault's History of Sexuality and the Colonial Order of Things*. London: Duke.

Sue, D. Patricia Arredodo and Roderick J. McDavis. 1992. "Multicultural Counselling Competencies and Standards: A Call to the Profession." *Journal of Multicultural Counselling and Development* 20: 64–88.

Sugiman, M. (ed.). 1992. Women's Book Committee, Chinese Canadian National

Council. *Jin Guo: Voices of Chinese Canadian Women*. Toronto: Women's Press.

Swift, E. 1945. Letter to A. Mosher, June 26. PAC, MG 28, I 215, Vol. 81, File—The Race Issue.

Tahon, M.B. 1996. "Regards croisés sur les <<musulmanes>> au Québec." In Khadiyatoulah Fall, Ratiba Hadj-Moussa and Daniel Simeoni (eds.), *Les convergences culturelles dans les sociétés pluriethniques*. Montréal: Presses de l'Université du Québec.

Tator, C. 1996. "Anti-Racism and the Human Service Delivery System." In C.A. James (ed.), *Perspectives on Racism and the Human Services Sector: A Case for Change*. Toronto: University of Toronto Press.

Thomas, B. 1987. *Multiculturalism at Work: A Guide to Organizational Change*. Toronto: YWCA of Metropolitan Toronto.

_____. 1994. "The Politics of Being White." In C. James and A. Shadd (eds.), *Encounters*. Toronto: Between the Lines.

Thompson, C. 1934. "The Conclusions of Scientists Relative to Racial Differences." *The Journal of Negro Education,* July 3(3): 494–512.

Tinker, H. *Separate And Unequal*. Vancouver: University of British Columbia Press.

Tobin, L. 1959. Letter to H. Craib, July 15. PAC, MG 28, I 173, Vol. 34.

Toronto Board of Education. 1919. "Report of Trustee (Mrs.) Groves on her Visit to Special Auxiliary Classes in American Cities." *Appendix to Minutes*. June 19.

_____. 1925. Minutes. 205.

Tremblay, R. 1994. "Le carcan intellectuel des *politically correct*. Un sujet crucial comme l'immigration n'a même pas été effleuré pendant la campagne électorale." *Le Devoir,* 27 sept.: A9.

Trésor de la langue française. Dictionnaire de la langue du XIXe et du XXe siècle (1789–1960). 1990. Paris: Editions du Centre nacional de le recherche scientifique. Gallimard, 1971–1994.

Trinh, Minh-ha T. 1989. *Woman, Native, Other*. Bloomington, Indiana: Indiana University Press.

Troper, H. 1972. "The Creek-Negroes and Canadian Immigration, 1909–1911." *Canadian Historical Review* (September) 53(3): 272–88.

Trudel, M. 1960. *L'esclavage au Canada français*. Québec: Les Presses de l'Université Laval.

UHWIGNA, Canadian Chapter. 1997. "Remembering the Past, Creating the Future, Making Changes, Taking Charge." Conference. Toronto, May 2–3.

United Way of Greater Toronto. 1991. *Action, Access, Diversity! A Guide to Anti-racist/ Multicultural Organizational Change for Social Service Agencies*. Toronto: United Way.

Valverde, M. 1991. *The Age of Light, Soap, and Water: Moral Reform in English Canada, 1885–1925*. Toronto: McClelland & Stewart.

_____. 1992. "When The Mother of the Race Is Free: Race, Reproduction, and Sexuality in First-Wave Feminism." In Franca Iacovetta and Mariana Valverde (eds.), *Gender Conflicts*. Toronto: University of Toronto Press.

van Dijk, T. 1988a. *News Analysis*. Hillsdale, New Jersey: Lawrence Erlbaum Associates.

_____. 1988b. "How 'They' Hit the Headlines: Ethnic Minorities in the Press." In Geneva Smitherman-Donaldson and Teun A. van Dijk (eds.), *Discourse and Discrimination*. Detroit: Wayne State University Press.

_____. 1988c. *News As Discourse*. Hillsdale, NJ: Lawrence Erlbaum Associates.

_____. 1991. *Racism and the Press*. London and New York: Routledge.

_____. 1993. *Elite Discourse and Racism*. London: Sage Publications.

Van Kirk, S. 1981. *Many Tender Ties: Women in Fur trade in Western Canada, 1670–1870*. Winnipeg: Watson and Dwyer.

_____. "The Impact of White Women on Fur Trade Society." In S. Mann and A. Prentice (eds.), *The Neglected Majority: Essays In Canadian Women's History, 1880–1920*. Toronto: McClelland & Stewart.

Vear, D. 1993. "Quatre fois moins d'actes antisémites à Montréal qu'à Toronto." *Le Devoir*, 3 mars: A3.

Vincent, S. 1992. "Terre québécoise, première nation et nation première: notes sur le discours québécois francophone au cours de l'été 1990." In Nadia Khouri (ed.), *Discours et mythes de l'ethnicité*. Montréal: Acfas.

Vizkelety, B. 1987. *Proving Discrimination in Canada*. Toronto: Carswell.

Walkerdine, Valerie. 1990. *School Girl Fictions*. New York: Verso.

Warburton, R. 1992. "Neglected Aspects of the Political Economy of Asian Racialization in British Columbia." In Vic Satzewich (ed.), *Deconstructing a Nation: Immigration, Multiculturalism and Racism in '90s Canada*. Halifax, NS: Fernwood Publishing.

Ward, W.P. 1978. *White Canada Forever: Popular Attitudes and Public Policy Towards Orientals In British Columbia*. Montreal: McGill-Queen's University Press.

Ware, V. 1992. *Beyond the Pale: White Women, Racism and History*. London: Verso Press.

Webster, P. 1992. "Toronto Social Workers' Skills Buried by New Urban Realities." *Now Magazine* (October) Toronto.

Werier, V. 1961. "Target of Fight is Equal Rights." *Winnipeg Tribune*. April 22.

West, C. 1987. "Race and Social Theory." In M. Davis (ed.), *The Year Left*.

_____. 1992. *Race Matters*. Boston: Beacon Press.

Wharf, B. 1990. *Social Work and Social Change in Canada*. Toronto: McClelland and Stewart.

Williams, L. 1957a. Letter to J. Diefenbaker, August 1. PAC, MG 28, I 215, Vol. 14.

_____. 1957b. Letter to C. Jodoin, October 4. PAC, MG 28, V75,Vol. 15, File 8.

_____. 1957c. Letter to M. Starr, November 8. PAC, MG 28, I 215, Vol. 15.

_____. 1958. Letter to M. Starr, March 15. PAC, MG 28, I 215, Vol. 14.

_____. 1961. Letter to S. Blum, May 12. PAC, MG 28, V75, Vol. 15.

Williams, L., L. Lewsey, E. Brisco, M. Crawford, G. Beckles, E. Bailey, E. Grant, E. Parsons and A. Tynes. 1963. Complaint to the Director. Canada FEP Act, July 5.

Williams, W. 1978. "The 'Sambo' Deception." *Phylon* 39(3): 261–63.

Williamson, J. 1986. *Rage for Order*. Oxford, U.K.: Oxford University Press.

Wilson, C. 1996a. *Racism: From Slavery to Advanced Capitalism*. Thousand Oaks: Sage.

Wilson, T. J. 1996. "Feminism and Institutionalized Racism." *Feminist Review* 52(Spring): 1–26.

Wilson, W.J. 1973. *Power, Racism and Privilege*. New York: Free Press.

Winant, H. 1994a. *Racial Conditions*. Minneapolis: University of Minnesota Press.

_____. 1994b. "Racial Formation and Hegemony: Local and Global Developments." In A. Rattansi and S. Westwood (eds.), *Racism, Modernity and Identity*. London: Polity Press.

Wolf, E.R. 1982. *Europe and the People Without History.* Berkeley and Los Angeles: University of California Press.

Woodsworth, J.S. 1972. *Strangers Within Our Gates.* Toronto: University of Toronto Press.

Wright, E. 1989. "Thoroughly Postmodern Feminist Criticism." In T. Brennan (ed.), *Between Feminism and Psychoanalysis.* New York: Routledge.

Wright, M. 1964. Letter to H. Walsh, May 25. PAC, MG 28, I 215, Vol. 14.

Yinger, J. 1994. *Ethnicity: Source of Strength and Source of Conflict.* New York: State University of New York Press.

Young, D. 1992. *The Donna Young Report.* Toronto: OHRC.

Young, D. and K. Liao. 1992. "The Treatment of Race at Arbitration." *Labour Arbitration Yearbook* 5: 57–79.